I0095298

WIRED FOR CHAOS

Origins of Personality Disorders and Coping Mechanisms

NAKEL W. A. NIKIEMA

© **Copyright 2025 - All rights reserved.**

The content contained within this book may not be reproduced, duplicated or transmitted without direct written permission from the author or the publisher.

Under no circumstances will any blame or legal responsibility be held against the publisher, or author, for any damages, reparation, or monetary loss due to the information contained within this book, either directly or indirectly.

Legal Notice:

This book is copyright protected. It is only for personal use. You cannot amend, distribute, sell, use, quote or paraphrase any part, or the content within this book, without the consent of the author or publisher.

Disclaimer Notice:

Please note the information contained within this document is for educational and entertainment purposes only. All effort has been executed to present accurate, up to date, reliable, complete information. No warranties of any kind are declared or implied. Readers acknowledge that the author is not engaged in the rendering of legal, financial, medical or professional advice. The content within this book has been derived from various sources. Please consult a licensed professional before attempting any techniques outlined in this book.

By reading this document, the reader agrees that under no circumstances is the author responsible for any losses, direct or indirect, that are incurred as a result of the use of the information contained within this document, including, but not limited to, errors, omissions, or inaccuracies.

CONTENTS

PART III
STRATEGIES IN MOTION

INTRODUCTION

We live beside it, sleep with it, and sometimes mistake it for our personality; chaos, hidden in patterns too familiar to question. It shows up as emotional outbursts that feel bigger than the moment, silences that last too long, and relationships that break and then return like clockwork. It isn't always loud. Often, it whispers through the rules we live by, the defenses we mistake for identity, and the reactions we don't remember choosing.

When people hear "personality disorder," most assume it's a clinical label reserved for someone else; someone extreme, someone unstable, someone not us. But that distance is a myth. These patterns aren't locked in a textbook. They show up in the friend who vanishes at the first sign of intimacy. The partner whose warmth flips into a rage without warning. The parent who needed control more than connection, or the part of ourselves we've learned to hide because it feels too messy, too much.

The goal of this book is not to pathologize personality, but to reclaim it. Personality disorders are extensions of human traits turned up too loud, repeated too often, and left unchallenged for too long. They are the stories we inherit, the reactions we practice, and the habits we mistake for who we are. They are survival patterns, written in a code our nervous systems learned long before we had words.

You may be reading this because you recognize something in yourself, or because you're trying to make sense of someone else. You may be reeling from a relationship that made you question your reality, or sitting with years of behaviors you don't quite understand. Or maybe you're just curious, wondering why the same dynamics keep repeating, no matter how much you grow or how many boundaries you set. Wherever you are, this book meets you there.

What you will not find here is judgment. What you will find is clarity.

This book is structured around three movements: understanding, identifying, and managing. First, we unpack what personality is and how it becomes disordered. Then, we look at how these patterns show up in everyday life: in subtle choices, in relationships, and in the way we talk to ourselves when no one is listening. Finally, we offer strategies—not quick fixes, but tools—for shifting the patterns that cause harm, whether they live in you or in the people around you.

You do not need a diagnosis to see yourself in these pages. In fact, most people who carry these patterns are never diagnosed. But their traits still shape how they love, work, parent, and connect. Understanding those patterns gives you a map. And when you have a map, you stop walking in circles.

We'll explore why some traits spiral under stress, and why others stay hidden until it's too late. We'll talk about the way childhood experiences wire our emotional responses. About the roles we play to feel safe. About how trauma doesn't always leave visible scars, but often leaves visible behaviors.

If you're looking for validation, insight, language, or just a different way of understanding the chaos you've lived through, you'll find it here. Not in the form of absolutes, but in the form of frameworks that honor complexity. Because there is no one-size-fits-all answer, but there is a path forward—one paved with recognition, responsibility, and choice.

You are not broken; you are patterned, and patterns can be rewired.

PART I

CHAPTER 1

WHAT ARE PERSONALITY DISORDERS

We've all heard someone called "toxic," but we rarely stop to ask what that means. Personality disorders aren't meant to be catchphrases or insults; they are complex, human responses to a lifetime of patterns. This chapter grounds the reader in what personality is, what makes it disordered, and why those distinctions matter.

DEFINING PERSONALITY

Before we jump into the disorder part, it helps to start with the basics: What exactly *is* personality? It's more than being the kind of person who alphabetizes their spice rack or has strong opinions about the correct way to load a dishwasher (you know who you are). In psychology, personality refers to the enduring patterns of thought, emotion, and behavior that make you... Well, you. And it's a lot more consistent than your morning mood swings or coffee-fueled brainstorms.

The Five-Factor Model: The Personality Playlist

Psychologists Costa and McCrae (1992) came up with a model that's still widely used today: the Five-Factor Model, also known as the Big Five. It includes:

- **Openness:** Are you creative and curious, or do you prefer the tried-and-true?
- **Conscientiousness:** Do you plan ahead or wing it (and forget your keys three times a week)?
- **Extraversion:** Do you thrive on social energy, or does small talk make your soul shrink?
- **Agreeableness:** Are you empathetic and cooperative, or blunt with a side of spicy?
- **Neuroticism:** Do you stay cool under pressure, or is your inner world one long anxiety playlist?

These five traits exist on a spectrum, and everyone has a unique mix. None of them are inherently good or bad. They just are. But when life throws curveballs, and let's face it—it always does, these traits can either help us adapt or send us spiraling.

Nature vs. Nurture

Is your personality a hand-me-down from your parents or a product of the chaos you grew up in? Spoiler: it's both. Genetics gives you the basic ingredients, but the environment is the chef.

Research shows that personality is moderately heritable, meaning there's a decent chance you inherited your dad's stubborn streak or your mom's anxiety-prone tendencies (Turkheimer, 2000). But experiences, especially early ones, play a major role in shaping how those traits play out.

HOW PERSONALITY SHOWS UP IN REAL LIFE

Your personality isn't something you switch on for job interviews and off when you're bingeing *Netflix*. It shows up in how you handle stress, how you relate to others, and how you talk to yourself when you spill coffee on your shirt before 9 a.m. The keyword here is *enduring*. Personality is relatively stable over time, not something that shifts every Tuesday.

The Building Blocks of Who We Are

Before we ever develop a "personality," we're shaped by a mix of things that have nothing to do with conscious choice. From our temperament at birth to the way our earliest caregivers responded to our needs, the blueprint of who we become starts early, and it starts deep.

Temperament

Temperament refers to the biological foundation of personality. Some babies are easygoing and quiet, while others come into the world loud and sensitive. These aren't choices, they're hardwired tendencies that influence how we experience the world.

Research shows that traits like emotional reactivity, activity level, and sociability have biological roots (Rothbart & Bates, 2006). These temperamental traits aren't destiny, but they lay the groundwork for how we'll interact with our environment.

Attachment

Then there's attachment. Our earliest relationships, especially with primary caregivers, shape how we see ourselves and others. Were our needs met consistently? Did we feel safe to explore, cry, and connect?

Attachment theory, pioneered by Bowlby and expanded by Ainsworth, identifies patterns such as secure, anxious, avoidant, and disorganized attachment (Bretherton, 1992). These styles influence how we form bonds, handle conflict, and interpret emotional safety later in life.

Environment

The environment is everything from our family dynamics and culture to traumatic events, stability, and stress. A child raised in a nurturing, predictable home will often have a very different developmental path than one raised in chaos, neglect, or emotional inconsistency.

While temperament is the seed, and attachment is the soil, the environment is the weather. A harsh storm early on doesn't guarantee dysfunction, but it increases the odds.

Understanding these building blocks helps us make sense of why certain traits emerge and why others harden into patterns that are tough to break.

WHEN PERSONALITY BECOMES A PROBLEM

Alright, so we've talked about what personality is, but when does it cross the line into something more serious? It's one thing to be a little dramatic under stress, but it's another thing entirely when those traits dig in their heels and start wrecking your relationships, career, or inner peace.

The Diagnostic and Statistical Manual of Mental Disorders, Fifth Edition, Text Revision (DSM-5-TR) defines a personality disorder as an enduring, inflexible pattern of thinking, feeling, and behaving that:

- deviates significantly from the expectations of your culture
- shows up across many areas of life (not just during family dinners or awkward office meetings)
- causes real distress or problems in daily functioning
- starts in adolescence or early adulthood and sticks around like that one friend who never takes the hint (American Psychiatric Association, 2022)

Think of it like this: Everyone has quirks. Maybe you're a perfectionist who triple-checks their emails, or you hate surprises with the passion of a thousand suns. That's not necessarily a disorder. It becomes a problem when it's extreme, inflexible, and leads to suffering, for you or the people around you.

Here's a quick comparison:

- **Trait:** You like things organized.
- **Disorder:** You can't function if your pens aren't lined up by color and type, and you melt down if someone moves one.

The key difference? Impairment, distress, and inflexibility.

And it's not just about what you *do*. It's also about whether these patterns are sticking around in *all* areas of life, not just in specific contexts. If you're hypercritical at work but laid-back at home, that's a personality *style*. If you're rigidly critical everywhere, all the time, that might be something deeper.

WHAT THE DSM-5-TR REALLY SAYS

So, what exactly qualifies as a personality disorder according to the experts? We touched on the basics earlier, but let's unpack this more clearly. The *Diagnostic and Statistical Manual of Mental Disorders, Fifth Edition, Text Revision* (DSM-5-TR) outlines specific criteria that need to be met. And no, being moody, dramatic, or irritating on occasion doesn't cut it.

Here's what actually makes something diagnosable:

1. Deviates from cultural expectations: The behavior has to be noticeable outside what's expected in the person's cultural context. That means we have to consider what's "normal" for the environment someone grew up in. For instance, emotional expressiveness in one culture might be seen as excessive in another. Context matters.

2. Pervasive across situations: This isn't about how someone acts on a bad Monday. These patterns show up in multiple areas of life, at work, in friendships, romantic relationships, and even internally. The consistency of dysfunction is what raises the red flag.

3. Causes distress or impairment: This one is big. The traits don't just exist; they interfere. Maybe the person can't hold a job, maintain relationships, or regulate their emotions. The dysfunction gets in the way of daily functioning.

4. Stable and long-standing: The patterns usually begin in early adulthood and stay pretty consistent over time. We're not talking about a six-month spiral. These are traits that have dug in and stuck around.

5. Not better explained by something else: Before diagnosing a personality disorder, clinicians rule out other possible causes, like brain injuries, medical conditions, or substance use. A disorder has to stand on its own, not ride the coattails of another issue.

The DSM also organizes personality disorders into three clusters:

- **Cluster A (odd or eccentric):** Paranoid, Schizoid, Schizotypal
- **Cluster B (dramatic or erratic):** Antisocial, Borderline, Histrionic, Narcissistic
- **Cluster C (anxious or fearful):** Avoidant, Dependent, Obsessive-Compulsive

These clusters aren't perfect categories, but they help group similar behavioral styles. Most people don't fit neatly into one, and comorbidity is common.

Case snapshot: Two people, same trait, different impact: Take perfectionism. For one person, it helps them deliver top-notch work. For another, it causes panic attacks, social withdrawal, and missed deadlines because nothing ever feels "good enough." Same root trait, but only one meets the threshold for a disorder.

The goal here is to grasp the depth behind a diagnosis. These disorders aren't handed out casually, and they're not trendy personality labels. They represent real, persistent struggles that deserve understanding, not oversimplification.

COMMON MISCONCEPTIONS

Just because someone drives you nuts doesn't mean they have a personality disorder. But thanks to TikTok, Twitter, and that one cousin who took a psych class ten years ago, everyone's suddenly an expert. Clinical terms like "narcissist" and "sociopath" are getting tossed around like confetti, usually in the middle of a breakup or group chat meltdown.

The Rise of Armchair Diagnosis

Social media has helped more people talk about mental health, which is great. But it's also created a culture where a moody moment or a bad habit gets mistaken for a full-blown disorder. And that's a problem.

In fact, a 2023 study found that while mental health content on TikTok reached billions of views, up to 60% of the videos contained misleading or exaggerated claims (Fontanella et al., 2023).

Not Everyone You Dislike Has a Disorder

Being manipulative, rude, or self-absorbed doesn't mean someone has a diagnosable condition. Sometimes people are just... difficult. A personality disorder isn't about a single argument or a bad week. There needs to be deep, long-standing patterns that disrupt lives and relationships.

Let's break it down:

- A friend who flakes on plans isn't necessarily Avoidant Personality Disorder.
- Your boss, who needs everything done *their* way, might not have Obsessive-Compulsive Personality Disorder.
- And your ex, who ghosted you? Probably not a sociopath. Just inconsiderate.

Why Misuse Matters

When we casually throw clinical terms around, it does real damage. It makes it harder for people with actual personality disorders to be taken seriously. It spreads stigma, fuels misinformation, and turns complex mental health issues into punchlines.

It's also worth saying: real diagnosis takes time, context, and professional training. Watching a few TikToks doesn't cut it.

So, before you play internet therapist, take a step back. Human behavior is messy. Flawed isn't the same thing as disordered.

THE SPECTRUM OF TRAITS

Personality disorders aren't some mysterious condition that only affect a few people; they're extreme expressions of traits we all carry to some degree. That fear of rejection? That tendency to avoid confrontation or obsess over details? Those live on the same spectrum; it's just a matter of degree, frequency, and fallout.

Think of traits like the volume knob on a radio. Most of us live in the middle: functional, flexible, occasionally neurotic. But when the dial gets stuck at full blast, and there's no way to turn it down, that's when things get tricky.

Personality Disorders Are Not All-or-Nothing

For a long time, psychology treated disorders like light switches, either you had it or you didn't. But modern research, especially the dimensional approach suggested by Widiger and Trull (2007), says it's more like a dimmer. Traits exist on a continuum. The same rigidity that makes someone a stickler for rules at work might become pathological when it sabotages their relationships, health, or sanity.

The dimensional model also helps explain why so many people relate to certain symptoms. You don't have to meet full diagnostic criteria to *feel* a little avoidant, obsessive, or dramatic sometimes.

The Everyday Mirror

Most of us have moments where we catch a glimpse of ourselves acting out; snapping at a loved one, ghosting a text, obsessing over what someone *really* meant in an email. These aren't personality disorders, but they do live on the same map.

For example:

- Someone with abandonment anxiety may not have Borderline Personality Disorder, but that fear might still influence how they act in relationships.
- A person who prefers isolation doesn't automatically have Schizoid Personality Disorder; they might just recharge better alone.
- And yes, your need to triple-check the stove doesn't make you disordered, but if it rules your life, it might be worth exploring.

Frequency, Intensity, and Impairment

The difference lies in how often it happens, how extreme it gets, and how much it disrupts your ability to live, love, and work. In psychology, those are the big three: frequency, intensity, and impairment. They separate quirks from disorders, and they're the litmus test for deciding when someone needs more than just a deep breath and a bubble bath.

CASE SNAPSHOTS AND SUBCLINICAL TRAITS

So far, we've talked about traits living on a spectrum. But what does that actually look like in real life? Let's put theory into practice with a few fictional, but realistic, case snapshots that show how common traits can show up differently depending on their intensity, frequency, and impact.

Avoidant Tendencies in Action

- *Rawa*, a 34-year-old graphic designer, turns down most social invitations, preferring solo time to recharge. He sometimes worries that people judge him, but he still maintains a few close friendships and functions well at work.
- *Leah*, a 29-year-old HR manager, avoids nearly all social interactions outside of work. She fears rejection so intensely that she cancels plans last minute and declines promotions that require visibility. Her loneliness causes distress, but she doesn't know how to change.

Same root trait, avoidance. But Leah's experience involves significant impairment and distress, nudging it toward clinical territory.

Control vs. Rigidity

- *Tariq* likes his space tidy. He organizes his desk every morning and uses spreadsheets to track household expenses. It helps him feel prepared and grounded.
- *Tenin* needs things a certain way, or she spirals. If someone moves a book on her shelf, she gets visibly agitated. Her routines are rigid, and she struggles in relationships where unpredictability is common.

Again, same core trait, conscientiousness and order. One is adaptive; the other becomes maladaptive.

Subclinical Doesn't Mean Subimportant

A person doesn't need to meet full diagnostic criteria for their struggles to be valid. Subclinical traits can still affect relationships, self-esteem, and decision-making. In fact, many people live in the grey zone, close enough to feel the weight, but not enough to qualify for a diagnosis.

The dimensional model proposed by Widiger and Trull (2007) supports this. It argues that rather than drawing a line between "sick" and "well," we should recognize where someone falls along the continuum. That lens allows for earlier support, more personalized care, and less stigma.

THE RISE OF DIMENSIONAL MODELS

For decades, personality disorders were diagnosed in a yes-or-no format. Either you met the criteria or you didn't. But mental health doesn't work like flipping a switch; it lives in nuance. That's why newer systems, like the ICD-11 and the Alternative Model for Personality Disorders (AMPD) in the DSM-5, are shifting toward dimensional models.

ICD-11: Focus on Severity, Not Just Symptoms

The International Classification of Diseases, 11th edition (ICD-11), released by the World Health Organization, takes a big-picture approach. Instead of asking, "Does this person have borderline or avoidant personality disorder?" it asks, "How severe is their personality dysfunction overall?"

The ICD-11 measures severity based on self-functioning (identity, self-direction) and interpersonal functioning (empathy, intimacy). Then it looks at *traits*, like negative affectivity, detachment, dissociality, disinhibition, and anankastia (a fancy word for obsessive perfectionism).

This model helps clinicians focus on the *impact* of traits, not just the label. It's less about fitting people into boxes and more about understanding the shape of their struggles.

AMPD: The DSM's Dimensional Cousin

The AMPD (Alternative Model for Personality Disorders) lives in Section III of the DSM-5. It's a framework for when the standard criteria don't quite fit. Like ICD-11, AMPD also focuses on *levels of personality functioning* and *trait domains*.

It breaks things down into:

- **Level of personality functioning scale (LPFS):** How well a person manages their identity and relationships
- **Pathological personality traits:** Grouped into five broad domains similar to ICD-11's

While not yet the primary system in clinical practice, the AMPD is gaining traction among researchers and therapists who want a more nuanced and less stigmatizing way to work with complex personalities.

If you're reading this book to understand yourself or someone you care about, dimensional models offer something incredibly valuable: they leave room for complexity. You're not "all better" or "totally disordered." You're on a spectrum of functioning, like everyone else.

THE FUNCTION OF DYSFUNCTION

It's easy to look at personality disorders and see only chaos, volatile moods, fractured relationships, and self-sabotage. But behind the dysfunction is often a deeper story: these patterns didn't come from nowhere. In fact, they usually served a purpose. At some point, they helped someone survive.

Personality disorders often begin as adaptations. A child growing up in an unpredictable or unsafe environment may learn to detach emotionally, control everything around them, or read every room like their life depends on it, because sometimes, it does. Those behaviors can become so ingrained that they stick around long after the threat is gone, like armor that's fused to the skin.

The Survival Strategy That Outstayed Its Welcome

When someone is emotionally guarded, hypervigilant, or intensely perfectionistic, it's not always about being "difficult." Sometimes, it's about safety. The rigidity we associate with personality disorders is often just an overdeveloped survival response, one that worked once but now causes more harm than good.

The goal isn't to label these behaviors as bad. It's to understand their origins. Because if we can understand *why* someone acts the way they do, we can replace judgment with empathy, and, more importantly, help them replace outdated strategies with healthier ones.

A Shift in Perspective

This is where things get hopeful. Understanding dysfunction as functional (at least at some point) opens the door to growth. It means we're not just dealing with brokenness, we're dealing with patterns that *used* to work, and now need updating.

When we move away from moral judgment and toward psychological understanding, we shift the focus from "what's wrong with you?" to "what happened to you?" And that shift changes everything.

EXERCISE: PERSONALITY MAPPING REFLECTION

This chapter might have stirred up a few realizations or maybe some questions. Either way, this is where we pause and turn the spotlight inward. The goal isn't to diagnose yourself or anyone else; it's to notice the patterns you live with every day, especially the ones that show up under pressure.

Step 1: Explore Your Trait Mix

Take a simplified Five Factor personality test (you can find free versions online, such as the one from Open Psychometrics: https://openpsychometrics.org/tests/IPIP-BFFM/. This gives you a snapshot of where you land on the spectrum of:

- openness
- conscientiousness
- extraversion
- agreeableness
- neuroticism

There's no right or wrong here. Just patterns.

Step 2: Under Stress, What Shifts?

Now reflect: how do these traits show up when you're stressed, overwhelmed, or emotionally triggered? Do you get more rigid, more reactive, more withdrawn? Personality is revealed in how we respond when life gets bumpy.

Step 3: Journal It Out

Grab a notebook or open a blank doc and respond to the following:

- What behaviors or reactions do I keep repeating, even when they don't serve me?
- In what situations do I feel most reactive, anxious, or avoidant?
- If these behaviors had a job, to protect me from something, what would that job be?

This is the beginning of insight.

Reminder: Patterns are powerful, but so is awareness. The goal here is curiosity. Understanding your own personality patterns is the first step toward compassion for yourself and others.

CHAPTER 2

A BRIEF HISTORY OF MADNESS

F rom ancient curses to asylum walls, the story of disordered personality has been one of fear, confusion, and slow evolution. To understand how far we've come, we must first see where we started.

MADNESS IN THE ANCIENT WORLD

Long before the DSM, before the word "diagnosis" even existed, people still struggled with what we now call personality disorders. But without neurology or psychology, ancient cultures had to explain these behaviors the best way they knew how: through spirit worlds, bodily fluids, or cosmic forces.

The Four Humors and the Greco-Roman Lens

Hippocrates (c. 460–370 BCE) proposed that human behavior was guided by four bodily fluids: blood, phlegm, black bile, and yellow bile. Mental imbalance, in his view, was a physical issue; too much black bile might make someone melancholic, while too much yellow bile could result in rage or impulsivity (Jackson, 1986). Galen later expanded on this, aligning temperament types with these humors. It was medicine, in a way, but with a mystical twist.

The Babylonian and Egyptian Models

In Mesopotamia and ancient Egypt, disordered thoughts or behaviors were often seen as the result of supernatural forces. The Babylonians believed that madness could be caused by the gods' wrath or by ghostly possession. Treatments involved rituals, incantations, and appeals to deities. Egyptian texts like the Ebers Papyrus describe symptoms resembling depression or hallucinations but frame them through spiritual and magical explanations (Scull, 2015).

Eastern Perspectives: Balance Over Battle

Meanwhile, Eastern traditions such as Ayurveda and Taoism saw mental distress through a more holistic lens. In Ayurveda, mental health was tied to dosha imbalances, vata, pitta, and kapha, and treatments involved herbs, meditation, and dietary shifts. Taoist philosophy emphasized harmony between yin and yang; mental unrest suggested a disharmony in life force energy, or qi (Kakar, 2013).

Healers, Shamans, and Spiritual Guides

In tribal and indigenous societies, mental and emotional struggles weren't necessarily seen as illness but as signs of spiritual crisis, or even potential. Shamans and spiritual guides were often people who had experienced altered states, visions, or behavioral extremes. Their "madness" wasn't treated; it was honored and guided into something useful for the community (Porter, 2002).

Across these diverse worldviews, one idea persists: when someone behaved in ways others couldn't understand, the explanation had to come from somewhere. Whether it was bodily fluids, angry spirits, or cosmic imbalance, the search for meaning began long before modern psychiatry arrived.

DEMONOLOGY AND THE DARK AGES

When the Roman Empire fell, much of the classical understanding of illness, however flawed, gave way to a different worldview. In medieval Europe, explanations for madness moved out of the physician's hands and into the church.

Madness as Sin and Possession

Christian theology became the dominant lens through which all suffering was seen. Strange behavior wasn't medical; it became spiritual. People showing signs of mental disturbance were often believed to be possessed by demons or to be punished for sin. This shift reframed madness as a moral failure, not a health issue (Rousseau et al., 1970).

Priests replaced doctors. Confession replaced treatment. And for those whose behavior strayed too far from the accepted norm, punishment often replaced care.

Exorcisms and Purification Rituals

One of the primary "treatments" was exorcism. The goal was cleansing. Emotional outbursts, hallucinations, or nonconformity could all be interpreted as evidence of demonic influence. In many cases, the more distressed the person became, the more convinced communities were that evil was present.

While some clergy offered compassion, others saw madness as a threat to spiritual order. Individuals might be isolated, whipped, or even starved in an effort to drive out the devil. For women, especially, emotional intensity or nonconformity was a dangerous thing to display.

The Witch Hunts: Misdiagnosis on a Grand Scale

The most tragic example of this era's misunderstanding came with the witch hunts. Women who were poor, unmarried, outspoken, or simply eccentric were accused of witchcraft, often for behavior that today might be seen as symptoms of trauma, neurodivergence, or mental illness (Porter, 2002).

A Legacy of Fear

These centuries left deep scars in how society views mental health. The association between disorder and danger, between emotion and evil, still lingers in how we talk about certain diagnoses today. The idea that someone must be "controlled," "fixed," or "punished" for their behavior echoes far beyond the medieval era.

ENLIGHTENMENT AND THE RISE OF INSTITUTIONS

By the 18th century, the grip of religious explanations on madness began to loosen. The Enlightenment brought with it a new emphasis on reason, science, and human rights. And with that shift came a radically different question: What if madness wasn't a sin or a curse, but an illness?

The Birth of the Asylum

In Europe, the first wave of mental institutions emerged primarily as places of containment. The goal was order, not treatment. People considered "mad" were removed from society and locked away in buildings like London's infamous Bedlam Hospital. Conditions were often brutal: chains, overcrowding, and public viewing for entertainment (Scull, 2015).

Still, the creation of asylums marked a change. Madness was now being physically separated from sin and crime. This separation laid the groundwork for a new kind of thinking: maybe the mind, like the body, could be treated.

Pinel and the Moral Treatment Movement

In 1793, the French physician Philippe Pinel famously ordered the removal of chains from patients at Bicêtre Hospital in Paris. Pinel believed that those labeled as insane should be treated with dignity, structure, and compassion, not fear (Porter, 2002).

This idea, later echoed by William Tuke in England, became the moral treatment movement. Patients were given fresh air, routines, and purposeful work. Though far from perfect, it marked a step toward more humane care.

The Enlightenment reframed madness as an illness. The mind became something to observe, study, and, possibly, heal. This marked the beginning of psychiatry as a medical discipline. Physicians began to look at patterns, causes, and classifications, planting the seeds that would eventually grow into diagnostic systems like the DSM.

Public Health and the "Problem" of Madness

As urban populations grew, governments started to see mental illness as a public health issue. Asylums expanded to manage growing social unrest. This dual purpose, care and control, would haunt institutions for centuries.

The Enlightenment didn't cure madness, but it changed its meaning. It opened the door to science, structure, and medical authority, but also to systems that, at times, confused order with healing.

FREUD, JUNG, AND THE INNER WORLD

By the early 20th century, mental illness was becoming a question of *why*. Why do we behave the way we do? Why do our thoughts sometimes betray us? Why do some patterns stick like glue, even when they hurt?

Enter Sigmund Freud and Carl Jung, two towering figures who helped shift the conversation from external behavior to internal life.

Freud: The Unconscious as Battleground

Freud's big idea was that much of what drives us lies outside our awareness. Childhood experiences, repressed desires, and unconscious conflicts were the hidden engines of personality. To Freud, the mind was a battlefield between the id (instincts), ego (reality), and superego (morals), all competing for control (Freud, 1923).

Symptoms were clues. Anxiety, obsession, and emotional outbursts pointed to unresolved inner tension. Freud's theories weren't always right (or subtle), but they paved the way for the idea that personality could be shaped by history and healed through insight.

Jung: Patterns, Archetypes, and the Collective Unconscious

Jung, once Freud's protégé, eventually broke away and built his own vision. He introduced the idea of the collective unconscious: a layer of the psyche shared by all humans, filled with archetypes like the Hero, the Shadow, and the Trickster (Jung, 1964).

Where Freud saw pathology, Jung saw meaning. He believed that people weren't just products of trauma, but carriers of deep, symbolic patterns. Dreams, myths, and even hallucinations could be messages from the unconscious, not just symptoms to silence.

Jung also developed early personality typologies that would later inspire tools like the Myers-Briggs Type Indicator (MBTI). He viewed personality as a dynamic interplay of opposing forces—introversion and extraversion, thinking and feeling.

The Legacy: Personality as a Living System

Together, Freud and Jung helped move mental health out of institutions and into therapy rooms. They treated the mind as layered, symbolic, and deeply personal. For all their flaws and eccentricities, they shifted the field toward introspection and laid the groundwork for the modern study of personality disorders.

In many ways, their work bridged the spiritual and the scientific. The human psyche was no longer just a broken machine to be fixed; it was a complex world to be explored.

FROM NEUROSIS TO DIAGNOSIS

As the 20th century progressed, psychology evolved from a mostly theoretical practice into a data-driven science. Freud and Jung cracked open the doors of the unconscious, but the mental health field soon wanted something more concrete. That desire for structure led to a new era.

The Shift to Science and Structure

In the early decades, clinicians still relied on loosely defined terms like "melancholia," "hysteria," or "neurosis." These labels were as much cultural as they were clinical, often reflecting societal anxieties more than individual pathology (Foucault, 1965).

By mid-century, psychiatry wanted legitimacy. It sought to align more closely with medicine: observable, measurable, and replicable. This push gave rise to structured diagnostic systems.

The Birth of the DSM

In 1952, the American Psychiatric Association released the first *Diagnostic and Statistical Manual of Mental Disorders* (DSM). It was slim, vague by today's standards, and heavily influenced by psychoanalysis. Still, it marked the start of a shift: madness could now be categorized.

The real leap came in 1980 with the DSM-III. It introduced a multi-axial system that treated personality disorders as distinct entities listed on Axis II. This separation helped define them as long-standing patterns, not just symptoms of something else (American Psychiatric Association, 1980).

The Medical Model Takes Over

The DSM-III and its successors brought structure, but also controversy. Critics argued that diagnoses became too rigid, reducing human experience to checklists. Personality disorders, in particular, were often stigmatized as untreatable or manipulative, reinforcing stereotypes rather than relieving suffering.

This "medicalization" of personality shifted the focus from context to criteria, and from meaning to measurement. And while it helped standardize care, it also narrowed how we understood distress.

Categorical vs. Dimensional: The Debate Continues

Modern editions like the DSM-5 (2013) and the ICD-11 (2022) have tried to strike a balance. There's growing support for dimensional models, which see traits on a continuum rather than in isolated categories. These frameworks aim to capture nuance, reduce stigma, and reflect the messy reality of human behavior.

Still, the debate persists. Is a label helpful or limiting? Are we diagnosing people, or pathologizing difference?

WHY HISTORY STILL SHAPES US

You might think we've outgrown the medieval shackles and humoral theories, but echoes of the past still shape how we talk about personality and mental health today. The language we use, the stigma we carry, even the way we diagnose, it's all got history baked into it.

Language Carries Luggage

Terms like "crazy," "insane," and "lunatic" still creep into everyday conversations. They show up in headlines, pop culture, and even casual jokes. These are relics of a time when mental illness was treated with chains or fire. When we use them uncritically, we carry forward centuries of shame and misunderstanding.

Stigma: A Long Shadow

The idea that personality disorders are "difficult," "dangerous," or "incurable" didn't come out of nowhere. It has roots in early models that viewed behavior through lenses of sin, fear, and social threat. Women were labeled hysterical. People of color were pathologized for not conforming to white, Western norms. And those outside the mainstream—queer, neurodivergent, emotionally intense, were often seen as morally or mentally defective (Scull, 2015).

Diagnosis as a Tool—and a Weapon

Throughout history, diagnosis has been used to control. Political dissidents, rebellious women, and people who refused to assimilate, many were often labeled "mad" to justify their exclusion or punishment.

Even today, marginalized communities are more likely to be misdiagnosed or underdiagnosed and less likely to receive adequate treatment (Snowden, 2001). Cultural bias still lingers in the way symptoms are interpreted, particularly when personality is involved.

Why Cultural Literacy Matters

Understanding where these ideas come from isn't just historical trivia. It's a form of mental health literacy. When we recognize that our ideas about "normal" and "abnormal" are shaped by culture, religion, race, and power, we get better at seeing people as they are, not just as they've been labeled.

EXERCISE: REWRITE THE NARRATIVE

We've come a long way from leeches and exorcisms, but that doesn't mean the old ideas are gone. Many of us still carry echoes of those outdated beliefs, quiet assumptions passed down through family, culture, media, or religion.

This exercise is your chance to pause and unpack them.

Step 1: Choose a Historical Narrative

Pick one old-school explanation of madness that stood out to you from this chapter. Maybe it was demonic possession, the four humors, or the idea that women were "hysterical" by nature. Whatever it is, sit with it for a moment.

Ask yourself:

- How did this narrative shape the way people were treated?
- Who benefited from this belief—and who suffered?
- Does anything about that thinking still show up today?

Step 2: Reflect on Your Own Beliefs

Now bring it closer to home. Think about how mental health has been talked about in your life. At school, at home, in your faith community, or in your culture.

- What messages did you absorb about emotion, control, or personality?
- Were certain behaviors labeled as "bad," "crazy," or "broken"?
- Where did those messages come from—and are they actually true?

Step 3: Journal Prompt

"What belief about mental health do I carry that might not be mine? Where did it come from?"

Let the question sit. You don't need to solve anything right now. Just notice what rises up.

Because rewriting the narrative doesn't start with history books—it starts with the stories we stop telling ourselves.

CHAPTER 3

PERSONALITY DISORDERS AFFECT EVERYONE

THE SPECTRUM OF PERSONALITY TRAITS

We've all got our quirks; some people color-code their closets, others need complete silence to fall asleep. That's personality in action. It's the blend of how we think, feel, and act across time. But when does that blend turn into something more serious? When do those quirks cross a line?

That's where this chapter begins, with the idea that personality disorders aren't some rare phenomenon, or some clearly defined disorder. They're just the extreme ends of traits we all carry. Think of it like turning the volume way up on behaviors that already exist in everyone. It's just a dial that's stuck too high.

MENTAL HEALTH ISN'T A LIGHT SWITCH

Mental health doesn't live in a yes-or-no world. It's a continuum. Not "healthy" or "sick", just different degrees of functioning. Most people sit somewhere in the middle, adjusting based on things like stress, sleep, and life chaos. But when traits become rigid, extreme, or disruptive, they start to veer into disorder territory.

Take perfectionism. A little can fuel success. Too much? It leads to paralysis. Or take sensitivity, great for empathy, tough when it turns into reactivity. These aren't random traits; they're regular human behaviors that got turned up too loud (Robitz, 2022).

When Familiar Traits Get Stuck on High

The traits that define personality disorders are familiar, but exaggerated. That's what makes them so sneaky. You recognize them, maybe even see them in yourself, but don't realize how much impact they can have when they harden into patterns.

Here's how that can look:

- **Perfectionism** becomes a constant internal drill sergeant.
- **Sensitivity** turns into a hair-trigger reaction to minor slights.
- **Assertiveness** morphs into dominance or control.

It's not that these traits are bad. It's the inflexibility, the inability to turn the volume down, that creates problems.

FREQUENCY, INTENSITY, AND FALLOUT

Everyone has rough days. We lash out. We shut down. We worry too much. But for someone living with a personality disorder, these reactions are persistent. And they come with real consequences.

Clinicians look at three key things (Cleveland Clinic, 2019):

- **Frequency:** How often does this happen?
- **Intensity:** How extreme is the reaction?
- **Impact:** How much damage does it cause to relationships, work, and personal peace?

It's the combo of those three that shifts a trait from a quirk to a clinical concern.

It's all about recognizing that we're all on the same map, some just live closer to the edge. And if we can stop thinking in terms of "normal" and "not normal," we can start looking at personality with more curiosity, less judgment.

Because of the line between trait and disorder, it's thinner than you think. And it's something we all walk, whether we know it or not.

SUBCLINICAL BUT SIGNIFICANT

Here's the thing most people don't realize: you don't need a diagnosis to be affected by disordered traits. There's a whole category of behavior that flies under the radar, just below the clinical threshold, but still makes life harder than it needs to be. Welcome to the world of subclinical traits.

When "Not Quite a Disorder," Still Hurts

Think of subclinical traits as the middle zone. These aren't the kinds of issues that would get someone a formal diagnosis, but they're still strong enough to cause friction. A partner who emotionally shuts down during conflict. A coworker who needs control over every detail (Furnham & Petropoulou, 2017). A friend who lashes out when they feel ignored. Not diagnosable, but definitely impactful.

These patterns can wear on relationships, affect decision-making, and chip away at emotional well-being, even if no one's using words like "personality disorder."

A Few Familiar Faces

Subclinical traits tend to show up in quiet, persistent ways. Here are a few that tend to pop up in everyday life (Frost et al., 1994):

- **Low empathy:** The person who steamrolls others emotionally and never seems to notice.
- **Emotional volatility:** One small comment can trigger a full-blown meltdown.
- **Rigid thinking:** Rules are rules, even when they no longer make sense.
- **Passive dependency:** Waiting for others to decide, act, or fix everything.

These traits might not scream "disorder," but they shape interactions in real and often painful ways.

Stress Turns the Volume Up

Dr. Theodore Millon, one of the foundational voices in personality theory, emphasized that stress doesn't create new traits; it amplifies what's already there. When life gets chaotic, people don't suddenly change. They lean harder into their defaults (Millon, 2011).

- The detail-obsessed person becomes a control freak.

- The independent friend disappears completely.
- The conflict-avoidant partner becomes invisible.

Stress acts like a magnifier, pulling those subclinical traits into the spotlight where they can suddenly look and feel a lot more serious.

Subclinical doesn't mean unimportant. These traits still affect people's lives in powerful ways. Because they don't meet the full diagnostic threshold, they often go unaddressed. But naming the pattern is the first step to changing it.

We don't need to wait for a disaster or a diagnosis to start paying attention.

PERSONALITY IN EVERYDAY LIFE

You don't have to sit in a therapist's office to witness personality patterns at work. In fact, you see them all the time, in your coworkers, your partner, your family, and your group chat. Personality disorders aren't rare exceptions; their traits are quietly woven into daily interactions. Once you know what to look for, the patterns become clear.

People You Know, Patterns You've Seen

Let's bring this down to earth. Below are some real-world examples that mirror common personality traits, not to label anyone, but to help you recognize the signs (Cleveland Clinic, 2019):

- **The boss who micromanages every email and spreadsheet:** This might reflect traits seen in Obsessive-Compulsive Personality Disorder (OCPD). It's not about being tidy, it's about needing total control to feel safe.

- **The friend who vanishes when conflict arises:** Classic avoidant traits. It's not laziness or indifference; it's fear of rejection or not knowing how to handle closeness.
- **The relative who turns every event into their personal spotlight:** Traits of narcissistic or histrionic patterns show up here. The attention isn't just desired, it feels necessary for their sense of self.
- **The partner who loves you one day, then pushes you away the next:** Borderline traits often involve emotional whiplash, idealization followed by devaluation. It's not manipulation; it's often fear of abandonment driving that pendulum swing.

One Moment Isn't the Whole Story

Here's the key: none of these behaviors, by themselves, mean someone has a personality disorder. Everyone has bad days. Everyone lashes out or withdraws sometimes. The real marker is consistency; these patterns show up across time and settings.

If your boss only micromanages during budget season, that's stress. But if they do it year round, across teams and tasks, that's a pattern. Personality disorders are about long-standing habits, not isolated events.

WE ARE ALL SHAPED BY THESE DYNAMICS

Before we ever know the words for trust, boundaries, or fear, we're learning them in real time, from the people who raise us. Our earliest environment isn't just background noise, and it's the blueprint. And when those caregivers carry unresolved issues, the house we grew up in can teach us things that echo for decades.

When Caregivers Set the Emotional Stage

If you were raised by someone with traits of a personality disorder, volatile moods, emotional withdrawal, need for control, you learned to adapt. Maybe you became hyper-aware of others' emotions, scanning every room for signs of danger. Maybe you kept your needs small so you wouldn't cause trouble. Maybe you became the fixer, the peacemaker, the emotional bodyguard.

These roles don't come out of nowhere. They're survival strategies in response to inconsistent or unsafe caregiving. And over time, they hardwire beliefs about what love, safety, and connection should feel like (Hoermann et al., 2024).

The Blueprint: Boundaries, Beliefs, and Bonding

When a child grows up with emotionally unpredictable or unresponsive caregivers, they build their world on shaky ground. They may struggle with (Cherry, 2025):

- **Boundaries:** Not knowing when to say no or how to protect their own emotional space
- **Self-concept:** Internalizing blame, shame, or the belief that they're "too much" or "not enough"
- **Attachment:** Either clinging too tightly or staying distant to avoid getting hurt

These patterns don't just fade with age. They often show up in adult relationships, romantic or otherwise, like old software running a new system.

Attachment Theory: The Emotional GPS

Attachment theory, developed by John Bowlby and later expanded by Mary Ainsworth, helps explain how early relationships set the stage for future ones. If a child's needs were met reliably, they likely developed a secure attachment style, they trust easily, ask for help, and feel safe in closeness.

But if love was conditional, absent, or overwhelming, they may have developed an insecure style (McGarvie, 2024):

- **Anxious:** Fear of abandonment, need for reassurance
- **Avoidant:** Discomfort with closeness, emotional distance as protection
- **Disorganized:** A push-pull between craving connection and fearing it

These styles aren't just labels. They're survival maps. And many adults still follow the one they built in childhood, even if it leads them in circles.

Your Patterns Are Not Your Fault (But They Are Your Responsibility)

If you recognize yourself here, take a breath. This isn't about blaming your parents or staying stuck in the past. It's about understanding that some of the ways you show up in the world were shaped by systems you didn't choose.

But here's the empowering part: you get to update the script. You get to question whether those old roles still serve you. You get to build new ways of connecting that reflect who you are now, not who you had to be to survive.

Because you're not broken, you're patterned. And patterns can be rewritten.

FROM JUDGMENT TO UNDERSTANDING

It's easy to write people off. To call someone manipulative, dramatic, cold, or toxic and walk away feeling justified. But what if those behaviors weren't about cruelty? What if they were just survival strategies dressed up as dysfunction? That's where real understanding begins.

Harm Isn't Always Hostile

Most people aren't trying to hurt others; they're trying to protect themselves. Traits that feel unbearable from the outside, emotional outbursts, stonewalling, and controlling behavior often began as defenses. Not chosen, not malicious, just inherited or developed in response to pain.

A person who lashes out may have learned early that anger was the only way to get noticed. A person who shuts down may have grown up in a home where feelings weren't safe. Seen through this lens, harmful behaviors start to look a lot more like wounded ones.

From "What's Wrong With You?" to "What Happened to You?"

This shift in question changes everything. Instead of seeing someone as broken, we begin to see them as burdened. That doesn't mean we excuse abusive behavior or drop our boundaries. It means we add compassion to the equation.

Asking what happened doesn't deny the damage; it expands our understanding of the why. It helps us step back from judgment long enough to glimpse the person beneath the pattern.

We All Carry Something

Nobody is immune to stress, fear, or trauma, which means that nobody is immune to acting in ways that mirror personality disorder traits from time to time. You don't have to be diagnosed to relate to the struggle.

- Have you ever lashed out and regretted it?
- Have you pulled away because you didn't know how to ask for what you needed?
- Have you tried to control something (or someone) because everything else felt out of control?

Welcome to the club. Awareness isn't about shaming ourselves. It's about being honest enough to say, "Yeah, I've been there. I get it."

Language Matters

Words are powerful. They shape perception, influence treatment, and either open or shut the door to empathy. Terms like "crazy," "psycho," or even casually thrown-around diagnoses like "narcissist" aren't just flippant, they're harmful.

Changing how we speak about mental health isn't about being politically correct. It's about making room for dignity, for healing, and for human complexity. When we replace labels with curiosity, we start seeing the whole person, not just the symptom.

Compassion Is a Skill

Understanding personality disorders doesn't mean letting people off the hook. It means holding space for both accountability and empathy. It means honoring your own boundaries while recognizing that some behaviors are echoes of deeper wounds.

If you walk away from this chapter with one thing, let it be this: most people aren't trying to be difficult. They're trying to survive something. And once we see that, our responses get softer, smarter, and a whole lot more effective.

EXERCISE: PATTERN RECOGNITION MAP

Let's bring this all home.

You've just explored how personality traits can go from everyday quirks to deeply embedded patterns, and how they often hide in plain sight. Now, it's time to take what you've learned and apply it to your own life. This isn't about diagnosing anyone. It's about making sense of the patterns that leave you feeling confused, drained, or unsure of yourself.

This is a gentle, judgment-free check-in.

Step 1: Who Comes to Mind?

Think of one person whose behavior has repeatedly confused, hurt, or unsettled you. Not just a one-off moment, but a recurring dynamic, something that feels like déjà vu in all the wrong ways.

It could be:

- A family member who always makes you feel like the bad guy.
- A partner who pulls you in close and then pushes you away.
- A friend who disappears when things get too real.

Step 2: What's the Pattern?

Now, get specific. What behaviors do you keep seeing?

Some examples:

- emotional withdrawal
- guilt-tripping or passive-aggressive comments
- explosive reactions over small things
- needing control over plans, decisions, or people

Write them down. Don't censor. Don't justify. Just notice.

Step 3: What Might Be Underneath It?

Here's where we shift the lens from "What's wrong with them?" to "What might be going on underneath?"

Ask yourself:

- What fears might be driving this behavior? (Abandonment, shame, rejection?)
- What needs might be going unmet? (Validation, safety, autonomy?)

You don't need to be a therapist to reflect with compassion. You just need to be curious.

Step 4: What's Yours to Learn?

Now, turn inward:

- What does this pattern stir up in you?

- Where do you tend to over-function, under-react, or lose your voice in this dynamic?
- What boundary might you need to hold more clearly?
- What insight do you want to carry forward?

Journal prompt: Think about what this person might be afraid of, or what kind of emotional armor they've built over time. Now ask yourself: what's one boundary you can hold, or one truth you can carry forward, that protects your peace without shutting down your compassion?

THE BIGGER PICTURE

This isn't about fixing anyone. It's about seeing clearly. When you map the patterns around you, you begin to understand the emotional terrain of your relationships. And that clarity? It's the first step toward healing.

CHAPTER 4

THE ROLE OF THERAPY AND INTERVENTION

Healing from a personality disorder is rarely fast, rarely easy, and almost never linear. For many, change feels like walking into the unknown without a map, while carrying the weight of everything they've ever used to survive. Therapy does not offer a quick fix, but it does offer a path—one that is slow, relational, and often uncomfortable, but deeply human.

Therapy is about recognizing patterns that once made sense and learning when they no longer serve. For people living with personality disorders, those patterns often run so deep that they feel inseparable from their identity. Therapy helps them step back, see the pattern, and ask: Do I still need this?

Now, you will explore how therapy supports that process. It begins with why therapy is particularly important for personality disorders, then breaks down leading approaches, expectations, barriers, and alternative supports. Each section builds on the idea that recovery is not just about becoming someone new, but about returning to what has always been possible, beneath the defenses, beyond the diagnoses, and back toward the self.

WHY THERAPY MATTERS FOR PERSONALITY DISORDERS

Before diving into treatment models or techniques, it's worth asking: Why therapy? Why not self-help, willpower, or just "learning to do better"? For individuals with personality disorders, the challenge isn't a lack of insight or effort. It's that the very tools they've used to survive—emotional withdrawal, control, avoidance, manipulation, and overachievement—have become so automatic that they feel like second nature. Therapy makes those patterns visible. And it offers something that most people with personality disorders have never experienced consistently: a safe, stable relationship where they can be fully human without performance or punishment.

The following sections will unpack why therapy matters, what makes it work, and how different approaches meet different needs. But it begins with one core idea: healing happens in relationship. And therapy, when done well, becomes the rehearsal space for the kind of connection that can truly change a life.

Externalizing the Pattern: "This Is Something I Learned"

One of the most powerful shifts in therapy for personality disorders comes when a person stops saying, "This is just who I am" and begins to understand, "This is something I learned." That moment, quiet, often hard-won, creates a space for change. It draws a line between the self and the behaviors, between identity and adaptation.

Many traits associated with personality disorders were not consciously chosen. They were picked up through repetition, reinforced by survival, and eventually mistaken for core personality. A child who learned to stay quiet to avoid punishment may grow into an adult who believes their needs are a burden. Someone who learned to manipulate for attention might grow up convinced that direct communication never works. These aren't random behaviors; they are learned responses to real conditions.

Therapy helps a person recognize that these patterns were once adaptive. They worked for a while. But as the context changes, the same strategies can become restrictive, even harmful. What once protected someone may now isolate them. What once offered control may now create chaos. When the person can identify a behavior as learned, they no longer feel trapped by it. They begin to ask: Is this still helping me?

This psychological distancing is called externalization. It doesn't mean avoiding accountability. In fact, it often leads to more responsibility, because the person now believes they can choose differently. Instead of saying, "I'm just difficult," they start saying, "I react this way when I feel unsafe." That shift opens the door to skill-building, emotional insight, and self-compassion.

According to the National Alliance on Mental Illness (NAMI), therapy encourages individuals to challenge ingrained beliefs and assumptions, many of which were formed in environments that no longer exist. This challenge isn't about blame; it's about ownership. When someone sees their behaviors as conditioned rather than fixed, they begin to reclaim their agency (National Alliance on Mental Illness, 2025).

Understanding that patterns were learned allows people to start unlearning them. And unlearning, while uncomfortable, is the beginning of healing.

The Therapist as a Relational Blueprint

For many people with personality disorders, trust is not assumed; it is earned slowly, if at all. Early relationships may have taught them that affection comes with conditions, safety can be revoked without warning, and vulnerability leads to rejection or punishment. In this context, therapy becomes more than a place to talk. It becomes the first space in which a different kind of relationship is possible.

Therapists working with personality disorders must become what some call a "corrective emotional experience." This doesn't mean acting as a surrogate parent or rescuer. Instead, it means showing up consistently, responding with boundaries instead of threats, and remaining emotionally present even when the client tests those limits. These moments, where the therapist does not abandon, retaliate, or collapse, become profoundly healing.

Over time, therapy can provide a template for how healthy relationships function. It models honesty without cruelty, disagreement without rupture, and connection without control. This consistent experience allows the client to internalize new relational patterns. They begin to expect calm instead of chaos, repair instead of rejection.

Ardito and Rabellino (2011) found that the strength of the therapeutic alliance is one of the most important predictors of success in psychotherapy, especially for individuals with relationally rooted disorders. It's not just about what technique is used; it's about how safe the person feels while using it. In cases of chronic emotional dysregulation, abandonment fears, or mistrust, the relationship is the intervention.

Eventually, the therapist is no longer needed to supply this safety. The client begins to offer it to themselves. But before that can happen, they must first feel it in the presence of another. Therapy provides that experience, steady, imperfect, human, and through it, the possibility of new relational patterns begins to take root.

Ardito, R. B., & Rabellino, D. (2011). Therapeutic alliance and outcome of psychotherapy: Historical excursus, measurements, and prospects for research. *Frontiers in Psychology*, *2*, 270 (Ardito & Rabellino, 2011).

Psychoeducation as Empowerment

Understanding what's happening is often the first moment of relief. For many people with personality disorders, their inner experience has long felt confusing, overwhelming, or shameful. They may have been told they were "too much," "too sensitive," or "impossible to deal with," but rarely offered any explanation for why they think or feel the way they do. Psychoeducation changes that.

In therapy, psychoeducation refers to the process of learning about symptoms, diagnoses, treatment options, and coping mechanisms. It's not a dry academic exercise. It's an act of self-respect. When clients can name their experiences, they can start understanding them. And when they understand them, they can start navigating them more skillfully.

This process also helps dismantle stigma. Instead of framing behaviors as moral failings or personality defects, psychoeducation shows how these traits developed. It offers context. For example, learning that black-and-white thinking is a common cognitive distortion in Borderline Personality Disorder doesn't excuse every outburst, but it does offer a framework. That knowledge becomes a map, not a justification, but even a basic map can make unfamiliar terrain easier to cross.

Knowledge also reduces shame. When someone sees their experience reflected in clinical descriptions or real-world examples, they stop feeling defective. They begin to realize they are not alone and not beyond help. According to a study published in *The Journal of Psychiatric and Mental Health Nursing*, psychoeducation improves treatment engagement and client outcomes by increasing self-efficacy and perceived control (CADDY et al., 2011).

When people understand the what and why of their patterns, they can make more intentional choices about how to respond. They start setting boundaries, asking better questions, and catching distortions in real time. Psychoeducation becomes the foundation for practical change.

EVIDENCE-BASED APPROACHES

Therapy is not one-size-fits-all. What works for one person may feel completely ineffective, or even harmful, for another. That's especially true when working with personality disorders, which often involve longstanding patterns, emotional sensitivity, and trust challenges. Choosing the right therapeutic approach requires nuance, patience, and often, trial and error.

The good news is that there are several evidence-based therapies developed specifically to address the complexities of personality disorders. These transcend casual frameworks or trends; they've been studied, refined, and validated through years of clinical research and lived experience.

Each approach offers something different: skills training, emotional regulation, deeper insight, behavioral change, or relational repair. Some clients benefit most from structured techniques. Others need space for reflection and meaning-making. What matters most is finding a model and a therapist that fits the person's needs, not forcing the person to fit the model.

Dialectical Behavior Therapy (DBT)

Dialectical Behavior Therapy, or DBT, was originally developed by psychologist Marsha Linehan to treat Borderline Personality Disorder. It has since become one of the most widely used and researched therapies for emotional dysregulation, impulsivity, and relationship instability, traits that commonly appear in Cluster B personality disorders.

What makes DBT unique is its balance between acceptance and change. Clients learn to hold two truths at once: "I'm doing the best I can" and "I need to do better." This approach reduces shame while encouraging growth. It doesn't ask the person to abandon their emotions. It teaches them how to work with those emotions skillfully.

DBT is structured and skills-based. Clients often participate in both individual therapy and group skills training. The treatment focuses on four core skill areas:

- **Mindfulness:** learning to observe thoughts and emotions without being overwhelmed by them
- **Distress tolerance:** Building tools to survive emotional crises without resorting to harmful behaviors
- **Emotion regulation:** Identifying, labeling, and managing intense emotional states
- **Interpersonal effectiveness:** Navigating relationships with more confidence and clarity

One of DBT's strengths is that it addresses the emotional reactivity that makes other forms of therapy difficult for some individuals with personality disorders. It helps people pause, reflect, and regulate before reacting, giving them more choice in how they respond to life.

According to the Mayo Clinic, DBT has been shown to reduce suicidal behavior, self-harm, and emotional instability in people with Borderline Personality Disorder and related conditions. It's especially effective when practiced consistently and supported by a strong therapeutic alliance (Mayo Clinic, 2024).

Cognitive Behavioral Therapy (CBT)

Cognitive Behavioral Therapy, or CBT, is one of the most widely used and studied forms of psychotherapy. While not originally designed for personality disorders, it has been adapted over time to help address the rigid thought patterns, emotional responses, and behavior loops that characterize many PDs.

At its core, CBT helps people examine the link between their thoughts, feelings, and actions. It's based on the idea that the way we interpret situations, often without realizing it, shapes how we feel and responds. For individuals with personality disorders, these interpretations can be distorted by early experiences, chronic stress, or trauma, leading to automatic reactions that feel justified but are ultimately self-defeating.

CBT invites clients to slow down those automatic reactions and asks: What am I telling myself right now? Is that story true? What might be another explanation? This practice, over time, builds self-awareness and cognitive flexibility.

A major strength of CBT is its structure. It often includes homework assignments, worksheets, and specific behavioral experiments. These give clients a way to test their assumptions in real-life situations and gather evidence for new perspectives. It's less about analyzing the past and more about changing what happens in the present.

For example, someone with Avoidant Personality Disorder might believe, "If I speak up, I'll be humiliated." CBT would help them challenge that belief, explore where it came from, and practice behaviors that disprove it. Over time, this process can reduce avoidance, build confidence, and create a sense of agency.

The American Psychological Association notes that CBT is effective for reducing anxiety, depression, and maladaptive behaviors in people with personality disorders. It's especially useful for clients who are ready to reflect, willing to track patterns, and motivated to engage with structured tasks (American Psychological Association, 2021).

Schema Therapy

Schema Therapy was developed by Dr. Jeffrey Young as an expansion of traditional CBT, designed to address deeper-rooted emotional patterns that begin in childhood. While CBT targets surface-level thoughts and behaviors, Schema Therapy goes further by exploring the core beliefs, or schemas, that shape a person's entire sense of self and their relationships.

Schemas are deeply embedded mental frameworks formed from unmet emotional needs, repeated early experiences, and internalized messages. For individuals with personality disorders, these schemas often revolve around themes like abandonment, mistrust, emotional deprivation, or unworthiness. They operate like invisible filters, coloring every interaction with assumptions that feel absolute: "People will always leave," "I can't trust anyone," or "I'll never be good enough."

Schema Therapy helps people identify these core beliefs and trace them back to their origins. Once a schema is recognized, the work becomes about disrupting its hold, using a combination of cognitive, experiential, and behavioral techniques. This might include imagery work, chair dialogues (where the person voices different parts of themselves), or reparenting techniques within the therapy relationship.

One of the key ideas in Schema Therapy is the concept of "modes." These are moment-to-moment emotional states that reflect different aspects of the personality. For example, someone might shift between a vulnerable child mode, a punitive inner critic, and an avoidant protector. Therapy helps the client learn to recognize these modes, reduce the power of harmful ones, and strengthen the healthy adult part of themselves.

Schema Therapy is particularly effective for Avoidant, Borderline, Narcissistic, and Dependent Personality Disorders. According to the International Society of Schema Therapy (ISST), this approach has shown significant clinical success in long-term treatment, especially for clients who haven't responded well to shorter-term therapies (Lockwood, 2008).

Mentalization-Based Therapy (MBT)

Mentalization-Based Therapy, or MBT, was developed by Peter Fonagy and Anthony Bateman to help individuals better understand their own minds and the minds of others. It focuses on a skill many people take for granted: the ability to reflect on internal states, emotions, thoughts, beliefs, and to recognize that other people have those inner experiences, too.

For individuals with personality disorders, especially Borderline Personality Disorder, this capacity, called "mentalizing," is often disrupted. Under emotional stress, people may lose the ability to interpret their own behavior or others' accurately. This can lead to assumptions, reactivity, and ruptured relationships. MBT is designed to restore and strengthen this capacity.

In practice, MBT is less about giving advice and more about creating space to think. The therapist helps the client pause, consider different perspectives, and tolerate uncertainty. Instead of assuming, "They ignored me because they hate me," the client is encouraged to explore multiple possibilities: "Were they distracted? Did I misread the situation? Could something else be going on?"

This process helps reduce impulsivity, defensiveness, and the kind of black-and-white thinking that often fuels conflict. Over time, clients develop more stable identities and more nuanced views of the people around them. This has a direct impact on emotional regulation and relationship health.

The American Psychiatric Association notes that MBT has shown strong results for individuals with severe relational instability and chronic emotional dysregulation. Its emphasis on slowing down, thinking things through, and engaging reflectively makes it especially effective for people who struggle with interpersonal sensitivity and confusion around motives, both their own and others' (American Psychological Association, 2021).

Transference-Focused Psychotherapy (TFP)

Transference-Focused Psychotherapy, or TFP, was developed by Dr. Otto Kernberg to treat individuals with severe personality disorders, particularly Borderline and Narcissistic Personality Disorders. It is rooted in psychodynamic theory, with a focus on how unconscious patterns from early relationships shape current behaviors, especially in close interpersonal contexts.

The heart of TFP lies in the therapeutic relationship itself. Clients often bring the same fears, defenses, and relational dynamics into therapy that they experience in daily life. For example, someone who struggles with abandonment may view the therapist's boundaries as rejection. A person with narcissistic traits might interpret feedback as an attack. Rather than dismissing these reactions, TFP uses them as real-time opportunities for growth.

In this model, the therapist pays close attention to the emotional shifts and assumptions that arise in the room. These are viewed not as obstacles, but as windows into how the client experiences the world. Through structured, consistent interpretation and exploration, the therapist helps the client understand where these patterns come from, what triggers them, and how they affect relationships.

TFP doesn't avoid conflict. Instead, it provides a safe space to explore it. By working through intense emotional reactions in the moment, often called "transference episodes," clients begin to develop a more cohesive sense of self and a more realistic view of others. Over time, this reduces splitting (seeing others as all good or all bad), builds emotional regulation, and supports healthier attachment.

Research highlighted by the American Psychological Association shows that TFP is effective in reducing symptom severity, improving interpersonal functioning, and supporting long-term personality integration for individuals with complex personality disorders (American Psychological Association, 2021).

Acceptance and Commitment Therapy (ACT)

Acceptance and Commitment Therapy, or ACT (pronounced "act"), is a mindfulness-based behavioral therapy that helps individuals build psychological flexibility. Rather than trying to eliminate uncomfortable thoughts or feelings, ACT focuses on changing the relationship we have with those experiences. For individuals with personality disorders, where internal experiences can be intense, confusing, or shame-laden, this shift can be transformative.

ACT begins with the idea that pain is a natural part of life, but suffering often comes from how we respond to that pain. When someone avoids, suppresses, or tries to control their internal world at all costs, they often end up more stuck, not less. ACT teaches people to notice their thoughts without being dominated by them, and to stay present even when that feels difficult.

A core technique in ACT is called "cognitive defusion." Instead of accepting every thought as truth, clients learn to step back and see thoughts as passing mental events. For example, instead of thinking, "I'm worthless," ACT encourages a person to recognize, "I'm having the thought that I'm worthless." This slight shift creates space, and in that space, new responses become possible.

ACT also places a strong emphasis on values. Clients are encouraged to identify what truly matters to them, not what they've been told should matter, but what makes life meaningful on a personal level. Therapy then becomes about taking committed action toward those values, even in the presence of discomfort. This approach helps move people from avoidance to engagement.

ACT has shown effectiveness in helping people with a range of personality disorder traits, especially when avoidance, emotional numbing, or rigid thinking are present. According to a 2021 review published in *Clinical Psychology Review*, ACT has demonstrated promising outcomes for reducing experiential avoidance and improving overall functioning in clients with personality disorders (Swain et al., 2013).

THERAPY GOALS AND EXPECTATIONS

People often come to therapy hoping for a quick fix, something that will erase the pain, resolve the chaos, and make life feel stable again. But therapy for personality disorders isn't about erasing anything. It's about learning to live differently with the patterns that once felt automatic, unchangeable, or overwhelming.

The goals in this kind of work are not perfection or symptom elimination. They're about increasing self-awareness, building emotional range, and expanding relational capacity. Therapy helps people notice their internal experience, understand how it influences behavior, and make more intentional choices, even when those choices are hard.

This section looks at what meaningful progress really means in therapy. It explores the time it takes, the setbacks that happen, and the importance of finding the right therapeutic match. Because real growth isn't just measured by what gets better, but by what finally starts to make sense.

Not to Eliminate All Symptoms, but to Build Flexibility and Awareness

In therapy for personality disorders, success lies in becoming someone who recognizes the struggle earlier, responds to it with more flexibility, and learns to navigate it with greater self-awareness. That might not sound dramatic, but for many, it's life-changing.

You will never make all the symptoms disappear. Some traits may always show up under stress. What changes is how much power they have. A person who used to lash out or shut down might still feel the impulse, but now they notice it, pause, and choose a different response. That shift, from automatic reaction to intentional choice, is what therapy aims to cultivate.

This kind of growth is built through repetition, emotional risk, and practice in real-life situations. Over time, people learn to name their patterns, recognize their triggers, and develop a broader emotional range. They also start understanding their own motivations and needs more clearly, which strengthens their sense of agency.

According to the National Institute of Mental Health, effective therapy for personality disorders focuses on improving emotional regulation, interpersonal effectiveness, and identity clarity, not erasing discomfort, but making it manageable and meaningful (NIMH, n.d.).

When clients understand that growth means building capacity, not achieving perfection, they often feel more motivated and less ashamed. That understanding becomes the foundation for sustainable, compassionate progress.

Treatment Can Be Long-Term, Especially for Cluster B Disorders

Therapy for personality disorders is often not a short-term project. For many, it can take years of steady work to see meaningful and sustained change. This is particularly true for Cluster B disorders, such as Borderline, Narcissistic, and Antisocial Personality Disorders, where emotional intensity, relational volatility, and defensive patterns tend to be deeply ingrained.

These traits didn't develop overnight, and they won't unravel overnight either. In fact, much of the early work in therapy is about building trust and emotional safety. Clients may need time just to feel secure enough to open up, let alone explore painful memories or challenge long-standing beliefs. Progress may appear slow from the outside, but internally, the person may be doing the hard work of unlearning survival strategies that once felt like truth.

Long-term therapy allows space for these layers to unfold. It gives clients room to regress and recover, to test new behaviors, and to return after setbacks without fear of being dismissed or pathologized. According to the National Institute for Health and Care Excellence (NICE), long-term therapy has been associated with better emotional stability, reduced risk behaviors, and improved quality of life for individuals with complex personality disorders (National Institute for Health and Care Excellence, 2009).

Therapy becomes less about fixing and more about building: building emotional regulation, relationship skills, identity coherence, and internal stability. Over time, these gains become durable, not because change was rushed, but because it was rooted.

Progress Is Non-Linear

In therapy, especially for personality disorders, progress rarely moves in a straight line. There are moments of clarity and relief, followed by setbacks that feel like a return to square one. This isn't a failure of the person or the process. It's a normal part of how change unfolds.

When a person begins to challenge long-standing patterns, they also stir up the fears, memories, and defenses that those patterns were built to manage. That can lead to emotional pushback. Someone who starts setting boundaries might suddenly feel guilt or shame. A client who begins trusting may experience a wave of panic and pull away. These aren't signs that therapy isn't working. They're signs that it's getting to the heart of the issue.

Non-linear progress also reflects the complexity of human behavior. A breakthrough in one area doesn't always mean immediate change across the board. A person might become better at managing anger, yet still struggle with abandonment fears. That unevenness is expected and often temporary.

Therapists help normalize these ups and downs. They track patterns over time, reinforce small wins, and support clients in riding out emotional turbulence. According to the *British Journal of Psychiatry*, understanding that setbacks are part of the recovery process improves client retention and helps prevent the dropouts that often derail long-term progress (BATEMAN & FONAGY, 2010).

Therapist-Client Fit Is Essential

No matter how effective a therapy model is on paper, it won't make an impact if the relationship between therapist and client doesn't work in practice. A strong therapeutic bond, sometimes called the working alliance, is one of the most consistent predictors of positive outcomes, especially for personality disorders, where trust and relational safety are central concerns.

Therapist-client fit doesn't mean finding someone who agrees with everything or makes therapy feel easy. It means finding someone who communicates in a way that feels respectful, understands your emotional language, and holds a safe space for both challenge and support. For many clients, especially those with histories of relational trauma, this is the first time they've experienced such a dynamic.

When the fit is right, therapy feels collaborative, even when it's difficult. The client feels seen, but also held accountable. Misattunements still happen, but they're addressed and repaired, not ignored or dismissed. These moments of repair are powerful in themselves. They model what healthy conflict resolution looks like, building trust not through perfection, but through consistency.

Research published in *Psychotherapy Research* shows that therapist-client match, particularly around communication style, cultural sensitivity, and emotional tone, can significantly influence both engagement and long-term treatment outcomes (Norcross & Wampold, 2011).

Finding the right therapist can take time, and switching therapists is not a failure; it's part of advocating for your needs. Therapy isn't about fitting yourself into someone else's method. It's about finding a guide who can meet you where you are and walk alongside you as you grow.

BARRIERS TO TREATMENT

If therapy were simply a matter of desire, more people would be in it, and staying in it. But many individuals who could benefit from treatment face real, persistent barriers. These obstacles aren't just personal; they're systemic, cultural, and financial. And they often hit hardest for those living with personality disorders, where the very symptoms of the condition can make accessing or trusting support more difficult.

Some barriers are visible, like cost, availability, or lack of nearby services. Others are harder to spot: a history of being dismissed by professionals, internal resistance to change, or growing up in an environment where mental health support was stigmatized or never even discussed.

Stigma Around Seeking Help for PDs

Stigma is one of the most enduring and invisible walls between people and the help they need. When it comes to personality disorders, the stigma can be especially harsh. These conditions are often misunderstood, even within clinical spaces. They're framed as "difficult," "manipulative," or "untreatable," rather than as legitimate and deeply rooted psychological patterns.

This judgment doesn't just come from outside. Many individuals internalize these labels long before ever entering a therapy room. If you've been told that your pain is just a character flaw or that your behaviors make you "too much," you may start to believe therapy isn't for people like you. That kind of internalized stigma creates shame, and shame shuts doors.

Misdiagnosis or Being Labeled "Untreatable"

A major barrier to care is misdiagnosis, or no diagnosis at all. Personality disorders can present in complex, overlapping ways. When clinicians aren't properly trained in assessment, people may be labeled with anxiety, depression, or trauma-related disorders without a deeper look into enduring personality patterns.

Even worse, some people are told outright that their disorder is "too difficult to treat." That phrase sticks. It leads many to stop trying, believing the problem isn't solvable. But newer evidence-based treatments, like DBT and Schema Therapy, are specifically designed to meet these challenges. The problem isn't the client; it's a mental health system that hasn't always caught up to the research.

Financial and Access Limitations

Even for those who want treatment, the cost can be prohibitive. Long-term therapy, often necessary for personality disorders, is rarely covered fully by insurance. Specialized treatments may not be available outside of urban centers. And in many places, waitlists are months long.

For marginalized communities, the problem is even more acute. Finding a therapist who understands your cultural context, language, or life experience shouldn't be a luxury, but it often is. These access barriers aren't just logistical; they're structural. And they require systemic solutions, not just personal resilience.

Resistance or Lack of Insight

Another layer of difficulty is that personality disorders often include defenses that make self-reflection difficult. This isn't denial, it's protection. Behaviors that push people away, shut down vulnerability, or avoid emotion may have once been necessary for survival.

Therapy asks people to touch the very places they've spent years avoiding. That takes time. Some individuals don't immediately recognize that their patterns are contributing to their distress. Others fear what will happen if they let go of control. Resistance isn't failure. It's often the clearest signal that the work is getting close to something important.

Cultural Mistrust of Mental Health Systems

For many people, especially in historically marginalized communities, the idea of therapy carries deep cultural mistrust. That mistrust isn't imagined. Mental health systems have excluded, misdiagnosed, or pathologized people of color, LGBTQ+ individuals, and those living in poverty for decades.

When the system itself has been unsafe, walking into a therapist's office can feel like a risk. It's not enough to say, "Get help." Help has to feel safe, accessible, and inclusive. Culturally competent care isn't a bonus; it's a basic requirement for treatment that works.

Recognizing these barriers doesn't excuse the lack of access, but it does validate why many people hesitate. The good news is that the field is evolving. Therapists are becoming more trauma-informed, more culturally aware, and more flexible in how they approach personality disorders. The more we name these barriers, the easier they are to challenge, and eventually, to dismantle.

SUPPORT SYSTEMS BEYOND THERAPY

Therapy is powerful, but it doesn't exist in a vacuum. What happens in the therapist's office needs to be supported, echoed, and reinforced in the rest of a person's life. For those living with personality disorders, healing often depends not just on internal insight but on external support, relationships, resources, and environments that reinforce safety and change.

Peer Support Groups

Sometimes the most healing words aren't "you're fine," they're "me too." Peer support groups offer something formal therapy can't: shared lived experience. Whether it's a DBT skills group, an ACA (Adult Children of Alcoholics) meeting, or a local NAMI (National Alliance on Mental Illness) chapter, these spaces normalize struggle and reduce isolation.

In groups like these, people learn to speak a common language. They practice setting boundaries, offering feedback, and holding space for others. For many, it's the first time they've felt understood without having to explain or defend themselves. That sense of connection alone can be stabilizing.

Psychoeducational Resources

Books, podcasts, online workshops, and guided journals can all deepen a person's understanding of their experience. These resources extend the work of therapy and give people ways to learn at their own pace. They're also a lifeline for those waiting for access to formal treatment or living in areas with limited mental health services.

Quality matters, though. With so much content available online, it's important to seek out resources grounded in evidence-based approaches and created by qualified professionals. A well-curated reading list can be just as transformative as a session, especially when it helps someone name what they've been feeling for years.

Skills-Based Groups

Skills groups, especially those rooted in DBT or CBT, provide practical tools for managing emotions, improving communication, and coping with stress. These are often offered in clinics, hospitals, or private practice settings. While they may not dive into personal history as deeply as individual therapy, they're invaluable for building emotional muscle.

Participants practice techniques in real time, get immediate feedback, and see their progress reflected in others. The accountability of the group setting can also help people stay consistent, especially when motivation dips or symptoms spike.

Family Therapy

Healing doesn't happen in isolation, and sometimes the most powerful shifts occur when the family system begins to change. Family therapy helps loved ones understand what the person is going through, how their behaviors might unknowingly reinforce patterns, and what healthier dynamics can look like.

This isn't about blame. It's about understanding. Many people with personality disorders come from environments where needs were ignored, emotions were unsafe, or boundaries were blurred. When the family is willing to examine its own role and grow alongside the individual, therapy gains traction faster.

Support systems don't replace therapy, but they do surround it. They offer reinforcement, accountability, and belonging. In the best cases, they become the scaffolding for a life that can hold the weight of real change.

REFLECTION EXERCISE: REWRITING WHAT THERAPY MEANS TO YOU

Therapy is often misunderstood. It's seen as something people turn to when they've "failed" to cope, or when things get so bad that there's no other option. But as this chapter has shown, therapy is not a last resort; it's a long-term investment in self-understanding, growth, and freedom from patterns that no longer serve you.

This exercise is designed to help you pause, look back on what you've learned, and begin reshaping your relationship with the idea of therapy.

Step 1: What Have You Believed?

Write down what you were taught, explicitly or implicitly, about therapy.

- Was it for people who are weak, dangerous, broken?
- Did your culture, family, or upbringing talk about therapy at all?
- Have you ever judged yourself for needing help?

Step 2: What Are You Rethinking?

Now reflect on what's shifted.

- After reading this chapter, what new truths feel possible?
- What ideas about therapy do you want to unlearn, or hold onto more firmly?
- Which therapy model or support system stood out to you, and why?

Step 3: Define Support on Your Terms

If therapy or healing didn't come with shame or fear, what kind of support would you seek?

- Describe what a healthy support system might look like for you now.
- Name at least one concrete step you could take in the next month to explore support, whether that's reading more, reaching out, or reflecting deeper.

This isn't about rushing into anything. It's about giving yourself permission to approach therapy and healing with curiosity, rather than judgment.

Reminder

You are not a problem to be solved. You are a person learning how to live, and therapy is one tool in that journey. The decision to reach out, stay with the work, or even just think about it differently is, in itself, a meaningful act of change.

PART II

THE DISORDERS IN FOCUS

Personality disorders are not abstract diagnoses; we should think of them as lived realities. They shape how people see themselves, how they connect with others, and how they respond to a world that often feels confusing, threatening, or out of reach. In Part 1, we explored the broader terrain: how personality develops, how it can become disordered, and how therapy opens the door to growth. Now we narrow the lens.

In this section, we examine each personality disorder individually —Not to reduce people to labels, but to understand the emotional logic behind the patterns. Every chapter in part 2 is structured to highlight the human experience behind the diagnosis. We'll explore the official clinical criteria, but we'll go further, into the fears, needs, behaviors, and histories that give those criteria meaning.

Each disorder is presented with real-world examples, treatment insights, and practical strategies. Whether you're reading to understand yourself, support someone you care about, or deepen your knowledge of human behavior, the goal here is clarity and compassion.

The chapters ahead are designed to be both honest and hopeful. Personality disorders are difficult, but they are not life sentences. With the right tools, the right support, and the right framing, change is possible, and dignity can be restored where shame once lived.

We begin with one of the most widely misunderstood diagnoses: Borderline Personality Disorder.

CHAPTER 5

BORDERLINE PERSONALITY DISORDER (BPD)

THE NERVOUS SYSTEM ON HIGH ALERT

I magine waking up every morning with the emotional volume turned to ten. A look, a pause, a delayed reply, all can feel like rejection. One moment you're craving closeness, the next you're pushing it away. You don't know who you are without the people around you, yet being around them feels like walking on eggshells. This is the daily reality for many people living with Borderline Personality Disorder.

Borderline Personality Disorder (BPD) is one of the most stigmatized and misunderstood mental health conditions. Often mistaken for attention-seeking or emotional instability, BPD is more accurately understood as a disorder of emotional regulation, attachment, and self-perception. It's like living with a nervous system that registers threat in places others see safety.

We'll break down what BPD is and what it isn't. We'll explore the roots of its symptoms, the experiences that shape it, and the strategies that help people manage and even thrive. Most importantly, we'll listen. Behind every symptom is a story. And behind every reaction is a person trying to survive a world that often feels too much, too fast, and too fragile.

DSM-5-TR DIAGNOSTIC FEATURES OF BPD

According to the DSM-5-TR, Borderline Personality Disorder is characterized by a pervasive pattern of instability that begins in early adulthood and presents across contexts. To meet the diagnostic threshold, a person must exhibit five or more of the following nine symptoms:

1. **Frantic efforts to avoid real or imagined abandonment**
2. **A pattern of unstable and intense interpersonal relationships**
3. **Identity disturbance**
4. **Impulsivity in at least two areas that are potentially self-damaging**
5. **Recurrent suicidal behavior or self-mutilation**
6. **Affective instability due to mood reactivity**
7. **Chronic feelings of emptiness**
8. **Inappropriate, intense anger or difficulty controlling anger**
9. **Transient stress-related paranoid ideation or dissociative symptoms**

But behind the list is a person navigating a world that often feels emotionally unsafe. These behaviors aren't random; they are adaptive strategies developed to manage fear, rejection, confusion, and emotional pain. For many, they are the residue of environments where connection was conditional, boundaries were unclear, or emotional expression was punished.

Case Snapshot: Tankuilga

Tankuilga, 35, has always struggled with relationships. He quickly attaches to people who show him kindness, but feels devastated when they don't respond to a message or cancel plans. One week, he's applying for new jobs with confidence. Next, he feels like a failure with no identity outside of his romantic partner. He drinks heavily some nights to cope with emptiness, and after an argument, he once impulsively drove for hours, unsure of where he was going. Therapy helped Tankuilga understand that these patterns weren't signs of being broken; they were patterns that made sense in the context of his early life, where emotional needs were consistently invalidated or ignored.

PREVALENCE OF BPD

Borderline Personality Disorder is more common than many people realize. The National Institute of Mental Health estimates that approximately 1.6% of the general population meets the criteria for BPD. However, some studies suggest the true prevalence may be closer to 5.9%, depending on the population studied and the assessment tools used (Grant et al., 2008).

In clinical settings, BPD is especially prevalent. Research suggests that up to 20% of psychiatric inpatients and around 10% of outpatients meet criteria for the disorder (APA, 2022). These figures underscore just how often BPD shows up where emotional pain runs deep, and how important it is for clinicians to recognize the signs early.

GENDER MYTHS

For decades, Borderline Personality Disorder has been stereotypically associated with women. Popular media and even some clinical literature have perpetuated the idea that BPD is a "female disorder," tied to emotional volatility or instability. But this belief is not supported by current research.

While it's true that women are more frequently diagnosed with BPD, studies suggest that the actual prevalence is similar across genders. The discrepancy lies more in how symptoms are interpreted. Men with BPD may express their distress through anger, substance use, or externalizing behaviors, traits that often lead to different diagnoses, such as Antisocial Personality Disorder or PTSD (Sansone & Sansone, 2011).

This diagnostic bias matters. It can delay treatment, skew research, and reinforce damaging stereotypes. It also places many men with BPD in clinical limbo, treated for surface symptoms, while the deeper disorder remains unrecognized.

Case Snapshot: Devon

Devon, 31, had been in and out of substance use programs for years. He was labeled as aggressive and resistant to treatment, especially when he lashed out during moments of perceived betrayal. It wasn't until a therapist began exploring his history of emotional neglect, abandonment fears, and unstable identity that the correct diagnosis emerged. With targeted support, Devon began to build emotional regulation skills and reframe his relationships, not just with others, but with himself.

LINK TO COMPLEX TRAUMA AND INVALIDATION

Borderline Personality Disorder doesn't emerge out of nowhere. While no single cause explains its development, a consistent pattern across research and clinical practice links BPD to early experiences of trauma, neglect, and emotional invalidation. Many individuals with BPD grew up in environments where their needs were ignored, their feelings were dismissed, or their safety was inconsistent.

This isn't always about overt abuse. Sometimes it's about growing up in a household where love was conditional, or emotions were seen as weaknesses. Invalidation can be subtle, being told to "toughen up," "stop overreacting," or that "nothing's wrong" when something clearly is. Over time, this can teach a child to doubt their internal experience, question their emotional reality, and suppress their needs to maintain connection.

Research supports this connection. A 2006 study published in *Child Abuse & Neglect* found that individuals with BPD were significantly more likely to report histories of childhood abuse, emotional neglect, or early loss compared to control groups (Zanarini et al., 2006).

Case Snapshot: Welhore

Welhore, 27, was the high-achieving daughter of emotionally distant parents. She learned early on that her success earned praise, but her sadness or fear earned silence. As an adult, Welhore found herself in relationships where she couldn't express anger without fearing abandonment. Therapy helped her connect the dots: her deep emotional responses weren't a flaw; they were the result of years spent hiding what she truly felt.

Understanding BPD through the lens of complex trauma shifts the conversation. It removes blame and brings compassion.

FEAR OF ABANDONMENT

Fear of abandonment is one of the most defining and painful traits of Borderline Personality Disorder. It's more than just feeling sad when someone leaves; this is when you experience the potential for disconnection as a threat to one's very sense of safety.

This fear can be triggered by small, everyday events: a delayed text, a partner seeming distracted, a friend rescheduling plans. For someone with BPD, these moments are loaded with meaning. The nervous system responds as if danger is imminent, activating a cascade of emotional and physical responses.

At the root of this fear is often a deep history of relational inconsistency. Many people with BPD grew up in environments where love and attention were unpredictable. As a result, the brain and body learned to monitor for signs of rejection constantly.

Case Snapshot: Noaga

Noaga, 24, recently started dating someone new. In the early weeks, the connection felt electric. But when his partner took a few hours to reply to a message, Noaga spiraled. He imagined being ghosted, felt waves of panic, and began drafting a breakup message just to feel in control. Later, he felt ashamed and confused. In therapy, Jordan realized his reaction wasn't about the message delay; it was a pattern. As a child, Noaga's caregivers frequently disappeared emotionally when he needed them most. That early absence wired his system to interpret uncertainty as abandonment.

Implementation Exercise: Reframing the Trigger

This reflective exercise is designed to help you slow down during a moment of perceived abandonment and bring clarity to what's actually happening.

1. **Recall a recent triggering moment:**
   - What event sparked a strong fear of being abandoned?
2. **Break it down:**
   - What was the exact trigger?
   - What thoughts immediately followed?
   - What physical or emotional reactions did you notice?
3. **Ask: What does this remind me of?**
   - Is there an earlier memory where you felt a similar fear or panic?
   - Was the reaction larger than the situation warranted?
4. **Reframe the narrative:**
   - How else could you interpret the event if abandonment weren't the explanation?
   - What would you say to a friend in your shoes?
5. **Ground yourself:**
   - Use a calming technique: deep breathing, holding something warm, or repeating a grounding statement like: "This feeling is old. The threat isn't real right now."

Practice doesn't erase the pattern, but it opens a window between feeling and action, long enough to choose something different.

BEHAVIORAL RESPONSES

When the fear of abandonment is activated, the response is often immediate and intense. For someone with BPD, the internal alarm system is wired to detect loss, rejection, or disconnection at high sensitivity.

Some individuals respond by clinging tightly. They may call repeatedly, text nonstop, or seek constant reassurance. Others react in the opposite direction, cutting people off abruptly, walking away first, or creating emotional distance.

Sometimes, the behavior is confusing even to the person acting it out. There may be a compulsion to test others: to see if someone will chase them, forgive them, or prove their loyalty.

Implementation Exercise: Pause Before the Push or Pull

This practice can help reduce reactive behavior during moments of fear or conflict.

1. **Notice the impulse:**
   - Are you about to send a long text, cut someone off, or say something sharp?
2. **Label what's happening:**
   - Ask yourself: "What am I feeling right now?"
   - Is it fear, shame, sadness, or loneliness?
3. **Ask: What am I trying to protect?**
   - Are you afraid of being hurt, ignored, or rejected?
4. **Try a holding response:**
   - Instead of acting immediately, commit to waiting 10 minutes.
   - Use a grounding technique or journal the urge.

5. **Return with clarity:**
    - After the pause, revisit the situation. What do you really want to say or do that reflects your deeper need?

Changing behavior takes repetition, not perfection. Each pause is a step toward safety without sabotage.

Craving Closeness But Fearing Its Loss

At the heart of BPD lies a paradox: an intense longing for closeness, paired with an equally intense fear that it will be taken away. This creates a relentless emotional tension. The need for connection is real and valid, but so is the fear that connection will eventually lead to pain.

This push-pull dynamic often leaves individuals exhausted and confused. They may idealize a friend or partner, feeling deeply bonded and emotionally fused. But the moment they sense emotional distance, even if imagined, fear kicks in. That fear can trigger anger, withdrawal, or panic, creating the very rupture they were trying to avoid.

Splitting (Idealization and Devaluation)

In Borderline Personality Disorder, relationships often feel like emotional roller coasters. One moment, someone feels like the safest person in the world; supportive, perfect, irreplaceable. Next, they seem cold, untrustworthy, or even cruel. This sudden shift isn't due to manipulation or a lack of gratitude. It's a psychological defense known as splitting.

Splitting refers to the inability to hold conflicting views of a person at the same time. Someone is either all good or all bad; there's little room for gray. This defense often develops in response to early relational trauma, where caregivers were inconsistent, unavailable, or abusive. For someone with BPD, learning to trust becomes complicated. It feels safer to idealize or devalue than to navigate the complex middle.

The emotional intensity behind splitting is real. When someone with BPD feels close, the connection feels absolute. But if they sense disappointment, rejection, or betrayal, the emotional whiplash can trigger panic or rage. It's not a conscious choice; it's a reflex meant to protect against pain.

Case Snapshot: Fatogoma

Fatogoma, 33, had a close relationship with their coworker, Tukum. They spent lunch breaks together, texted outside of work, and shared personal stories. One day, Tukum had to cancel plans due to a family emergency. Fatogoma felt crushed. Within hours, the narrative shifted: Tukum was selfish, unreliable, and fake. Fatogoma stopped speaking to her and unfollowed her on social media. A week later, Fatogoma regretted it, but didn't know how to explain the emotional shift without sounding irrational.

In therapy, Fatogoma explored how past experiences with abandonment shaped their all-or-nothing responses. Learning to recognize and name the split, rather than act on it, became the first step in developing emotional balance.

Implementation Exercise: The Gray Map

This tool helps individuals recognize black-and-white thinking in relationships and begin practicing emotional nuance.

1. **Choose a recent conflict or rupture:**
   o Who was involved?

- What triggered the emotional shift?
2. **List all the positive traits you associate with this person:**
   - Be honest about what you valued or admired.
3. **Now, list the negative traits or behaviors you've focused on since the rupture:**
   - Include the feelings those traits triggered.
4. **Identify the middle ground:**
   - What do both lists reveal about the complexity of this person?
   - What might explain the behavior without canceling the connection?
5. **Reframe with balance:**
   - Write one statement that includes both the good and the difficult. For example: "Maddie let me down when she canceled, but she's also been a supportive friend overall."

Emotional Intensity and Dysregulation

People with BPD absorb and amplify emotions, and often find themselves flooded by them. Emotional intensity is a core experience of the disorder. A seemingly small comment, delay, or shift in tone can unleash a wave of anger, panic, shame, or despair.

Research shows that individuals with BPD often have heightened sensitivity to emotional stimuli, paired with a slower return to emotional baseline (Glenn & Klonsky, 2009). In other words, they feel more, more quickly, and for longer periods.

Without the internal tools to regulate these spikes, emotions can become overwhelming. That's when dysregulation sets in. It might show up as lashing out, shutting down, withdrawing suddenly, or engaging in impulsive behaviors just to find relief.

Case Snapshot: Alyssa

Alyssa, 29, had always been described as "too sensitive" by her family. She would cry at minor criticisms and often felt emotionally raw even days after a small argument. During a team meeting, a coworker questioned her idea. Alyssa felt a surge of heat, her heart racing, and tears forming. She abruptly left the room. Later, she was filled with embarrassment, but couldn't explain why her reaction felt so out of proportion. In therapy, Alyssa began learning how quickly her emotional system became activated, and that this didn't mean she was weak. It meant her system had never learned how to recover.

Implementation Exercise: Name It to Regulate It

This exercise helps the reader begin identifying and labeling their emotional states as a first step toward regulation.

1. **Catch the moment:**
   - Reflect on a time when your emotional response felt overwhelming.
2. **Name the feeling:**
   - Was it anger, fear, shame, sadness, or a blend?
   - Use specific words (e.g., "embarrassed" instead of "bad").
3. **Rate the intensity:**
   - On a scale from 1 to 10, how strong was the emotion?
4. **What was the trigger?**
   - Try to pinpoint what happened just before the emotion surged.
5. **What helped, or what might have helped?**
   - Identify one strategy you used (or could use) to reduce the emotional load.

MOOD REACTIVITY

Mood reactivity is confusing to both clinicians and loved ones. It refers to the rapid, intense emotional shifts triggered by what others might see as minor events. These shifts aren't random; they are deeply tied to how a person with BPD experiences interpersonal stress, perceived rejection, or internal shame.

A neutral comment can lead to despair. A missed call might spark a full emotional collapse. These emotional states can be intense but short-lived, often changing within hours or even minutes.

For someone with BPD, the external world feels deeply personal. Validation can bring joy, but perceived slights or ambiguity can unleash a storm.

Case Snapshot: Poko

Poko, 22, was excited to see their friends after a long week. When they arrived at the restaurant and saw everyone already mid-conversation, they immediately felt excluded. Within minutes, Poko's mood plummeted. They stopped talking, avoided eye contact, and later left abruptly. That night, Poko cried for hours, convinced the group secretly disliked them. In reality, the friends had arrived just a few minutes earlier and didn't mean any harm, but Poko's emotional state was already overwhelmed.

Through therapy, Poko began to recognize that their mood shifts were often tied to perception rather than reality. Learning to slow down, ask clarifying questions, and regulate their nervous system became essential tools for rebalancing quickly.

Implementation Exercise: Mood Mapping

Use this exercise to track emotional shifts and identify the triggers behind them.

1. **Pick a three-day window:**
   ◦ Use a journal or phone notes to track emotional highs and lows.
2. **Label the emotions:**
   ◦ Each time you notice a change, name the new emotion.
   ◦ Rate its intensity on a scale from 1–10.
3. **Note the context:**
   ◦ What happened just before the shift?
   ◦ Who was around? What were you thinking?
4. **Look for patterns:**
   ◦ Were there common triggers?
   ◦ Were there moments you misread a situation?
5. **Reflect on recovery:**
   ◦ What helped your mood stabilize?
   ◦ What could you try next time?

Struggles With Emotional Modulation

Emotional modulation refers to the ability to shift, contain, or calm emotional responses in a healthy way. For many people with BPD, this process feels inaccessible. Once an emotion floods in, whether it's shame, anger, fear, or sadness, it can take over completely.

This difficulty regulating emotions doesn't mean a person is weak or unwilling. It often means they never had the chance to build the necessary tools. Many individuals with BPD grew up in environments where emotions weren't modeled, named, or accepted.

Instead of learning how to process feelings, they learned to avoid, suppress, or act them out.

Without reliable coping strategies, people may turn to impulsive behavior, yelling, isolating, self-harming, or substance use as a way to escape the internal storm.

Case Snapshot: Raogo

Raogo, 25, often found themselves overwhelmed by shame after small mistakes. After misplacing a work file, they panicked, left the office early, and spent the evening drinking alone. The next day, Raogo felt even worse, ashamed of their reaction but unsure how else to manage it. In therapy, Raogo began exploring how their childhood home lacked emotional safety. They had never been taught that distress could be tolerated without collapse.

As Raogo learned basic regulation techniques, like paced breathing, naming emotions, and checking the facts, they began to experience intense emotions without spiraling. It didn't erase the feelings, but it changed how those feelings were handled.

Implementation Exercise: The Regulation Toolkit

This activity helps readers begin to build a personal menu of emotional regulation tools.

1. **List three recent situations where you felt emotionally overwhelmed:**
   - What emotion did you feel?
   - What did you do in response?
2. **Now, imagine responding differently:**
   - What would it look like to stay with the feeling instead of acting on it?

- Could you pause, label the emotion, or speak it aloud?
3. **Write out three strategies that helped or could help:**
   - Examples: cold water on wrists, naming the feeling, walking away for five minutes.
4. **Create a calming routine:**
   - Design a 5–10 minute routine you can use when emotions start to rise.
   - Include at least one grounding technique and one validation statement (e.g., "I'm allowed to feel this. It won't last forever.")

Biological Roots

While BPD is shaped by environment and experience, there's growing evidence that biology also plays a role. Emotional sensitivity, impulsivity, and difficulty regulating mood are not only psychological; they're also linked to how the brain processes emotion.

Neuroscientific research has identified differences in brain structure and function in individuals with BPD. One of the most consistently studied areas is the amygdala, the part of the brain responsible for detecting threat and processing fear. People with BPD often have a hyperactive amygdala, which means they're more reactive to perceived danger or emotional cues (Silbersweig et al., 2007).

Meanwhile, the prefrontal cortex, which helps with reasoning, impulse control, and emotional regulation, may be underactive. This imbalance means the brain's alarm system fires quickly, while the parts responsible for calming it down and take longer to engage.

There are also links to serotonin imbalances, which affect mood stability, impulse control, and emotional reactivity. These biological vulnerabilities don't cause BPD on their own, but when combined with early relational trauma or invalidating environments, they can significantly increase the risk.

Impact on Relationships

For people living with BPD, relationships often feel like both a lifeline and a battlefield. The emotional intensity that characterizes BPD doesn't just stay inside; it spills into connections with friends, family members, partners, and coworkers. The highs can be euphoric, full of idealization, and emotional fusion. The lows, however, can be devastating.

BPD-related emotional dysregulation, mood reactivity, and fear of abandonment often make it difficult to sustain stable, reciprocal relationships. A small misstep can feel like betrayal. A missed message or a change in tone can spiral into panic or rage. These reactions may appear out of proportion to outsiders, but for the person with BPD, they reflect real, deeply rooted fears.

Case Snapshot: Shayla

Shayla, 34, had been in a romantic relationship for six months. She loved intensely, checking in frequently, planning surprises, and sharing everything. But if her partner seemed quiet or distracted, she would immediately assume something was wrong. She might accuse him of losing interest or withdraw completely to protect herself. This led to a cycle of conflict and confusion that neither of them knew how to stop.

Through therapy, Shayla learned that she was reenacting patterns from her childhood, when attention and love were unpredictable.

As she developed emotional awareness and practiced communication, she began to notice her own reactions before acting on them. Over time, her relationship stabilized, not because it became perfect, but because she became more grounded in herself.

Implementation Exercise: Repairing the Pattern

This exercise helps the reader reflect on relational patterns and build new responses.

1. **Think of a recent relationship conflict:**
   - What triggered the reaction?
   - How did you respond?
2. **Break the moment into parts:**
   - What emotion came up first?
   - What story did you tell yourself about the other person's behavior?
3. **Was it fact or fear?**
   - Ask: Was this reaction based on what actually happened, or on past experiences resurfacing?
4. **Name what you needed:**
   - What would have helped in that moment? Reassurance? Space? A clear boundary?
5. **Write one new way you could respond next time:**
   - For example: "When I feel ignored, I will pause before reacting and ask for clarification instead."

IDENTITY CONFUSION AND INNER EMPTINESS

People with BPD often describe a disorienting sense of not knowing who they are. Their self-image may shift from day-to-day, or even hour to hour, depending on who they're with or how secure they feel. Without a stable core identity, emotions tend to take the lead. Values may change based on the people around them. Beliefs, goals, and even tastes can fluctuate. This can make relationships complicated, careers unstable, and personal growth feel like walking on shifting ground.

Compounding this is a chronic sense of emptiness. Many people with BPD report feeling hollow, numb, or emotionally detached, not just during difficult times, but as a baseline state. This emptiness isn't boredom. It's the absence of self.

Case Snapshot: Yidi

Yidi, 27, had always adapted to fit in. In high school, she was artistic and introspective. In college, she became driven and competitive. In relationships, she mirrored her partner's values. But underneath all of it, Yidi felt like she was performing. When alone, she struggled to define what she wanted or believed. The more she tried to fill the void with roles, the deeper her sense of disconnection became.

Therapy helped Yidi begin naming what felt real versus what was shaped by fear or adaptation. By reconnecting with her core values and tolerating the discomfort of not knowing, she began to build a more stable sense of self.

Implementation Exercise: Building a Self-Map

This activity helps readers begin defining who they are, beyond external validation.

1. **Make two lists:**
   - List A: Things you've done, believed, or liked because others expected you to.
   - List B: Things you've done, believed, or liked that felt authentic, even if they weren't accepted.
2. **Compare and reflect:**
   - Which list feels more familiar? Which one feels more like you?
3. **Choose three items from List B:**
   - Why do these feel meaningful to you?
   - How might you nurture or expand them?
4. **Create a values snapshot:**
   - Write three words that describe the kind of person you want to be, regardless of how others respond.

Self-Harm and Impulsivity

Self-harming behaviors and impulsivity are often the most visible and alarming features of Borderline Personality Disorder, but they are also some of the most misunderstood. Self-harm, such as cutting or burning, may serve as a way to escape numbness, reduce emotional overload, or externalize invisible pain. Impulsive behaviors, like binge eating, reckless driving, substance use, or risky sex, are often acts of desperation to either feel something or stop feeling too much.

These behaviors typically emerge in moments of emotional crisis. They are survival strategies, not moral failures.

EXERCISE: EMOTIONAL TRIGGER JOURNAL

Understanding a trigger is the first step to disarming it. For people with BPD, emotional reactions often feel like explosions that go off without warning. But with practice, those moments can become less mysterious and more manageable.

This exercise is not about judgment or suppression. It's about observation. By tracing the thread between trigger, thought, emotion, and action, you can begin to see the map underneath the chaos. That map becomes the starting point for change.

Use this exercise regularly, once a day or after difficult emotional moments, to build self-awareness and emotional clarity over time.

1. **Describe the triggering moment**
   - What happened?
   - Who was involved?
   - Where were you?
2. **Name the thought that followed**
   - What story did your mind tell you in response?
   - Example: "They don't care," "I always mess things up," "I'm too much."
3. **Identify the emotion**
   - What were you feeling in that moment?
   - Try to be specific: shame, panic, anger, disappointment, fear.
4. **What action did you take?**
   - Did you lash out, shut down, cry, leave, text, or self-harm?
5. **Ask: What did I actually need?**
   - Rewind the moment and ask what might have helped instead.
   - Was it reassurance? Space? A reminder that you're safe?

6. **Try a reframe**
   - What might you say to yourself next time this happens?
   - Example: "This feels like abandonment, but maybe it's just silence."
7. **Optional reflection**
   - What pattern do you notice over time?
   - What coping tool would you like to try when this happens again?

CHAPTER 6

NARCISSISTIC PERSONALITY DISORDER

Narcissistic Personality Disorder is sold as arrogance or vanity. The truth is, it's about the hidden wounds beneath the surface, wounds that create a constant need for admiration and an unbearable sensitivity to shame.

We throw the word "narcissist" around casually. It shows up in gossip columns, breakup rants, and social media soundbites. But the clinical reality of Narcissistic Personality Disorder (NPD) is far more complex and far more painful. Behind the mask of superiority lies a fragile self-concept, one that depends heavily on external validation to stay intact. What looks like confidence on the surface is often a protective shell, an adaptation built to guard against emotional vulnerability.

Let's take a look at what NPD really is, how it develops, the many ways it shows up in people's lives, and most importantly, how healing and accountability can coexist.

WHAT IS NARCISSISTIC PERSONALITY DISORDER?

DSM-5-TR Diagnostic Features

Narcissistic Personality Disorder (NPD) is defined by a pattern of grandiosity, a deep need for admiration, and a marked lack of empathy. But unlike the popular caricature of a person who simply "loves themselves too much," NPD reflects a more fragile internal world. These individuals often experience significant fluctuations in self-esteem, depending almost entirely on how others see them.

The DSM-5-TR outlines several key features:

- a grandiose sense of self-importance
- preoccupation with fantasies of unlimited success, power, brilliance, or beauty
- belief in being special and unique
- excessive need for admiration
- a sense of entitlement
- interpersonally exploitative behavior
- lack of empathy
- envy of others or the belief that others are envious of them
- arrogant or haughty behavior

To meet diagnostic criteria, these traits must be pervasive, inflexible, and cause functional impairment in multiple areas of life, such as relationships, work, or emotional well-being. The disorder typically emerges in early adulthood and is often ego-syntonic, meaning that individuals may not see their behavior as problematic.

This is a framework for understanding persistent, patterned behavior that causes distress for the individual and those around them.

Prevalence

Estimates suggest that between 0.5% and 1% of the general population may meet the criteria for Narcissistic Personality Disorder (NPD), though findings vary depending on methodology and population sample (Stinson et al., 2008).

Part of the challenge in measuring prevalence is the nature of the disorder itself. Individuals with NPD rarely seek treatment on their own unless prompted by a crisis, like a breakup, job loss, or legal issue. Even in therapy, many struggle with self-awareness, making underreporting likely. In structured interviews, prevalence tends to be higher than in self-report surveys, pointing to denial or lack of insight as contributing factors.

Gender distribution also shows mixed results. Some studies suggest NPD is more frequently diagnosed in men, but this may reflect biases in diagnostic practices rather than true differences in prevalence. Cultural norms around assertiveness, emotion, and identity can shape how narcissistic traits present and how they are perceived.

Ultimately, prevalence is only a small part of the picture.

Differentiating NPD From Confidence

It's easy to confuse narcissistic traits with confidence, especially in a world that prizes charisma, assertiveness, and self-promotion. But the difference lies in what fuels those traits. Healthy confidence is rooted in internal security. It doesn't collapse when criticized or when someone else succeeds.

In contrast, Narcissistic Personality Disorder (NPD) relies heavily on external validation. Praise, admiration, and attention become emotional oxygen. Without it, the person may feel invisible, ashamed, or enraged. What looks like confidence may actually be a defense against deep self-doubt (Mayo Clinic, 2023).

A confident person can admit mistakes and tolerate being wrong. They can celebrate others' achievements without feeling diminished. Someone with NPD, however, may struggle with even minor criticism, interpret disagreement as betrayal, and need to control the narrative to preserve their fragile self-image.

This distinction is critical, especially in leadership roles, therapy settings, or relationships where surface traits can be misleading. The presence of assertiveness or ambition alone isn't enough to signal a problem; it's the rigidity, reactivity, and relational fallout that mark the difference.

Cultural Stereotypes vs. Clinical Reality

Narcissism has become a buzzword. It's used to describe ex-partners, celebrities, or anyone who posts too many selfies. But these cultural stereotypes often distort the clinical reality of Narcissistic Personality Disorder (NPD), reducing it to a caricature and missing the depth of psychological pain underneath.

Media portrayals typically spotlight over traits: arrogance, vanity, and manipulation. While these behaviors may appear in some individuals with NPD, they don't represent the full picture. Many people with narcissistic traits feel empty, ashamed, or chronically insecure. Their outward behavior may mask a deep fear of inadequacy that's difficult even for them to admit.

The clinical profile is nuanced. Not all individuals with NPD are flashy or dominant. Some may be quiet, self-effacing, or even socially withdrawn. The unifying thread is the fragility of the self and the need to manage that fragility through attention, control, or idealization (Ronningstam, 2023).

These realities are often lost in public discourse. When the term "narcissist" is used casually or just to drive a knife in the ribs, it adds stigma and blocks meaningful understanding.

THE FRAGILE SELF BEHIND THE MASK

People with Narcissistic Personality Disorder (NPD) didn't develop these patterns by choice. They're the result of early emotional experiences, experiences that shaped their sense of self, safety, and worth.

Developmental Origins

NPD, like most deeply rooted traits, often begins in childhood, but don't go blaming your parents just yet; peers play a role as well. The building blocks of narcissistic defenses are usually laid down early, sometimes in homes that look fine from the outside but are emotionally barren on the inside.

When emotional mirroring is inconsistent or absent, especially in environments marked by excessive criticism, unpredictable approval, or conditional love, the child learns to build an identity out of performance (Ronningstam, 2023).

Some grow up hearing that they're special, but only when they succeed. Others are shamed for showing vulnerability or need. In both cases, the message is the same: your worth depends on how well you mask your discomfort and meet someone else's emotional expectations.

Over time, this can create a survival strategy that sounds like: "If I act like I'm fine, if I appear successful, no one can hurt me." That mask becomes the personality, and the personality becomes the armor. What's underneath often remains unexplored, even to the person wearing it.

Humor can be a part of that armor, too. Many individuals with narcissistic traits have a sharp wit or magnetic charm. But these tools, while socially effective, often serve to deflect real intimacy.

Defense Mechanisms

When the emotional core feels unsteady, the mind gets to work building defenses. For someone with Narcissistic Personality Disorder, those defenses are purposeful, practiced, and often invisible to the person using them.

Denial is one of the most common. It allows the person to reject uncomfortable truths: "I'm not upset," "That didn't hurt," "I don't care what they think." Then there's projection. This is when someone attributes their own unacceptable feelings to someone else. If they feel insecure, they may accuse others of being weak. If they feel shame, they might call someone else pathetic. It's an emotional sleight of hand: if I can't tolerate it in me, I'll see it in you.

Superiority and control are also common. They help regulate an unstable self-image. By staying in control of others or appearing above them, the person avoids the vulnerability of being seen as ordinary, flawed, or dependent. Ironically, this drive for control often alienates others and creates the very disconnection the person fears most.

What makes these defenses so persistent is that they work, at least temporarily. They create a buffer between the person and their unprocessed pain. But over time, that buffer becomes a barrier. It blocks intimacy, growth, and emotional truth. What protected them in the past now prevents them from being fully present.

Case Snapshot: Lalle

Lalle, a successful consultant in his late 30s, prides himself on being the smartest person in the room. He often interrupts others in meetings and dismisses opposing views. When a colleague points out a minor error in his report, Lalle lashes out, calling it "nitpicking." Later, he jokes that the colleague must be jealous of his success. What others see as arrogance is Lalle's defense system at work, protecting against a deep fear of being exposed as incompetent.

Exercise: Noticing the Shield

Use this journaling prompt to explore your own defenses:

- Think of a moment recently when you felt judged, embarrassed, or rejected.
- What did you do in response: withdraw, lash out, make a joke, change the subject?
- Looking back, what might that reaction have been protecting?

Understanding the purpose of your defenses is the first step in softening them.

Narcissistic Injury

Beneath the inflated ego, and all the charm, lies something rarely talked about: a hair-trigger sensitivity to shame. This is known as narcissistic injury, the deep emotional wound triggered when someone with NPD feels criticized, overlooked, or exposed.

It doesn't take much. A missed compliment, a suggestion for improvement, or a moment of being outshone can all register as personal attacks. The emotional response can be swift and intense: anger, withdrawal, blame, or icy detachment. To an outsider, it might seem disproportionate.

Over time, this pattern can create a paradox: the more someone protects themselves from shame, the more disconnected they become from others. Authentic feedback, closeness, and growth all get sacrificed to avoid emotional exposure.

Case Snapshot: Wendinso

Wendinso, a mid-level executive, is known for her confidence and high standards. In a quarterly review, her supervisor praised the team but offered Wendinso a small piece of constructive feedback about delegation. Wendinso went silent, avoided eye contact for the rest of the meeting, and called in sick the next day. In her mind, she hadn't received feedback; she'd been humiliated. Her withdrawal wasn't calculated; it was a reflexive response to a wound she didn't know she had.

Narcissistic Rage

When someone with Narcissistic Personality Disorder experiences a narcissistic injury, what often follows is a surge of intense anger. This is known as narcissistic rage, a response that often seems disproportionate or sudden. It's not always explosive, though. It can present as a sharp outburst, a cutting remark, or a cold silence that stretches for days. The reaction is not really about the external event; it's about the internal meaning assigned to it. The individual may feel belittled, unworthy, or invisible, and the rage acts as an alarm bell: "Don't come any closer."

When you find yourself on the wrong side of this, the impact can be emotionally destabilizing. The suddenness of the reaction and the refusal to process it together can leave others feeling like they're walking on eggshells.

Case Snapshot: Marcus

Marcus, a creative director, appeared composed and in control until someone questioned the originality of one of his ad campaigns. Though the comment was framed constructively, Marcus felt deeply insulted. He raised his voice, accused the team of undermining him, and stormed out. For the next week, he ignored emails and refused to speak during meetings. To him, the critique felt like betrayal, not collaboration. His outburst wasn't just anger; it was the sound of a self-image under siege.

Exercise: The Reaction Journal

Next time you feel a strong emotional reaction to someone's words or actions, take five minutes to reflect before responding. Use the following questions:

- What did I feel the moment it happened: anger, fear, or embarrassment?
- What part of me felt threatened or dismissed?
- Could my reaction be protecting me from a deeper feeling?

You don't have to share the answers. The value lies in noticing the moment before it turns into a storm.

TYPES OF NARCISSISM

Narcissism is quite a nuanced trait, with distinct styles that can look and feel very different. Understanding these types helps avoid blanket assumptions and allows for more nuanced awareness, especially when navigating relationships or working toward self-understanding.

Let's explore the key subtypes: overt, covert, and vulnerable narcissism, followed by how these patterns can overlap with other personality disorders.

Overt Narcissism

This is the most recognizable form. People with overt narcissistic traits often appear confident, outgoing, and unapologetically assertive. They may seek admiration openly and feel entitled to special treatment. In social settings, they often dominate conversations, name-drop, or boast about achievements.

But beneath the surface, overt narcissism still revolves around emotional insecurity. The need for praise and recognition is a form of self-preservation. Criticism can quickly turn to defensiveness or disdain, and empathy may take a backseat to self-image.

Case Snapshot: Jamal

Jamal, a personal trainer, built his reputation on confidence and charm. Clients loved his energy, but colleagues noticed he struggled with feedback. When a client left a neutral review, Jamal publicly mocked them and posted his workout stats as proof of his superiority. His need to be admired wasn't just a habit; it was a buffer against feeling insignificant.

Covert Narcissism

Covert narcissism hides in plain sight. Instead of the loud charm and obvious entitlement seen in overt types, covert narcissists may come across as shy, self-effacing, or even fragile. But the core structure is still the same: a deep need for validation, paired with difficulty tolerating criticism or emotional discomfort.

These individuals may feel underappreciated, misunderstood, or resentful. They might not demand admiration openly, but they long for recognition nonetheless. When it doesn't come, the reaction is often withdrawal, passive-aggression, or internal rumination. Covert narcissism is sometimes described as "quiet suffering with a loud inner world."

Unlike overt narcissism, which pushes outward, covert narcissism pulls inward. But both are fueled by the same fear: that without admiration or control, the self might collapse.

Case Snapshot: Tessa

Tessa, a university student, avoided group discussions but often felt dismissed by peers. When her professor praised another student's work, Tessa spiraled into days of self-doubt and resentment. She didn't lash out, but her diary entries were filled with bitter observations and comparisons. To others, she seemed sensitive. Internally, she struggled with an unmet need to feel exceptional.

Vulnerable Narcissism

Vulnerable narcissism is often overlooked because it doesn't fit the typical mold. These individuals may appear anxious, sensitive, or even self-loathing on the surface. But underneath is the same core of fragile self-worth and desperate need for affirmation.

Unlike covert narcissism, which leans toward passive reactions, vulnerable narcissism often involves emotional volatility, hypersensitivity to rejection, and a heightened need for reassurance. They may seek constant validation while struggling with deep feelings of inadequacy.

This type can be especially confusing in relationships. The person might present as needy or dependent, yet still exhibit controlling or manipulative behaviors when their insecurities are triggered. It's not about grandiosity, but about emotional instability wrapped in longing.

Case Snapshot: Gorko

Gorko, a high school teacher, is kind and thoughtful, but deeply reactive. When his partner forgets to text during a busy day, Gorko spirals into insecurity and assumes abandonment. He responds with guilt-tripping and dramatic messages, followed by remorse. He craves closeness but feels perpetually unsafe in it. His vulnerability doesn't protect others from harm; it often pulls them into emotional storms.

Overlap with Other Personality Disorders

Narcissistic traits rarely operate in a vacuum. It's common for individuals to exhibit overlapping features from multiple personality disorders, which can complicate both diagnosis and treatment. When it comes to Narcissistic Personality Disorder (NPD), certain patterns frequently intersect with those seen in Borderline and Antisocial Personality Disorders.

Blurred Lines With Borderline Traits

Some individuals with NPD also show traits associated with Borderline Personality Disorder (BPD), such as emotional instability, fear of abandonment, and intense, rapidly shifting relationships. While BPD is typically marked by deep vulnerability and identity disturbance, narcissistic defenses may mask that vulnerability with anger, blame, or detachment.

In these cases, the person might appear grandiose and self-assured one moment, then spiral into panic or shame the next. This emotional whiplash can confuse loved ones and clinicians alike.

Antisocial Overlap

Others may show traits consistent with Antisocial Personality Disorder (ASPD), particularly in cases where manipulation, deceit, or lack of remorse are present. This subtype of narcissism is often more exploitative and callous, prioritizing dominance over connection. The person may violate others' boundaries with little regard, justifying their actions through entitlement or perceived superiority.

While not all individuals with NPD exhibit antisocial traits, the overlap can lead to increased relational harm and reduced treatment responsiveness.

Why This Matters

Overlapping traits highlight the need for careful, individualized assessment. Treating someone as a "narcissist" without acknowledging the full range of symptoms can miss the mark, and miss the person beneath the patterns.

Understanding these crossovers also supports more effective intervention strategies. A person with BPD traits may respond well to emotion regulation skills. Someone with antisocial tendencies might benefit from boundaries and accountability frameworks. One size does not fit all.

Case Snapshot: Kyle

Kyle is charismatic in meetings and often takes credit for group wins. He also lashes out when challenged, blames others for his mistakes, and has a history of unreliable relationships. In therapy, he shows both entitlement and a fear of being exposed. His therapist notes narcissistic and borderline traits but avoids pigeonholing him, choosing instead to focus on emotional insight, trust-building, and impulse control.

HOW IT AFFECTS OTHERS

Friends, family members, romantic partners, and coworkers often find themselves riding an emotional rollercoaster: one moment elevated, the next discarded.

Idealization and Devaluation

Relationships with someone who has NPD often begin with a rush of admiration and connection. This phase, known as idealization, can feel intoxicating. The individual with narcissistic traits may shower their partner with praise, attention, and what appears to be deep emotional intimacy. They may call you the best thing that's ever happened to them or place you on a pedestal so high it feels surreal.

But over time, that pedestal can wobble. Once flaws are noticed, or the admiration isn't reciprocated in exactly the right way, the shift begins. Devaluation creeps in. Criticism replaces compliments. The person once idealized may now feel like they can't do anything right. The warmth fades into coldness, often without warning.

This cycle creates confusion, anxiety, and a growing sense of instability for the person on the receiving end. They may begin to question themselves, wondering how they went from adored to dismissed so quickly.

Case Snapshot: Minampa

Minampa met Alex at a community art class. He was magnetic, charming, complimentary, and full of plans. Within weeks, he was talking about moving in together and describing her as "the only person who truly gets me." But when Minampa began asserting boundaries, Alex became distant. He criticized her choices, questioned her loyalty, and stopped replying to texts for hours, sometimes days. Minampa was left clinging to the version of Alex who once saw her as extraordinary, not the one who now made her feel invisible.

Manipulation and Gaslighting

Manipulation and gaslighting are two of the most destabilizing experiences reported by people close to someone with NPD.

These words have also gained popularity in modern culture. These tactics are not always conscious or malicious. Manipulation may involve guilt-tripping, shifting blame, or using emotional intimacy to gain influence. A person with NPD might portray themselves as the victim in every conflict or insist that others are responsible for their distress. Over time, these dynamics can erode the other person's confidence, making it harder to trust their own instincts.

Gaslighting takes this one step further. It involves distorting reality, questioning facts, denying past statements, or rewriting shared experiences, in a way that makes the other person feel confused or even "crazy." The intent may not be overt deception but a reflexive need to reshape the narrative when shame or vulnerability surfaces.

Case Snapshot: Priya

Priya had always been confident in her decisions until she started dating Jordan. When she brought up concerns, he'd say, "That never happened" or "You're too sensitive." Over time, Priya began doubting her memory, questioning whether she was overreacting. She found herself apologizing more, withdrawing from friends, and second-guessing her every move. What began as small contradictions turned into a full-blown identity fog.

IMPACT ON LOVED ONES

Living in the orbit of someone with narcissistic traits can lead to long-term emotional strain. The constant ups and downs create a psychological environment that's hard to navigate. Over time, loved ones may feel like they're losing touch with their own thoughts, needs, or identity.

Partners may feel emotionally drained, never quite sure where they stand. Children raised in such households may develop hypervigilance, always scanning for emotional cues to avoid conflict. Friends and coworkers often report feeling devalued, dismissed, or used.

The results can include burnout, chronic anxiety, low self-esteem, and even symptoms of trauma. The emotional cost of maintaining a relationship with someone who fluctuates between charm and control is real, and it often goes unspoken.

Case Snapshot: Danielle

Danielle's sister had always been the star of the family. When she was in a good mood, she was generous, funny, and warm. But when things didn't go her way, she lashed out, accusing others of betrayal or incompetence. Danielle often felt like she was walking on eggshells, trying not to trigger another storm. Over time, she noticed herself becoming quieter, second-guessing her words, and avoiding family gatherings altogether.

Exercise: Emotional Cost Inventory

If you've spent time in a relationship where your needs took a backseat to someone else's volatility, take a moment to reflect:

- What did you give up to maintain peace?
- When did you start silencing your voice or doubting your value?
- What boundaries do you need to reestablish to reconnect with your own emotional clarity?

There's power in naming what you've carried. It's the first step toward letting go of what was never yours to hold.

Emotional Exhaustion and Identity Erosion

Spending time around someone with narcissistic traits can slowly wear away your sense of self. Emotional exhaustion is the kind of weariness that sinks into your bones, often without you realizing it until you're depleted.

You might begin by making small compromises: letting things slide, avoiding conflict, or tiptoeing around certain topics. But those compromises pile up. Over time, you start to shrink, your laughter feels quieter, your needs feel inconvenient, and your instincts feel suspect.

This erosion of identity happens in subtle, repeated moments of invalidation, where your voice is minimized, your truth is questioned, and your presence feels like a burden.

Exercise: Restoring Emotional Resilience

When emotional exhaustion sets in, your mind and body are no longer working together in harmony. This kind of fatigue reflects a loss of emotional bandwidth, the depletion that comes from prolonged tension, people-pleasing, or walking on eggshells.

To begin replenishing that energy, try this structured reset:

- **Name your fatigue:** Write down the last three situations that left you feeling emotionally drained. What were the patterns? Were you over-giving, silencing yourself, or managing someone else's emotions?

NARCISSISTIC PERSONALITY DISORDER   123

- **Locate your body's signal:** Where do you feel this exhaustion? In your chest? Your jaw? Your stomach? Noticing it helps bring awareness back to your body's needs.
- **Schedule a self-return moment:** Choose a 30-minute window this week to do something just for yourself. No multitasking, no screens. Just one activity that makes you feel like you. Walking, painting, journaling, gardening, anything that reconnects you to your internal rhythm.
- **Ask this: What part of me have I been ignoring to keep the peace?** Let the answer guide a boundary, a conversation, or a habit shift.

Managing Narcissism, From Both Sides

Not every relationship is doomed, but managing these dynamics requires a different set of tools. You can't fix a person with NPD or win an emotional tug-of-war with them. You need to learn how to protect your own well-being while navigating the complexities of a narcissistic dynamic. And for those who identify with narcissistic traits themselves, this is an opportunity to build insight, increase emotional flexibility, and explore change without shame.

EXPLORING THERAPY OPTIONS THAT WORK

Many therapists today use integrative approaches tailored to the individual, but some evidence-based models stand out for their structure, practicality, and results.

Let's look at a few that are frequently used, not in abstract terms, but as real-world tools.

Schema Therapy: Healing Old Wounds

Schema therapy helps clients identify long-standing emotional patterns (schemas) that were shaped by unmet needs in childhood. People with narcissistic traits often carry schemas of defectiveness, entitlement, or emotional deprivation. These deep beliefs drive behaviors like grandiosity or avoidance of vulnerability.

In therapy, the goal isn't to shame these beliefs; it's to trace them back to their origin and teach healthier ways to meet emotional needs. A therapist may use imagery, journaling, and dialogue to help the client connect with their "child modes" and nurture those parts, rather than ignoring or overcompensating.

Real-Life Example: Jordan struggled with explosive anger and a constant need for validation. Through schema therapy, he discovered a core belief that he was only lovable if he succeeded. The therapist helped him explore where that belief started and how he could meet his emotional needs without chasing approval.

Try This: Write down one belief you carry about yourself that feels unshakable. Then ask: Where might that belief have started? Whose voice do you hear when it plays in your mind?

CBT: Restructuring Thought Patterns

Cognitive Behavioral Therapy (CBT) helps people identify and change unhelpful thoughts and behaviors. For someone with narcissistic traits, this could involve:

- Challenging automatic thoughts like "They're attacking me," or "I'm right and they're wrong"
- Learning how to tolerate disagreement without taking it personally

- Reframing criticism as information, not rejection

CBT is especially useful for increasing emotional regulation and self-awareness. It's practical, skills-based, and time-limited, making it accessible for those who may be skeptical of long-term therapy.

Case snapshot: Julian often left arguments feeling misunderstood and angry. In CBT, he tracked his thought patterns and learned how his mind jumped to extremes. Over time, he practiced pausing before reacting, checking for alternative explanations, and asking clarifying questions instead of accusing.

CBT Exercise: The next time you feel triggered, write down:

- the situation
- your first thought
- your emotional response
- a more balanced thought that could replace the original one

Psychodynamic Therapy: Understanding the "Why"

Psychodynamic therapy focuses on unconscious patterns that drive current behavior. It explores early relationships, hidden motivations, and internal conflicts. This can be especially powerful for clients with NPD, who may not recognize how past wounds shape present interactions.

This approach can be intense, but for those ready to dig deep, it offers lasting change. It also emphasizes the therapeutic relationship itself as a window into how the person relates to others.

Real-life example: Marcus entered therapy after being accused of emotional manipulation in his marriage. He didn't see it. But after months of reflection and feedback from his therapist, he began to recognize how his fear of rejection led him to control conversations and dominate emotionally. That insight became the turning point.

BUILDING BOUNDARIES WITHOUT THE BLOWBACK

Boundaries can feel like battle lines when you're dealing with someone who has narcissistic traits. But they don't have to be combative. A healthy boundary is a clear line that protects your time, energy, and self-respect. And when done calmly and consistently, it can change the entire tone of a relationship.

This section focuses on creating boundaries that are realistic, enforceable, and rooted in clarity rather than control. It also includes strategies for those who struggle to respect others' boundaries, something that people with narcissistic traits may not recognize until it's spelled out clearly.

Clarify Your Non-Negotiables

Before you try to set a boundary, you have to know what really matters to you. Ask:

- What behaviors leave me feeling drained, disrespected, or unsafe?
- What am I constantly justifying, excusing, or tolerating?
- What patterns make me feel small?

Write down your top three non-negotiables. These are the lines you no longer want to blur.

Use the Calm Formula

When delivering a boundary, emotion may be high, but the message should be calm and structured. Try this four-part formula:

C = Clear (state the behavior)
A = Assertive (express your need without apology)
L = Limit (define your boundary)
M = Meaning (explain the consequence or reasoning)

Example: "When I'm interrupted repeatedly (Clear), I feel disrespected, and it shuts me down (Assertive). I need to be allowed to finish speaking (Limit). If that doesn't happen, I'll step out of the conversation until it does (Meaning)."

Practice Non-Reactivity

People with narcissistic traits may test boundaries, push back, or accuse you of being selfish. The key is to avoid reacting emotionally or defending yourself at length.

Tips:

- Repeat your boundary without escalation: "That's not okay with me."
- Avoid over-explaining: Clarity is stronger than justification.
- Step back if needed: Silence is sometimes the most powerful response.

Case Snapshot: Eliza

Eliza had always said yes to her brother's demands, even when they left her drained and resentful. After learning boundary skills in therapy, she tried something new. When he demanded that she cancel her weekend plans to help him move, she calmly said, "I'm not available this weekend. I understand you're frustrated, but this is important to me." When he pushed back, she didn't argue. She repeated her message and stuck to it. The backlash passed, and for the first time, she felt in control of her own time.

SUPPORTING SOMEONE WITH NARCISSISTIC TRAITS

Living with or caring about someone who shows narcissistic behaviors can be confusing, painful, and draining. But it can also be an opportunity to reclaim your voice, restore balance, and choose how you want to show up. Support doesn't mean self-sacrifice. In this workshop, we focus on strategies that center your well-being while offering realistic ways to engage with someone who struggles with empathy, accountability, or emotional regulation.

Reclaim Your Reality

Gaslighting and emotional invalidation are common in relationships marked by narcissistic traits. Over time, you might start to doubt your own memory, reactions, or feelings.

Try this: Keep a private validation journal. Each day, write down:

- One interaction that left you confused, frustrated, or dismissed.
- What you observed (facts).

- What you felt (emotions).
- What you needed or wanted that didn't happen.

Seeing your truth on paper builds clarity and self-trust.

Compassionate Detachment

Detaching doesn't mean you stop caring. It means you stop trying to control, fix, or be responsible for someone else's emotional world. This shift can protect you from burnout.

Practice:

- Limit your emotional investment in their reactions.
- Focus on how you want to respond, not how they should change.
- Remind yourself: "I am responsible for my energy, not their emotions."

Case Snapshot: Miwa

Miwa's adult daughter had long struggled with emotional outbursts and manipulation. Miwa used to bend over backwards to keep the peace, but it left her resentful and exhausted. After working with a therapist, she began practicing detachment with compassion. When her daughter accused her of being cold, Miwa calmly replied, "I love you, but I won't participate in yelling. I'm here when you're ready to talk respectfully." That boundary helped both of them reset.

CHAPTER 7

ANTISOCIAL PERSONALITY
DISORDER

I t's tempting to think of Antisocial Personality Disorder
(ASPD) as the stuff of true crime podcasts or courtroom
thrillers. The term conjures images of cold-hearted manipulators
or emotionless criminals. But in reality, ASPD is a complex
disorder rooted in early disruption, emotional detachment, and
impaired connections with others.

This chapter begins by stripping away the myths. "Antisocial"
doesn't mean someone who avoids parties or prefers solitude. It
refers to a chronic disregard for the rights, needs, and boundaries
of others. That disregard often masks a deeper struggle with
empathy, impulse control, and emotional bonding.

Our goal here is twofold: to understand ASPD from a humanizing,
clinical perspective, and to offer guidance for those navigating its
impact, whether in themselves, in someone they love, or in
someone they've had to walk away from.

WHAT IS ANTISOCIAL PERSONALITY DISORDER?

According to the *Diagnostic and Statistical Manual of Mental Disorders, Fifth Edition, Text Revision* (DSM-5-TR), Antisocial Personality Disorder is characterized by a pattern of disregard for and violation of the rights of others, beginning in childhood or early adolescence and continuing into adulthood (American Psychiatric Association, 2022). It includes:

- deceitfulness (repeated lying, conning others for pleasure or gain)
- impulsivity or failure to plan ahead
- irritability and aggressiveness
- reckless disregard for the safety of self or others
- consistent irresponsibility (e.g., job loss, unpaid debts)
- lack of remorse for harm caused

To qualify for diagnosis the person must be at least 18 years old and must have shown symptoms of conduct disorder before the age of 15.

ASPD is estimated to affect between 0.2% and 3.3% of the general population. However, rates are far higher in certain settings, particularly among incarcerated individuals, where estimates range from 40% to 70% (Fisher et al., 2024).

Sociopathy, Psychopathy, and ASPD

ASPD is often conflated with sociopathy and psychopathy. Here's how they differ (Wiginton, 2020):

- **ASPD** is the official diagnosis in the DSM-5-TR.

- **Sociopathy** is an informal term, often used to describe chronic rule-breaking and emotional instability.
- **Psychopathy** is not a DSM diagnosis but refers to traits such as superficial charm, manipulativeness, lack of empathy, and shallow emotions, often measured by tools like the Hare Psychopathy Checklist.

All three exist on the same behavioral spectrum but differ in presentation and severity.

THE DEVELOPMENTAL PATHWAY

Antisocial behavior begins with a trail of red flags in childhood, clues that something deeper may be forming beneath the surface. This section explores how environmental stressors, trauma, and early attachment disruptions interact with biological vulnerabilities to shape what eventually becomes Antisocial Personality Disorder.

Early Signs: The Childhood Signal Flares

Before someone is ever diagnosed with ASPD, there is typically a long-standing history of conduct problems during childhood. These signs are not always taken seriously or may be misinterpreted as "just a phase," but they often point to deeper emotional dysregulation.

Common early behaviors include:

- chronic lying
- aggression or cruelty toward others or animals
- repeated rule-breaking
- property destruction or theft

- truancy and defiance of authority

These symptoms, collectively recognized as conduct disorder, must be present before age 15 for an ASPD diagnosis later in life (Fisher et al., 2024).

Case Snapshot: Nanga

At age 10, Nanga had already been suspended three times for aggressive behavior and theft. His teachers described him as intelligent but "explosive." At home, he was withdrawn and rarely expressed emotion. His mother, a single parent, worked multiple jobs and struggled to maintain consistent discipline. When Nanga was referred to a child psychologist, he was found to have significant trauma exposure from early neglect and domestic violence. Despite early warning signs, his behavior was dismissed as "troublemaking." By age 19, he had been arrested twice for violent offenses. His story reflects the way early behaviors, left unaddressed, can become part of a larger pattern.

NEGLECT, TRAUMA, AND GENETICS

Behind many cases of Antisocial Personality Disorder lies a blend of biological sensitivity and environmental hardship. No one is born destined to disregard others, but certain early experiences can create a perfect storm of emotional detachment, impulsivity, and relational dysfunction. This section explores how trauma, neglect, and genetic predispositions shape the antisocial trajectory.

The Role of Neglect and Trauma

Children who grow up in chaotic, unstable environments often learn that the world is unpredictable and unsafe. When their caregivers are neglectful, abusive, or inconsistent, these children may begin to form protective behaviors that harden over time: distrust, emotional numbing, aggression, and withdrawal.

Research shows that children exposed to chronic maltreatment or emotional neglect are more likely to develop conduct problems, particularly if they lack stable attachment figures (Fisher et al., 2024). Without attuned caregivers, the child's capacity for empathy, emotional regulation, and moral reasoning often stalls or fragments.

Trauma can further disrupt development by altering the brain's stress response system. For example, early adversity is linked to heightened amygdala reactivity and impaired functioning in the prefrontal cortex, two areas involved in impulse control and emotional awareness (Teicher & Samson, 2016).

Genetic Vulnerability

While the environment plays a powerful role, it's not the only factor. Some individuals are born with a heightened risk for antisocial behavior, particularly if they inherit traits such as:

- high novelty seeking
- low fear or harm avoidance
- reduced emotional reactivity

Twin and adoption studies suggest that ASPD has moderate heritability, with estimates ranging from 38% to 69% (Rhee & Waldman, 2002). But genes don't determine destiny. They create a susceptibility that is shaped, and either amplified or buffered, by experience.

Case Snapshot: Ninalowo

Ninalowo's early childhood was marked by instability. His father was incarcerated, and his mother struggled with addiction. By age seven, he had been placed in three foster homes. Teachers described him as "fearless" but defiant. At 14, he was diagnosed with conduct disorder. His biological uncle had a history of criminal behavior, and Ninalowo often said he "felt nothing" when he hurt others. Later, genetic testing and neurological assessments revealed a high-risk temperament and reduced emotional responsivity. His case illustrates how biology and environment can interact to derail empathy and regulation.

Exercise: Understanding the Roots

If you're trying to make sense of someone's antisocial patterns or your own past, this reflection can help:

- What early environmental stressors or traumas might have shaped your worldview?
- Was safety or consistency present in your early caregiving?
- Do certain patterns in your family history reflect emotional disconnection, impulsivity, or aggression?

ATTACHMENT DISRUPTIONS AND CHRONIC STRESS

Human development thrives on connection. When that connection is broken or never formed, core psychological capacities like empathy, emotional regulation, and trust can erode. In children vulnerable to antisocial behavior, attachment disruptions act as both a cause and amplifier. This section explores how early relational breakdowns and ongoing stress contribute to the development of Antisocial Personality Disorder.

The Attachment Wound

Attachment theory tells us that the quality of our earliest relationships, particularly with caregivers, shapes our internal models of safety, worthiness, and connection. When caregivers are emotionally unavailable, unpredictable, or frightening, children often adapt by becoming emotionally guarded or detached.

Research has shown that children with disorganized attachment styles, those who experience caregivers as both a source of comfort and fear, are more likely to develop externalizing behaviors like aggression and defiance (Lyons-Ruth et al., 1993). These adaptations may protect the child in the short term, but over time, they reduce the capacity for trust, empathy, and guilt.

The inability to form secure bonds may also contribute to a worldview where others are perceived as tools, threats, or irrelevant. In this psychological landscape, manipulating or exploiting others may feel less like a choice and more like a survival strategy.

Chronic Stress and Emotional Blunting

When a child is constantly on edge, navigating conflict, poverty, neglect, or violence, their nervous system adapts by staying in a heightened state of alert. This chronic stress floods the brain with cortisol, which, over time can damage neural structures involved in emotional processing and impulse control (McEwen, 2003).

Eventually, the body begins to numb itself. Emotional blunting sets in as a biological shield. For children predisposed to ASPD, this blunting contributes to their limited responsiveness to others' emotions, poor frustration tolerance, and shallow affect.

Case Snapshot: Pamiral

Pamiral's earliest memories involved dodging conflict between her parents, who often fought violently. She described her home as a "war zone" and learned to survive by shutting down emotionally. In school, she was aggressive toward peers and often seemed indifferent to punishment. Therapists noted she showed no guilt after hurting others, but also no real joy. At 17, Pamiral was placed in a residential program where she began exploring how her early environment shaped her worldview. Slowly, she started recognizing emotional responses in others, and eventually in herself. Her progress wasn't fast, but it was real.

Exercise: Tracing Emotional Patterns

This activity is for those who want to better understand their emotional wiring:

- Think of your earliest relationships. Were they safe, consistent, and emotionally warm, or chaotic, unpredictable, or cold?
- When someone expresses sadness or anger, what do you feel? Do you tend to care, freeze, or feel nothing at all?
- How do you respond when you're overwhelmed? Do you lash out, withdraw, or go numb?

THE EMPATHY DEFICIT

Not everyone feels the world in the same way. For people with antisocial personality disorder (ASPD), the gap between what others feel and what they register can be striking. Where most people instinctively mirror distress, show compassion, or feel pangs of guilt, those with ASPD may seem unmoved. This is often rooted in deep neurological and emotional differences that blunt their ability to relate to the emotional states of others. This section breaks down the key components of that empathy deficit, beginning with emotional blunting.

Emotional Blunting

People with ASPD often display what's called emotional blunting, a noticeable flatness in their emotional life. This doesn't mean they feel nothing, but the range and intensity of their emotions are diminished, particularly when it comes to the experiences of others. They may seem indifferent when someone is hurt, dismissive during a moment of crisis, or unfazed by suffering that would deeply move most people. This emotional detachment is not the same as being calm or stoic; it's a chronic absence of empathy.

Where most individuals would feel a natural emotional pull to comfort someone crying or express concern in the face of distress, individuals with ASPD may shrug, laugh, or show no visible reaction. This disconnect can be confusing to others and damaging in relationships, often mistaken for cruelty when it may actually stem from a genuine lack of emotional resonance.

Neurologically, emotional blunting is believed to stem from impairments in the brain's limbic system, especially the amygdala. The amygdala plays a key role in processing emotional stimuli, including fear and empathy. When this part of the brain is underactive, as research has consistently shown in individuals with ASPD, emotional responses are dulled or absent (Fisher et al., 2024).

In everyday life, this might look like someone appearing "cool under pressure", but not in a healthy or grounded way. Instead, they may remain impassive during emotionally charged events, not because they're regulated, but because the internal emotional cues that drive concern or compassion are muted.

This emotional flatness can contribute to repeated interpersonal conflicts, job loss, or legal issues, as the person may fail to recognize or care about the social consequences of their behavior. Their inability to resonate emotionally with others can lead to a pattern of actions that come off as callous, manipulative, or cruel, even when those actions are more automatic than calculated.

Neurological Differences

The empathy deficit in ASPD happens on a biological level. A growing body of neuroscientific research shows that individuals with ASPD often exhibit structural and functional abnormalities in specific brain regions associated with emotional regulation, empathy, and impulse control.

One of the most consistently implicated areas is the amygdala, a small, almond-shaped structure deep within the brain that plays a central role in processing emotions, particularly fear and distress in others. Studies using functional MRI scans have found that individuals with ASPD show significantly reduced amygdala activity when exposed to images of suffering or emotionally charged stimuli. This muted response helps explain why many with ASPD appear indifferent to pain or unmotivated by guilt (Marsh et al., 2008).

In addition to the amygdala, research points to impairments in the ventromedial prefrontal cortex (vmPFC), a region critical for decision-making, emotional judgment, and the integration of empathy into behavior. Damage or dysfunction in the vmPFC has been linked to risk-taking, poor moral judgment, and a disregard for social norms, all of which are hallmark traits of ASPD (Blair, 2007).

Importantly, these brain differences are not necessarily caused by one single factor. Genetics, early trauma, chronic stress, and even exposure to violence in childhood can alter neural development in ways that predispose someone to these patterns. In other words, while ASPD traits may look cold or malicious on the outside, there is often an underlying neurological explanation for why emotional processing and empathy are so profoundly impaired.

Understanding these neurological mechanisms doesn't excuse harmful behavior, but it does challenge simplistic moral explanations. It shifts the lens from "bad" to "broken", from punishment to a more complex view rooted in brain science.

Limited Remorse or Guilt

A defining feature of ASPD is the absence of remorse or meaningful guilt. This helps the person avoid apologies, but it's a deeper disconnect from the emotional consequences of one's actions. Individuals with ASPD often commit harmful acts without experiencing the inner discomfort, regret, or moral conflict that typically follows such behavior.

They may justify what they've done, downplay the harm caused, or shift blame onto others. For example, instead of acknowledging they hurt someone, they might say, "They were asking for it," or, "That's just how the world works." This rationalization replaces reflection with detachment, allowing repeated violations of others' boundaries without internal resistance.

This lack of remorse has roots in both psychological development and neurobiology. The underactivity in areas like the amygdala and ventromedial prefrontal cortex, discussed earlier, means that the emotional signals most people associate with wrongdoing, like guilt, shame, or empathy, are weak or absent in those with ASPD. Without these internal signals, behavior is guided more by self-interest than by any sense of relational or societal responsibility.

It's important to note that some individuals with ASPD may learn to mimic regret when socially convenient. They might say the right things, appear apologetic, or even cry if it serves a goal, but these displays are often superficial and disconnected from actual emotional experience. This capacity for performative remorse can make it difficult for others to distinguish between genuine accountability and manipulation.

Ultimately, the limited experience of remorse in ASPD isn't about defiance or arrogance. It's often a byproduct of an impaired emotional system, one that doesn't register harm in the same way, and therefore doesn't generate the same internal cues to prevent it.

Control and Manipulation

Manipulation becomes a tool for navigating relationships, not necessarily out of malice, but because it provides predictability, advantage, and a sense of power in a world they often experience as hostile or transactional.

Unlike overt aggression, manipulation in ASPD can be subtle and highly calculated. Tactics may include lying, guilt-tripping, gaslighting, or exploiting vulnerabilities. These behaviors serve a psychological function: to neutralize perceived threats, dominate social dynamics, or extract something of value, whether emotional, financial, or physical.

What makes this manipulation particularly damaging is that it's often cloaked in charm or rationalization. The person may appear charismatic or persuasive, masking their coercion with humor, logic, or false vulnerability. It's not uncommon for victims to second-guess themselves, unsure whether they were misled or simply misunderstood the interaction.

The underlying driver of this behavior is often an impaired capacity for trust and reciprocity. Without empathy, relationships become strategic rather than mutual. Rather than seeking connection, individuals with ASPD tend to assess what others can offer and then shape interactions to maintain control.

Case Snapshot

Coubel, a 42-year-old woman in a long-term relationship with a partner diagnosed with ASPD, described a recurring pattern: "Every time I tried to set a boundary, he'd flip the script. Suddenly, I was the selfish one. He'd remind me of things I did wrong, and somehow I'd be the one apologizing by the end." Over time, she found herself questioning her memory, isolating herself from friends, and feeling emotionally worn down. What she initially interpreted as assertiveness in her partner slowly revealed itself as calculated dominance, enabled by gaslighting and emotional coercion.

THE IMPACT ON OTHERS

Being in a relationship with someone who has ASPD can feel like being trapped in a maze without an exit. The emotional terrain is often unstable, one moment charged with charisma, the next disorienting and unsafe. The harm caused is not always dramatic or violent. More often, it's slow, psychological, and cumulative.

People with ASPD can be remarkably charismatic. Their exploitative charm often draws others in before warning signs appear. Early interactions may be filled with flattery, intense focus, or expressions of shared values. But over time, these surface-level connections reveal themselves as tools of manipulation, designed to disarm suspicion and establish control. As one partner described it: "He was magnetic at first, until I realized he never really listened. Everything was about the performance."

This initial charm can mask deeper patterns of gaslighting and psychological harm. Victims may begin to doubt their own memories, instincts, or worth. Emotional abuse might be brushed off as "miscommunication." Cruelty may be disguised as honesty. With repeated boundary violations, victims often begin to internalize blame, asking themselves what they did to provoke the behavior.

Relationships with individuals with ASPD often become chronically strained, not because of isolated incidents, but because of the consistent erosion of trust and emotional safety. Friends, family members, and romantic partners report feeling emotionally diminished, like their needs are inconvenient or irrelevant. Over time, they may become isolated, exhausted, and unsure of what is real. This is especially true in long-term relationships, where subtle abuse is normalized and rationalized.

The most painful aspect of this dynamic is the rationalization and repetition of harm. People with ASPD often deflect responsibility by reframing their actions as justified, deserved, or exaggerated. "You're too sensitive," "It was a joke," or "You made me do it" are common refrains. This constant rewriting of reality not only distorts the truth, but also conditions others to accept mistreatment as normal.

Case study

Lobel, a 36-year-old professional, described how her two-year relationship with someone exhibiting ASPD traits left her feeling like a "ghost in her own life." She said, "At first, he seemed like the most confident man I'd ever met. But over time, everything was my fault. If I brought up a concern, he'd mock me or flip it back on me. I lost friends, I stopped trusting my own feelings, and by the end, I didn't recognize myself."

Her experience echoed what many survivors of ASPD relationships report: a slow unraveling of self-worth, masked behind moments of affection, promises of change, and manipulative reasoning.

MANAGING RELATIONSHIPS AND SAFETY

While many interpersonal conflicts benefit from empathy, compromise, or vulnerability, these tools often backfire with individuals who exhibit persistent manipulation, aggression, or emotional detachment. Safety, both emotional and physical, must become the guiding principle.

One of the first hard truths is that emotional appeals often fail. Trying to reason with someone high in ASPD traits may result in blame-shifting, defensiveness, or increased hostility. Vulnerability is frequently met with exploitation, not compassion. This can be disorienting, especially for people who are wired to seek resolution through honesty or emotional expression. The result is often confusion and burnout.

Because of this, boundaries must be clear, firm, and consistently enforced. They should not be debated or negotiated, as doing so only invites more manipulation. The person with ASPD may test limits, argue technicalities, or charm their way around the rules. Calm repetition of expectations and consequences is essential, and outside support may be needed to maintain clarity and strength.

In many situations, safety must take priority over resolution. Some relationships cannot be repaired, not because the other person is incapable of change, but because they are not willing or motivated to pursue it. Seeking peace or closure with someone who does not recognize your needs can keep you stuck in cycles of harm. In such cases, protecting your emotional and physical well-being must come first.

Learning to disengage is also a key survival skill. Not every battle needs to be fought. When patterns of harm persist despite boundaries and consequences, it may be necessary to walk away. You're not giving up here; you are just reclaiming your right to peace. Trust your instincts. Persistent gaslighting, control, or emotional abuse is justification enough to leave.

Finally, it's important to understand that therapy only works when self-motivated. Lasting change is rare unless the individual with ASPD is actively seeking help and possesses some capacity for introspection. Mandated or coerced therapy often leads to surface-level compliance without meaningful transformation.

Case study

Yoro, a 29-year-old man, had spent three years trying to help his older brother, who had a history of violent outbursts, legal trouble, and repeated deception. "I kept thinking I could reach him if I just explained things better. I tried everything: therapy referrals, interventions, and even moving him into my home. But every time, it ended with more lies or threats. Eventually, I realized that I wasn't helping him, I was enabling him, and it was costing me my health."

Yoro's turning point came when he stopped trying to fix the relationship and started protecting his own boundaries. "I had to choose peace over guilt," he said. "And that changed everything."

CHAPTER 8

HISTRIONIC PERSONALITY DISORDER

A person with Histrionic Personality Disorder (HPD) might be the life of the party, charismatic, expressive, flirtatious, and dramatic. To some, they seem attention-seeking or manipulative. But under the surface lies something more complex: a person trying to be seen, valued, and loved, often in the only way they were ever taught. HPD comes across as vanity or superficial charm. The individual may have learned early on that visibility was survival; if they weren't captivating, they were invisible.

WHAT IS HPD

According to the *Diagnostic and Statistical Manual of Mental Disorders* (5th ed., text rev.; DSM-5-TR), HPD is defined as a pervasive pattern of excessive emotionality and attention-seeking behavior. To meet the diagnostic criteria, individuals must display at least five of the following:

- discomfort in situations where they are not the center of attention

- interaction with others is often characterized by inappropriate, sexually seductive, or provocative behavior
- rapidly shifting and shallow expression of emotions
- consistent use of physical appearance to draw attention
- speech that is excessively impressionistic and lacking in detail
- self-dramatization, theatricality, and exaggerated expression of emotion
- is suggestible (easily influenced by others or circumstances)
- considers relationships to be more intimate than they actually are

The prevalence of HPD is relatively low in the general population, with estimates ranging between 0.4% and 1.8%, depending on the study and sample demographics (French & Shrestha, 2019). Though uncommon, the disorder has been disproportionately discussed and misrepresented in both clinical and popular narratives, often reduced to stereotypes of the "dramatic" or "flirtatious" woman.

HPD is diagnosed far more often in women than in men, yet research suggests this may reflect cultural and clinical bias more than actual differences in prevalence. Societal expectations often position women as more emotionally expressive, and behaviors considered symptomatic of HPD in women, like flirtatiousness or expressiveness, may be normalized or even valorized in men (French & Shrestha, 2019).

CHILDHOOD REINFORCEMENT

Emotional Expression as Survival

For someone with Histrionic Personality Disorder, emotions are magnified, projected, and often performed. But this amplification is a survival response. When a person grows up in an environment where subtle emotional cues are ignored, overlooked, or punished, they may learn that only exaggerated emotional displays will be noticed. As a child, tears had to be louder, laughter more vibrant, and charm more captivating to break through the emotional noise or indifference of their surroundings.

This early conditioning can evolve into an adult pattern in which emotions are still expressed in sweeping, theatrical ways. A casual disappointment may elicit visible despair while a compliment may inspire seemingly outsized joy. These reactions may seem confusing or disproportionate to outsiders, but for the individual with HPD, it's a continuation of the only emotional language they ever learned, a language designed to be loud enough to be heard (*Histrionic Personality Disorder: Causes, Symptoms, Treatment*, 2023).

What makes this cycle more complex is that the strategy often works, at least temporarily. People do respond to emotional intensity. The person with HPD may receive comfort, concern, or attention, which reinforces the behavior. But the relief is short-lived. Over time, others may begin to feel overwhelmed, manipulated, or confused by the drama.

Confusion Between Attention and Affection

HPD makes attention feel indistinguishable from love. When a person's early experiences have taught them that visibility equals value, they may begin to associate being looked at, complimented, or admired with being cared for. This is obviously a big problem.

As adults, individuals with HPD may find themselves chasing attention in all its forms: dramatic storytelling, provocative behavior, theatrical expression. This leads to an exhausting loop. If attention starts to feel like love, then the absence of attention feels like rejection. A partner distracted by a phone, a friend canceling plans, or a colleague not offering a compliment may trigger disproportionate emotional distress.

Loss of Authentic Self

Somewhere along the line, the person who constantly entertains, captivates, or flirts may lose track of who they are beneath it all. The need for external validation becomes so central that the authentic self is often buried under layers of adaptive performance. They may change their tone, style, or opinions to match the room without realizing it. Their preferences and beliefs may shift depending on the people around them. The question, "Who am I when no one is watching?" becomes difficult, sometimes even painful, to answer. Without this external mirroring, the person may feel hollow, disconnected, or even panicked. Moments of solitude or quiet can feel unbearable.

Case snapshot: Lila, 32, was known for her bold personality. She could command a room, adapt to any crowd, and always seemed effortlessly vibrant. But in therapy, she confessed that she often didn't know what she actually liked or wanted. Her choices, from clothing to career moves, were shaped by what others admired in her. Alone, she felt anxious and disoriented, like a performer without a script. Through therapeutic work, Lila began experimenting with silence, introspection, and authenticity. It felt awkward at first, but slowly, she began to recognize her own voice beneath the performance.

Implementation Exercise: Authenticity Inventory

Use this reflection exercise to begin separating your inner self from the roles you feel obligated to perform.

1. **Recall a moment of performance:** Think of a recent situation where you acted or spoke in a way that wasn't fully aligned with how you actually felt. What was the setting? Who was there?
2. **Ask: What did I need?** What were you hoping to achieve through that behavior: approval, affection, security, or inclusion?
3. **List three ways you adapt to others:** These might include tone, dress, opinions, or humor. Where did you learn these adaptations?
4. **Imagine a pause:** If you had given yourself permission to be completely honest in that moment, what would you have said or done differently?
5. **Write a grounding statement:** Choose one sentence to affirm your worth without performance. For example: "I am valuable even when I am quiet."

RELATIONSHIP DYNAMICS

Relationships are often where the traits of Histrionic Personality Disorder come into sharpest focus. The very strategies that once helped the individual feel noticed, charm, expressiveness, intensity can become obstacles to connection when they are misunderstood, overused, or misinterpreted.

For individuals with HPD, the pursuit of intimacy is often para-doxical. They want closeness, but the only tools they trust to create that closeness are ones rooted in performance. The result is often a cycle of connection and rupture, of emotional highs that lack depth and lows that feel devastating.

Intensity Without Depth

When suffering from HPD, new relationships can feel like instant intimacy, an emotional spark that flares within hours or days. They might share personal details quickly, express deep affection early on, or speak of fate and soulmates before truly knowing the other person. The warmth is real. So is the urgency.

Individuals with HPD feel a strong need for closeness and emotional resonance. But the way they pursue it tends to be shaped by learned habits. Without the foundation of genuine emotional depth, relationships may falter when real conflict, boundaries, or differences emerge. The person with HPD may feel hurt, confused, or rejected when the intensity wanes. The shift from "everything" to "nothing" can feel like abandonment, even if the other person simply needs space or time.

In long-term relationships, this pattern often leads to cycles of highs and lows. The emotional energy may be captivating, but it can also be exhausting for both partners. The individual with HPD may feel like they're doing everything to stay close, while the other party may feel overwhelmed by the demand for attention or reas-surance. This creates a paradox: the more intensity is used to secure a connection, the more it can push others away.

Case snapshot: Lobo, 28, often described her friendships as "instant besties." Within days of meeting someone new, she would be planning trips together, sharing vulnerable stories, and expressing how deeply she felt connected. But after a few weeks, things would shift. If the friend didn't reciprocate her intensity, Lobo felt betrayed or abandoned. She'd then end the friendship abruptly or accuse the person of being fake. In therapy, Lobo realized that her early emotional bonds had been inconsistent; love had come in bursts, not steady streams. Her quick bonding was less about the other person and more about her need to feel safe and wanted immediately.

Implementation Exercise: Slowing the Bond

This reflection helps explore how quickly you attach to others and invites more deliberate emotional pacing.

1. **Think of a recent relationship:** How quickly did you feel emotionally attached?
2. **List three behaviors you engaged in early on:** Examples: sharing personal stories, expressing strong affection, fantasizing about the future.
3. **Ask: What need was driving that behavior?** Were you seeking security, validation, or relief from loneliness?
4. **Write a new relational mantra:** For example: "Closeness grows over time. I can be curious without rushing."
5. **Challenge yourself:** In your next relationship or friendship, try holding back one layer of emotional intensity. Instead of revealing everything early on, observe how it feels to build slowly.

This doesn't mean withholding your true self; instead, give connection the room to deepen naturally, without needing it to prove something right away.

Flirtation and Dramatization

When it comes to HPD, interpersonal behaviour is often marked by flirtation, theatrical speech, and dramatic emotional expression. These behaviors can be misinterpreted as manipulative or inappropriate, but for the person with HPD, they are often instinctual ways of relating, tools for gaining connection, attention, and affirmation.

Flirtation doesn't always stem from romantic or sexual intent. Instead, it may be the default method for engaging others, rooted in a belief that charm and allure are necessary to secure approval. Compliments may be lavish, physical proximity close, and conversations filled with humor, touch, or innuendo. Similarly, dramatization plays a central role. The person with HPD might speak in sweeping statements, use vivid language, or recount events with high emotional intensity.

Case snapshot: Mateo, 30, often used playful teasing, compliments, and suggestive remarks in his interactions with coworkers and friends. He thought of himself as outgoing and fun. But over time, he noticed some people started to distance themselves. One colleague told him his behavior felt inappropriate, even though Mateo never intended harm. In therapy, he explored how his charm had been a survival skill growing up in a chaotic home; he had learned early that being entertaining earned him affection. Slowly, he began practicing ways of expressing himself that felt genuine without needing to be provocative.

Difficulty With Intimacy

People with Histrionic Personality Disorder often appear socially gifted, outgoing, emotionally expressive, and quick to form bonds. But more often than not, the opposite is true. A difficulty with intimacy steps forward, stems from early relational experiences. If the person learned that being emotionally honest led to punishment, rejection, or indifference, they may have developed strategies to appear close while keeping their core self guarded. As a result, relationships can feel one-sided or superficial.

Healing begins when the individual recognizes that intimacy doesn't have to be earned through charm or performance. It can be built through mutual trust, honest sharing, and the willingness to stay present, even when connection feels uncertain or imperfect. Therapy offers a space to practice this slow unveiling, to test whether it's possible to be accepted without the act.

Case snapshot: Pinda, 33, was known for her infectious energy and flirtatious charm. She had no trouble attracting romantic partners and often described new relationships as "instant soul connections." But after a few months, she would begin to feel bored, suffocated, or panicked. Her partners would ask for deeper emotional engagement, and she would either deflect with humor or start dramatic arguments. In therapy, Pinda realized that she had never seen emotional intimacy modeled in her childhood home. Her caregivers valued appearances, not feelings. For the first time, Pinda began practicing emotional honesty, staying with discomfort instead of escaping it.

Craving Attention While Fearing Rejection

One of the most painful paradoxes for individuals with Histrionic Personality Disorder is the deep craving for attention paired with an equally intense fear of rejection. The need to be seen, validated, and admired is rooted in a legitimate human longing for connection. But for those with HPD, that longing often comes with a cost; the closer they get to others, the more they fear they'll be left.

This dynamic plays out in subtle and overt ways. A person may light up a room with charm and expressiveness, then privately spiral if their texts go unanswered or if a friend seems distracted.

Because of this, they may engage in behavior that ensures they stay center stage, telling dramatic stories, dressing provocatively, or generating emotional intensity. But these strategies can exhaust or confuse others, sometimes leading to the very rejection the person hoped to avoid. When that happens, the internal story gets reinforced: "People always leave."

Case snapshot: Jason, 35, was the life of every party. He was funny, stylish, and effortlessly engaging. People gravitated toward him, but he rarely felt secure in his relationships. If someone canceled plans or didn't respond quickly, he panicked, sometimes sending a string of anxious messages, other times cutting them off preemptively. Through therapy, Jason came to understand that his childhood was marked by emotional inconsistency. A parent's approval could vanish without explanation, leaving him desperate to stay noticed. By naming these patterns and slowly tolerating small moments of silence or distance, Jason began building relationships that didn't rely on constant performance.

Implementation Exercise: Safety Beyond the Spotlight

This reflection helps challenge the idea that attention is the only form of safety.

1. **Think of a recent moment when you felt rejected or ignored:** What happened? How did you interpret it?
2. **Notice your emotional response:** Was it fear, shame, anger, or something else?
3. **Ask: What did I fear losing?** Was it connection, approval, or a sense of self-worth?

4. **Write a grounding truth:** For example: "I am still safe even when I am not the center of attention."

5. **Create a non-performative connection goal:** Choose one relationship where you'll practice being present without trying to impress. Observe what it feels like to just be.

This exercise helps separate identity from image, reminding you that your presence, not your performance, is what makes you worthy of love.

IMPACT ON OTHERS

Living with Histrionic Personality Disorder doesn't happen in a vacuum. It affects everyone around the individual.

Mixed Signals

To the outside world, someone with Histrionic Personality Disorder can seem warm, enthusiastic, and inviting one moment, then distant, critical, or withdrawn the next. This emotional variability often sends mixed signals to others. Emotions often move quickly and dramatically. They might feel sincerely connected to someone, then suddenly perceive rejection or distance, even in neutral situations. This pattern can erode trust in relationships. Partners, friends, or coworkers may feel like they're being tested, manipulated, or kept at arm's length. They may worry that the relationship is unstable or that they're being held to invisible standards. Over time, the unpredictable emotional climate can lead to misunderstandings, tension, and even avoidance.

Case snapshot: Belko, 29, was known for being outgoing and attentive, always complimenting coworkers, offering help, and organizing team lunches. But when he felt overlooked or excluded, his mood would suddenly shift. He'd become sarcastic, withdrawn, or emotionally distant. One colleague described it as "walking into a different weather system every day." In therapy, Belko began to understand how quickly he interpreted minor slights as rejection. By learning to pause before reacting, he started to communicate his needs instead of acting them out.

Implementation Exercise: Clarifying Communication

This reflection helps reduce emotional misfires and improve clarity in relationships.

1. **Think of a recent interaction that ended in confusion:** What did you say, and how might it have been interpreted?
2. **Identify the emotion you were feeling:** Were you hurt, anxious, frustrated, or seeking reassurance?
3. **Ask: What did I need in that moment?** Did you need recognition, space, validation, or support?
4. **Write one clear statement you could have said:** For example: "I felt left out earlier. Can we talk about it?"
5. **Practice using that statement in a future moment:** The goal is not to be perfect, but to move from hinting or reacting toward honest, direct expression.

Strained Friendships

Friendships with individuals who have Histrionic Personality Disorder can begin with a bang and develop quickly, but they come under strain before either party realizes it.

This strain often emerges when emotional demands become too high or expectations feel unreasonable. A person with HPD might expect frequent check-ins, constant affirmation, or exclusive loyalty. Needy, right? If a friend pulls back or becomes less available, it may trigger emotional outbursts, silent treatment, or sudden accusations. The friend, caught off guard, may feel manipulated or drained, unsure how to meet the emotional expectations being placed on them. Additionally, their friends tend to feel like they are riding an emotional rollercoaster.

The individual with HPD is often unaware of how exhausting this pattern can be for others. Their behavior is typically driven by fear of being forgotten or left out, not by a desire to control. But if this fear isn't addressed directly, it can wear down even the most well-intentioned relationships. Friends may gradually distance themselves, creating a painful cycle of connection and loss.

Case snapshot: Layla, 24, had a tight-knit group of friends she loved deeply. But she often felt sidelined if someone made plans without her. She'd send long messages expressing how hurt she was or withdraw dramatically, waiting to be checked on. Over time, her friends began inviting her to fewer events, not because they didn't care, but because they feared conflict. In therapy, Layla explored how her early experiences of being overlooked by caregivers had made her hypersensitive to exclusion. Learning to express her feelings calmly, without ultimatums, helped her friendships become more sustainable.

Implementation Exercise: Friendship Filter

Use this tool to examine the expectations you bring into friendships and how they affect connection.

1. **List three recent moments you felt let down by a friend:** What happened, and what did it mean to you?
2. **Ask: What did I assume about their behavior?** Did you

assume they didn't care, were avoiding you, or didn't value the friendship?

3. **Identify what you actually needed:** Did you want more inclusion, reassurance, or honesty?

4. **Write a clear, non-accusatory message:** Example: "When I heard about the get-together, I felt a little left out. Can we talk about that?"

5. **Reflect on your friendship expectations:** Are they mutual, flexible, and realistic? Or are they rooted in fear?

This exercise supports the transition from reactive disappointment to thoughtful communication, laying the groundwork for stronger, more balanced friendships.

Misinterpreted Intentions

The intent behind their actions is often misunderstood. Because many individuals with HPD use emotional expressiveness, flirtation, or dramatization to feel seen and valued, others might assume their behavior is calculated. A heartfelt story told with intensity may be dismissed as attention-seeking. An affectionate gesture may be read as flirtation. A genuine emotional response may be labeled "too much." The result is a profound sense of being unseen or judged. The person with HPD may begin to believe that no matter what they do, they will be misunderstood. This creates a feedback loop where behaviors become more exaggerated in an attempt to clarify emotion or secure validation, leading to even more misunderstanding.

What's often missed is the vulnerability underneath. These behaviors usually stem from early experiences where the person had to "perform" to be loved, heard, or safe. In adulthood, the same habits emerge, but without a conscious awareness of their origins. When others assume bad intent, it reinforces old wounds of rejection and emotional invisibility.

Case snapshot: Marisol, 26, had a vibrant personality and loved telling animated stories. In her workplace, some colleagues saw her as dramatic or "fake," even though she was sincere in her enthusiasm. One supervisor assumed she was manipulating others for attention and gave her a poor review, citing a lack of professionalism. In therapy, Marisol explored how she had learned to be expressive to stay close to an emotionally distant parent. By learning to communicate her needs more directly and adjusting her tone in certain environments, she found new ways to express herself without being misunderstood.

NAVIGATING HPD TRAITS

Living with Histrionic Personality Disorder requires you to understand the patterns beneath your behaviors, the fears that drive them, the needs they reflect, and the origins they may be rooted in. When those patterns are seen clearly and approached with compassion, they can be reshaped.

Building Emotional Awareness

Emotions are often expressed before they're understood. A sudden burst of tears, laughter, or frustration may pour out before the underlying feeling is even recognized. When emotional expression was once the only path to connection, the habit of reacting instantly became second nature.

Building emotional awareness is the first step toward regaining control. It involves slowing down the emotional process long enough to identify what you're truly feeling, and why. This awareness helps create a gap between emotion and action, a space in which choice becomes possible.

Developing a richer emotional vocabulary also helps. Instead of defaulting to general terms like "bad" or "fine," individuals learn to use precise language: frustrated, hurt, embarrassed, hopeful. This not only deepens self-understanding but also improves communication with others, reducing misunderstandings and strengthening connections (Lovering, 2017).

Mindfulness practices can also be valuable. Learning to observe feelings without immediately reacting, through breath work, body scans, or simple self-inquiry, builds internal resilience. Over time, the emotional system becomes less reactive and more reflective.

Case snapshot: Omolara, 31, frequently described herself as being "too emotional." In conflicts, she'd cry quickly or escalate situations with dramatic exits. But she couldn't always explain what she was feeling. In therapy, Omolara began using a daily emotion journal, tracking not only what she felt but what triggered it and what helped her calm down. Over time, she began to notice patterns: embarrassment often showed up as anger, and sadness emerged when she felt excluded. With practice, Omolara started naming her emotions before expressing them, bringing more stability to her reactions and her relationships.

Implementation Exercise: Emotion Labeling Log

This tool helps you slow down, observe your feelings, and respond with clarity.

1. **At the end of each day, list three emotional moments:**
   What happened? How did you react?

2. **Name the primary emotion:** Use specific words, e.g., "disappointed," "anxious," "hopeful."
3. **Explore the trigger:** What led to this feeling? What thoughts or fears were activated?
4. **Notice your response:** Did you react immediately? Did it help or harm the situation?
5. **Write one alternative response for the future:** Example: "Next time I feel ignored, I'll ask for a moment to check in instead of withdrawing."

The more familiar you become with your internal world, the less it controls you, and the more empowered you become in every emotional exchange.

Encouraging Depth Over Performance

One of the most significant internal shifts for individuals with Histrionic Personality Disorder is learning to value emotional depth over dramatic performance. Expressiveness is not the problem; it's when that expressiveness becomes a shield, a show, or a shortcut to connection that it begins to obscure true emotional presence.

The goal should not be to silence emotion, but to allow space for quieter truths. This means noticing when you feel the urge to exaggerate, impress, or entertain, and gently asking what's underneath. Are you feeling insecure? Unseen? Nervous? Instead of amplifying expression to win attention, you begin to build comfort with simply being.

Encouraging depth involves slowing down conversations, resisting the urge to perform, and practicing emotional honesty, even if it feels awkward at first. It means tolerating the silence between words, the pauses in connection, and the discomfort of not always being the most captivating person in the room.

THERAPEUTIC APPROACHES

There's no one-size-fits-all treatment for Histrionic Personality Disorder, but several therapeutic approaches have shown strong promise in helping individuals build self-awareness, emotional regulation, and deeper relational connections. Each approach offers tools not to erase someone's personality, but to stabilize the emotional terrain that often drives reactive behavior.

Psychodynamic Therapy: Psychodynamic therapy helps individuals explore how early life experiences shaped their current emotional patterns and relationships. For people with HPD, this often means uncovering where the performative self was first formed, usually in environments where love felt conditional or only available when they were entertaining, pleasing, or impressive. By understanding these unconscious dynamics, clients begin to disentangle their identity from their coping strategies and reclaim a more authentic self.

Cognitive behavioral therapy (CBT): CBT is effective in helping individuals with HPD recognize the thoughts that fuel their emotional reactivity and relationship difficulties. For instance, beliefs like "If I'm not interesting, I'll be abandoned" or "I must always be charming to be liked" are explored and challenged. Clients learn to replace automatic thoughts with more balanced, grounded beliefs, reducing emotional overreactions and impulsive social behavior.

Dialectical behavior therapy (DBT): Although DBT was originally developed for Borderline Personality Disorder, its emphasis on emotional regulation, interpersonal effectiveness, and mindfulness makes it particularly useful for people with HPD as well. DBT teaches skills like distress tolerance, identifying emotions before acting on them, and maintaining boundaries in relationships, all of which are valuable for navigating the emotional intensity that characterizes HPD.

Mindfulness-based approaches: Mindfulness practices help individuals become more attuned to their internal states without reacting immediately. For someone with HPD, this could mean noticing the urge to seek reassurance and choosing instead to sit with that discomfort. Breathwork, grounding exercises, and body awareness techniques support a slower, more reflective response to emotional stimuli.

Implementation Exercise: Finding Your Therapeutic Fit

Use this exercise to reflect on which therapeutic path might support your growth.

1. **What do you notice about your emotional patterns?** Do you react quickly, seek constant affirmation, or feel uncertain about your identity?
2. **Which of these approaches feels most aligned with your needs?**
   - Psychodynamic: Want to explore your past and relational patterns?
   - CBT: Interested in changing thought patterns that fuel your behavior?
   - DBT: Need help with emotion regulation and relationship skills?
   - Mindfulness: Want to be more present and less reactive?

3. **Set one intention for therapy:** Example: "I want to stop feeling like I have to perform in every relationship."

4. **Write down a question you could ask a therapist:** Example: "What experience do you have working with people who use performance as a coping strategy?"

Choosing a therapeutic path is not about fixing yourself. It's about supporting your growth in ways that respect who you are and who you're becoming.

SUPPORT FOR LOVED ONES

Loving someone with Histrionic Personality Disorder can feel like being caught in a constant current of emotional highs and lows. One moment, you're pulled close with warmth, affection, and intensity. Next, you may find yourself navigating drama, insecurity, or unexpected emotional storms.

Providing effective support requires a balance of empathy and boundaries. Being compassionate doesn't mean being consumed. In fact, healthy support often means knowing when to step back, when to speak up, and how to avoid reinforcing reactive patterns. It's not about fixing the other person; it's about showing up in ways that are clear, consistent, and sustainable.

Therapy isn't just for the person with HPD. Involving loved ones in therapy, through family sessions, psychoeducation, or support groups, can dramatically improve understanding and communication. It gives everyone in the relationship tools for navigating emotional intensity without losing connection.

Case snapshot: Alex and Mira, 28, had been in a relationship with Alex for three years. She often felt overwhelmed by his emotional needs; he needed constant praise, became upset if she didn't respond immediately to messages, and often accused her of losing interest if she spent time alone. Mira started attending therapy on her own and learned about HPD. With her therapist, she developed scripts for setting boundaries and practiced validating Alex without taking responsibility for his emotional state. Eventually, Alex joined her for a few sessions. Together, they began shifting their patterns, less blame, more clarity, and room for both people's emotional needs.

Implementation Exercise: The Steady Support Checklist

Use this checklist to reflect on how you can support someone with HPD while protecting your own well-being.

1. **Am I trying to fix or rescue?** Support doesn't mean solving, ask yourself if you're over-functioning in the relationship.
2. **Have I named my boundaries?** What's okay and not okay in terms of emotional demands, time, and space?
3. **Am I reinforcing reactive behavior?** Do I give extra attention when the person escalates emotionally? If so, how can I shift toward reinforcing calm, direct communication instead?
4. **Do I have emotional outlets of my own?** Ensure you're receiving support from friends, therapy, or peer groups.
5. **Can I stay kind and firm at the same time?** Practice saying, "I care about you, and I need to pause this conversation until we can both speak calmly."

Loving someone with HPD doesn't mean abandoning yourself. It means learning how to stay grounded while offering real support, support that helps them grow instead of spinning in cycles.

EXERCISE: AUTHENTICITY INVENTORY

For many people with Histrionic Personality Disorder, the line between genuine expression and performance has been blurred for years. When connection has been historically tied to how entertaining, charming, or emotionally dramatic one can be, it becomes difficult to know what it means to simply be.

This exercise is designed to help you begin untangling that line. It's not about self-criticism, it's about self-discovery. The goal isn't to eliminate expression, but to root it more deeply in authenticity. When you show up as you truly are, you don't have to chase connection. You attract it naturally.

Authenticity Inventory

Use this journaling exercise regularly to reconnect with your emotional truth.

1. **Recall a recent moment when you exaggerated or performed.**
   - What happened?
   - Who was involved?
   - What did you say or do?
2. **What were you feeling underneath?**
   - Were you anxious about being ignored?
   - Did you want to feel important, admired, or loved?
3. **Ask yourself: What would I have done differently if I felt safe to just be me?**
   - How would your tone, words, or body language have changed?

4. **Name the fear that drives performance:**
   - What do you think will happen if you're not "on" all the time?
5. **Try it in real time:**
   - Choose a safe interaction (e.g., with a close friend, therapist, or journal).
   - Share a thought or feeling without embellishing.
   - Notice how it feels in your body. Was it harder? Easier? More vulnerable?
6. **Reflection prompt:** "What would it feel like to show up as I am, without needing to impress, entertain, or exaggerate?"

By making space for your unfiltered self, you begin to rebuild trust in your own presence. You don't have to be larger than life to matter; you just have to be real.

CHAPTER 9

AVOIDANT PERSONALITY DISORDER

I magine living with a constant internal alarm that goes off every time someone looks your way, asks your opinion, or invites you into a conversation. You long to connect, but connection feels like exposure. You crave closeness, yet every step toward it feels like walking a tightrope over humiliation. That's the hidden world of Avoidant Personality Disorder (AvPD).

AvPD is marked by a chronic, deeply ingrained fear of rejection that colors every social interaction with the threat of shame. Unlike temporary nervousness or situational anxiety, this fear lives under the skin. It shapes how a person sees themselves, what they believe others think of them, and whether they dare to risk showing up at all.

WHAT IS AVOIDANT PERSONALITY DISORDER?

Avoidant Personality Disorder (AvPD) is often branded as just introversion or social discomfort. In reality, it's a deeply rooted psychological pattern that centers on fear of rejection, feelings of inadequacy, and extreme sensitivity to perceived criticism. The Diagnostic and Statistical Manual of Mental Disorders (DSM-5-TR) defines AvPD as a pervasive pattern of social inhibition, low self-esteem, and hypersensitivity to negative evaluation that begins by early adulthood and is present across contexts (Fariba & Sapra, 2021).

Individuals with AvPD often assume that others are constantly judging them, even in neutral settings. Compliments may be dismissed as pity; silence may be interpreted as disapproval. These perceptions represent persistent beliefs that shape behavior and self-worth. The world feels like a stage where every move risks embarrassment.

Research suggests that AvPD affects approximately 2.4% of the general population, though some studies report slightly lower or higher rates depending on the diagnostic criteria and population sampled (Zimmerman, 2021). Despite this, AvPD remains under-diagnosed or confused with other conditions like social anxiety disorder.

Differentiating AvPD From Social Anxiety

While AvPD shares features with social anxiety disorder, the two are not identical. Social anxiety tends to be more situational; someone might fear public speaking or large parties but function comfortably in other social settings. In contrast, AvPD is more pervasive. The fear isn't just of judgment in specific situations; it's the belief that one is inherently inadequate and will be rejected if truly known (Nichols, 2023).

At the core of AvPD is a deeply painful inner narrative: "I am not enough." This often stems from a childhood history marked by emotional neglect, criticism, or bullying. As a result, the person begins to avoid not just situations, but entire dimensions of life, relationships, goals, visibility, anything that might invite scrutiny or disappointment.

This inner world is often filled with chronic shame and hypervigilance. Individuals may second-guess every word they say, replay conversations obsessively, and withdraw from opportunities that might reveal their perceived flaws. Ironically, the efforts to avoid rejection often lead to isolation, creating the very loneliness they feared in the first place.

CORE REJECTIONS AND DRIVERS

At the center of Avoidant Personality Disorder lies a fear of being disliked, it's the expectation of humiliation, the assumption of failure, and the haunting certainty that any exposure will lead to emotional harm.

Hypervigilance to Signs of Disapproval

Imagine being in a conversation where every word, glance, or silence is scrutinized, not by others, but by your own mind. For individuals with Avoidant Personality Disorder, this isn't occasional social anxiety. It's a relentless internal monitoring system, constantly scanning for the possibility of rejection, ridicule, or disapproval.

This hypervigilance is often automatic. Someone may replay a passing look as a judgment, or interpret a neutral comment as a veiled criticism. Compliments might be distrusted and assumed to be sarcastic or obligatory. Even casual social interactions become high-stakes emotional minefields, where every detail is analyzed through the lens of perceived inadequacy. What makes this vigilance particularly distressing is that it's self-perpetuating. The more someone watches for rejection, the more they interpret ambiguous social cues as negative, reinforcing the belief that they are disliked, unworthy, or socially incompetent. These thought patterns become deeply embedded, shaping not just social behavior but also self-identity.

Case snapshot: Leah, 31, avoided casual interactions at work. Even a co-worker saying, "You're quiet today," would spiral her into self-doubt. She'd spend hours wondering if she seemed rude or awkward. In therapy, she discovered this hyperawareness began in adolescence, when peer bullying made her feel constantly judged. Learning to slow down her thoughts and reality-check her assumptions helped Leah start to differentiate between actual criticism and perceived threat.

Implementation Exercise: Decoding the Moment

This exercise helps reduce misinterpretation by bringing awareness to real-time social triggers.

1. **Recall a recent interaction that left you feeling judged:** What was said or done?
2. **Describe your internal reaction:** What did you think the other person meant?
3. **Ask: What's another possible explanation?** Could they have been tired, distracted, or thinking about something unrelated?
4. **Reality-check the moment:** Would someone else interpret it the same way?
5. **Practice grounding:** Take three deep breaths, name five things you see, or repeat a statement like: "This is a reaction, not a fact."

Over time, decoding these moments reduces the emotional load and weakens the reflex to assume rejection.

Anticipating Criticism and Abandonment

Criticism becomes a looming certainty. Even in seemingly safe interactions, the mind leaps ahead, preparing for the moment when someone will pull away, roll their eyes, or expose their inadequacy. This anticipation of disapproval becomes a silent, but constant, force. The fear is about being fundamentally unworthy of love or belonging. This belief often leads to preemptive self-editing, avoiding conversations, withholding opinions, and staying out of the spotlight. The logic is clear but heartbreaking: if no one sees the real me, they can't reject me.

This pattern is especially damaging in relationships. People with AvPD may test others by withdrawing or downplaying their needs to see if anyone notices. When others don't respond as hoped, often because the signals are too subtle, the avoidant person takes this as confirmation that rejection is inevitable. The pain of disconnection, though self-imposed, still feels deeply real.

Fear of abandonment doesn't always come from dramatic betrayals. Often, it grows out of smaller but consistent relational wounds: caregivers who were emotionally absent, peers who mocked vulnerability, or family systems that discouraged authenticity. These experiences teach a powerful lesson: being yourself is too risky.

Case snapshot: Damian, 34, had a history of ghosting friends after minor disagreements. Even gentle feedback would trigger overwhelming shame. He assumed people were just being polite and didn't actually like him. In therapy, Damian uncovered memories of being criticized by a parent for "talking too much" or "needing attention." As an adult, he defaulted to silence, convinced any need would be met with judgment. Through relational repair work, Damian slowly practiced naming his needs out loud and learned that healthy relationships could hold disagreement without abandonment.

The Role of Early Invalidation

Behind the layers of avoidance, silence, and self-protection in Avoidant Personality Disorder often lies a childhood story defined by quiet hurt. Invalidation, whether through neglect, ridicule, or emotional unavailability, creates the fertile ground in which AvPD takes root.

Emotional invalidation sometimes stems from the chronic experience of having one's feelings minimized, dismissed, or ignored. When a child expresses sadness and is told to "stop being dramatic," or shares joy and is met with indifference, the lesson becomes clear: your emotions are too much, too wrong, or not worth hearing.

Repeated invalidation conditions a child to doubt their inner world. Over time, they learn that sharing their thoughts or feelings leads not to connection, but to embarrassment or isolation. As adults, these individuals internalize the idea that being seen means being shamed. So they shrink. They adapt. They hide the parts of themselves that once reached out and were hurt. AvPD grows from this adaptation.

Case snapshot: Sagdo, 28, was praised as a "quiet, easy child" growing up. But behind her calm exterior was a girl who had learned early that her parents had little tolerance for emotions. When she cried, she was ignored. When she showed excitement, she was told to "calm down." As an adult, Sagdo felt invisible in relationships but couldn't articulate what she needed. In therapy, she began to trace her emotional numbness back to those moments of childhood dismissal. Reconnecting with her emotional self became the first step in healing.

Internalized Belief: If I Show Who I Am, I'll Be Rejected

Avoidant Personality Disorder begins with a belief. A deep, often unspoken conviction that says, "If people knew the real me, they'd walk away." This belief doesn't arise overnight. It forms through thousands of subtle moments: a joke that landed poorly, a parent who mocked vulnerability, a peer who rolled their eyes at enthusiasm.

Over time, these moments form a pattern, a story about the self that feels permanent. And that story becomes the lens through which all new experiences are filtered. Compliments are met with suspicion. The connection feels unsafe. Vulnerability becomes synonymous with danger.

The tragedy of this belief is that it creates the very outcome it fears. In trying to avoid rejection, individuals hide their authentic selves. They withdraw, mask, or over-accommodate. And in doing so, they prevent others from forming a real connection with them, not because they're unworthy, but because they've become invisible.

This concealment doesn't mean apathy. In fact, the opposite is true. People with AvPD often care deeply about relationships, meaning, and being seen. But the pain of past rejection leaves them frozen between two truths: "I want to be known," and "Being known will break me."

Case snapshot: Kieran, 25, had a close group of friends but rarely shared his personal thoughts. He played the role of the agreeable one, always nodding, always deflecting. When someone praised his artwork, he changed the subject. In therapy, Kieran explored how childhood ridicule around his interests made self-expression feel unsafe. He realized he had been editing himself out of fear. With support, he practiced naming one feeling per day in conversations, a small but radical act of reclaiming visibility.

Implementation Exercise: Identity Check-In

This exercise helps you reconnect with parts of yourself that have been hidden for safety.

1. **List three parts of yourself you tend to hide in social settings:** Examples: creative hobbies, strong opinions, emotional vulnerability.
2. **Write why you believe these parts might be rejected:** What past experiences influenced that belief?
3. **Ask: What might it feel like to show just 10% more of this part?** How could you try that safely, through a conversation, a post, or a small act?
4. **Reflection prompt:** "If someone saw this part of me and stayed, what would that mean?"

Each small act of self-expression is a challenge to the old belief, and a step toward building a new one.

THE DOUBLE BIND OF AVOIDANCE

Avoidant Personality Disorder is built on a paradox: the desire for connection is just as strong as the fear of it. This creates an impossible bind. To move toward people feels dangerous, but staying away feels unbearable. The result is a life suspended between craving intimacy and fearing the exposure it demands.

This isn't laziness or disinterest. It's also not about being antisocial or cold. It's about living with a nervous system wired to equate visibility with pain. The more someone wants to be close, the more they fear being found out, flawed, awkward, or simply not enough. So they stay hidden, and loneliness becomes the price of safety.

Desire for Connection vs. Fear of Exposure

People with Avoidant Personality Disorder often feel torn between two powerful forces: the longing to connect and the terror of being seen. It might look like a random preference for solitude, but in reality, it's an emotional paradox. Deep down, they want closeness, intimacy, and belonging. But the prospect of letting someone in, of being known in their fullness, feels too dangerous to risk.

This fear doesn't stem from arrogance or an inflated sense of personal flaws. It's born from lived experiences where vulnerability led to pain. For many, opening up in the past has meant being laughed at, criticized, or ignored. And so, connection becomes synonymous with exposure, and exposure becomes unbearable.

What results is a life filled with silent yearning. People with AvPD may observe others laughing, bonding, and sharing openly while quietly grieving their own isolation. They may fantasize about relationships they're too afraid to initiate. They imagine being close to others while building walls to ensure it never happens.

Even when relationships are formed, the fear doesn't go away. It often shows up as self-sabotage, canceling plans last-minute, deflecting compliments, or withholding opinions out of fear they'll be judged. The individual may test their partner's affection by staying emotionally distant, waiting to be rejected. When rejection doesn't come, it feels confusing. When it does, it feels like proof that they were right to hide.

Case snapshot: Yara, 32, longed for a partner but avoided dating. On the rare occasions she went out, she carefully rehearsed every sentence, avoided personal questions, and left early. She later told her therapist she was terrified of someone discovering how "boring and broken" she was. Together, they unpacked how her childhood, where emotional openness was mocked, had created the belief that love required performance. Through gentle exposure work and journaling, Yara began to tolerate small acts of realness: sharing an honest feeling, letting someone see her art, staying one minute longer in a vulnerable moment.

Implementation Exercise: Holding Both Truths

This exercise helps name and navigate the internal conflict between wanting closeness and fearing it.

1. **Write two truths about your social experience:** One that reflects your desire (e.g., "I want deeper friendships") and one that reflects your fear (e.g., "I'm scared I'll be rejected").
2. **Visualize them side by side:** Imagine both truths sitting in the same room, neither erased, neither dominant.
3. **Ask: What would a small act of connection look like that honors both truths?** It might be texting a friend, commenting honestly in a meeting, or sharing a personal story.
4. **Reflection prompt:** "What does it feel like to be scared and still reach out?"

Healing doesn't mean the fear goes away. It means learning to move with it, rather than against it.

Avoidance as Protection

To someone on the outside, avoidant behaviors might look like indifference, aloofness, or even arrogance. But for those living with Avoidant Personality Disorder, these behaviors are not about apathy; they are shields. Avoidance becomes a carefully constructed system of protection, designed to prevent the emotional bruises that feel inevitable in social life.

At its core, avoidance is a form of emotional armor. If you don't speak, you can't say the wrong thing. If you don't try, you can't fail. If you don't get close, you can't be abandoned. This logic, while painful, makes emotional sense to someone who has been hurt simply for existing.

Avoidance can take many forms: skipping events, ghosting friends, hesitating to make eye contact, refusing compliments, or procrastinating on opportunities that might lead to exposure. Each behavior says: "If I don't engage, I can't be wounded." But while this defense reduces the risk of immediate harm, it also diminishes the chance of joy, connection, and growth.

Over time, the safety that avoidance provides begins to suffocate. What once offered relief now contributes to chronic loneliness, regret, and stalled potential. The world grows smaller. Relationships fade. Dreams go unexplored. And beneath it all lies a quiet grief, not just for missed opportunities, but for the parts of the self never given room to breathe.

Case snapshot: Niko, 40, passed on a major promotion because it involved leading team meetings. Despite being qualified and respected, he convinced himself others would see him as incompetent. He chose the safety of invisibility over the risk of rejection. In therapy, Niko realized he wasn't afraid of the job; he was afraid of being *seen* in the job. Through graduated exposure and self-compassion work, he began speaking up in low-risk situations, eventually finding confidence in sharing his ideas without the old sense of threat.

Implementation Exercise: Protective Behaviors Inventory

This exercise helps identify and explore avoidant patterns that are rooted in self-protection.

1. **List three common ways you avoid social or emotional discomfort:** Not replying to texts, over-preparing for meetings, staying silent in groups.
2. **Ask: What are these behaviors protecting me from?** Identify the perceived threat (e.g., embarrassment, rejection, being misunderstood).
3. **Evaluate the cost.** What has each behavior helped you avoid? What opportunities or experiences might it have also blocked?
4. **Name one area where you're ready to risk a little more:** Start small: say "thank you" when complimented, share an opinion in a group, or attend a social gathering for ten minutes.

Avoidance may have once saved you. But healing begins when you ask if it's still serving you now.

Emotional Cost

Avoidance may offer short-term safety, but it comes at a steep emotional price. Over time, the very strategies used to prevent pain can become the source of it. Individuals with Avoidant Personality Disorder often carry a quiet burden, a persistent ache that stems not from what happened, but from what never got the chance to.

The emotional cost of AvPD often looks like chronic loneliness. Even in the presence of others, individuals may feel like outsiders. They might sit through gatherings silently, smiling while internally bracing for missteps, or keeping conversation light to avoid vulnerability. And when the night ends, they return home with the same question: "Why can't I connect like everyone else?"

There is also grief, the kind that accumulates when life is lived at a distance. Friendships fade, not from conflict, but from silence. Opportunities go unpursued. Praise is deflected. Dreams are shelved. With each missed chance, the avoidant person becomes more convinced that they don't belong in the world they secretly long for.

These experiences often lead to depression, low self-worth, and intense self-criticism. The emotional isolation can feel like punishment, even though it was chosen for self-preservation.

Case snapshot: Chioma, 29, rarely left her apartment outside of work. She scrolled through social media, watching others share milestones, inside jokes, and memories. She felt invisible. When a friend texted to invite her out, Chioma always declined, terrified she'd say something wrong or be too awkward. But later, the loneliness was unbearable. In therapy, she began to name the cost of her choices, not as self-blame, but as clarity. From that awareness, she created a plan to re-engage with life, one manageable step at a time.

Implementation Exercise: Naming the Cost

This reflection helps make the emotional impact of avoidance more visible, without judgment.

184 WIRED FOR CHAOS

1. **List three recent situations you avoided:** Social, professional, or emotional.
2. **Ask: What did I feel in the moment of avoidance?** Relief? Shame? Sadness? Numbness?
3. **Explore the aftereffects:** What feelings followed? Loneliness, regret, or a sense of safety?
4. **Name the opportunity lost:** Was it a connection, a learning moment, or a sense of pride?
5. **Reflection prompt:** "What is the emotional toll of staying safe?"

Acknowledging the cost doesn't mean shaming the strategy; it means honoring your desire for more.

Self-Sabotage

In Avoidant Personality Disorder, self-sabotage often masquerades as self-preservation. It's not always obvious or dramatic; sometimes, it's as subtle as not returning a call, missing a deadline, or declining an opportunity that was deeply desired. These actions rarely stem from laziness or disinterest. Instead, they come from a deep-seated belief: "If I try, I'll fail. If I speak, I'll embarrass myself. If I show up, I'll be rejected." For someone with AvPD, success can feel threatening. The idea of being seen, even positively, can stir anxiety. Praise may feel like pressure. Achievement may invite scrutiny. And connection may awaken old fears of exposure and rejection. As a result, individuals may unconsciously derail their own progress, not because they don't want growth, but because they're terrified of what growth might cost them.

This can show up in many forms: procrastinating on important tasks, sabotaging relationships just as they become meaningful, or setting impossibly high standards and then retreating when they can't be met. Each instance is a way of managing the unbearable tension between desire and fear.

The internal dialogue is often harsh. "I knew I'd mess it up," "They probably didn't want me there anyway," or "Why bother?" These narratives don't reflect the truth; they reflect the protective logic of someone who has been wounded by exposure in the past.

Case snapshot: Obiora, 36, was offered a spot in a creative fellowship he'd dreamed about for years. But instead of accepting, he delayed his reply until the deadline passed. When asked why, he said, "I figured they sent the email by mistake." In therapy, Obiora traced this reflex back to a school experience where his teacher publicly dismissed his writing. That moment, long buried, had shaped a belief that he didn't deserve recognition. Naming the fear helped him begin to separate his past from his present.

IMPACT ON RELATIONSHIPS AND WORK

Avoidant Personality Disorder profoundly affects how individuals navigate relationships and professional spaces. From romantic intimacy to casual workplace interactions, AvPD can quietly undermine connection, communication, and confidence.

Withdrawal From Group Settings

People with AvPD often approach relationships with a deep-seated fear of rejection. Even when they care deeply, they may hold back, fearing that vulnerability will lead to abandonment or judgment. They may appear reserved, uninvested, or overly agreeable, not because they don't have strong feelings, but because they've learned to mask them as a form of self-protection. In group settings, this leads to silence, absence, and a painful sense of invisibility.

Case snapshot: Darius, 38, was known among coworkers as reliable but distant. He never attended office social events and declined every invitation with polite excuses. In his relationship, he avoided conflict to the point where small frustrations festered into resentment. When his partner asked for more emotional openness, Darius panicked, fearing rejection if he said the wrong thing. In therapy, he uncovered a belief that expressing needs would make him a burden. With support, he began practicing simple assertive statements, like saying, "I'm not sure how to answer that, but I want to try."

Difficulty Asserting Needs or Accepting Praise

In the workplace, AvPD often looks like over-apologizing, under-sharing, or shrinking away from leadership opportunities. A person with AvPD may avoid speaking up in meetings, hesitate to advocate for themselves, or brush off praise. These behaviors aren't about modesty; they're driven by a fear that visibility invites scrutiny and that any spotlight will reveal their perceived flaws.

Case snapshot: Noogo, 26, excelled at her job but downplayed her contributions. When praised, she'd deflect: "I just got lucky." She worried that accepting credit would make her a target for criticism. Her therapist helped her track the impulse to deflect and replace it with a simple "thank you." Over time, Noogo began to internalize her worth instead of hiding it.

Implementation Exercise: Receiving Practice

1. Identify three compliments or positive feedback you've received recently.
2. Instead of deflecting or minimizing, write down what it would feel like to fully receive each one.

3. Practice saying "thank you" aloud without explanation.
4. Reflect: "What story do I tell myself about being praised, and is it still serving me?"

Overanalyzing Feedback

Individuals with AvPD may ruminate on even neutral comments, interpreting them as veiled criticism. A brief glance, a missed word, or a slightly altered tone can spiral into hours of self-doubt. Feedback, instead of being constructive, becomes confirmation of their internal fears.

Fear of Intimacy

Romantic relationships can be particularly challenging for people with AvPD. The closer someone gets, the more exposed the avoidant person feels. They may long for intimacy but fear its emotional risks. Partners may feel shut out or burdened by the avoidant person's silence or emotional withholding.

Case snapshot: Lena, 34, often feared her partner would leave her. But instead of expressing this, she became distant and withdrawn. This confused her partner, who interpreted it as disinterest. Through therapy, Lena learned to name her fear directly: "I feel like I'm too much or not enough, and that makes me want to hide." This honesty deepened their connection rather than damaging it.

PATHWAYS TO RECONNECTION

Cognitive Restructuring

At the core of Avoidant Personality Disorder is a belief system shaped by shame, fear, and self-doubt. These beliefs aren't just thoughts; they feel like facts. "I'm unlikable." "If people knew the real me, they'd walk away." "I will always be rejected." Over time, these ideas become internal rules that govern behavior, decision-making, and self-worth.

Cognitive restructuring helps challenge and rewire these distorted beliefs. It's not about toxic positivity or repeating empty affirmations. It's about examining where those beliefs came from, asking whether they still serve a purpose, and gradually replacing them with narratives that reflect a more balanced reality.

This process often begins in therapy, where individuals learn to spot automatic negative thoughts and question their accuracy. It's a shift from assumption to investigation: "What evidence do I have for this thought? Is it always true? What's an alternative explanation?" With time, the inner critic begins to lose its grip.

Importantly, cognitive restructuring doesn't erase fear; it gives a person options beyond it. When the belief "I'll ruin everything if I try" becomes "I might struggle, but that doesn't mean I'm a failure," space opens up for action, connection, and growth.

Case snapshot: Lara, 30, avoided applying for a job promotion she wanted. Her thought: "They'll laugh if I even try." In therapy, she traced this belief to a childhood memory, being mocked for speaking up in class. That one moment became a rule: visibility equals humiliation. With support, she began challenging that rule. She drafted her application and asked a trusted friend to review it. When she submitted it, the result didn't just change her job prospects; it began to shift her entire self-concept.

Implementation Exercise: Thought Reframe Journal

This tool supports the daily practice of identifying and challenging negative self-beliefs.

1. **Record the situation:** What triggered the negative thought?
2. **Identify the thought:** What belief or assumption came up?
3. **Question the evidence:** What supports this belief? What contradicts it?
4. **Reframe the thought:** What would a more balanced, compassionate statement sound like?
5. **Reflect:** How did this shift in thinking impact your emotional response or behavior?

Exposure Therapy

Avoidant Personality Disorder convinces people that retreat equals safety. But in truth, the longer someone avoids what they fear, the more powerful that fear becomes. Exposure therapy gently interrupts this cycle, not by flooding someone with anxiety, but by introducing manageable, structured doses of discomfort. It is the practice of proving, over and over again, that feared outcomes are often survivable, or don't happen at all.

Unlike the avoidance instinct, which says "don't even try," exposure therapy says, "try, just a little." It works by gradually placing individuals in anxiety-provoking situations while helping them regulate their responses. Over time, the brain learns that social interactions don't always lead to shame, and that vulnerability can coexist with safety.

Effective exposure doesn't mean throwing someone into their worst nightmare. It means building a ladder: from low-stakes moments like asking a stranger for the time, to bigger steps like sharing an opinion at work or initiating a conversation with someone new. Each rung climbed becomes evidence that the avoidant narrative isn't the only truth.

Case snapshot: Aiden, 28, avoided all networking events, convinced he'd say something awkward and be remembered for it forever. In therapy, he began with micro-exposures, sending one message a week to a colleague, then staying five minutes longer at team meetings. Each action sparked anxiety, but with coaching and journaling, Aiden began to notice: no one recoiled, no one ridiculed him. Eventually, he attended a professional gathering and introduced himself to three people. His fear didn't disappear, but his confidence grew louder.

Implementation Exercise: Exposure Ladder

Use this tool to build your own hierarchy of social risks and face them step by step.

1. **List five social situations you usually avoid**: Example: making a phone call, starting a conversation, giving an opinion.
2. **Rank them from least to most anxiety-inducing**: Should feel mildly uncomfortable, not terrifying.
3. **Design one exposure per week**: For example, week one: say hello to a neighbor.
4. **Track the outcome**: What happened? How did you feel before, during, and after?
5. **Reflect**: "What did I learn about my fear, and about myself?"

Self-Compassion

For people living with Avoidant Personality Disorder, the inner voice is rarely kind. It is often filled with shame, criticism, and self-blame, an echo of earlier experiences where vulnerability was punished or ignored. Self-compassion doesn't come naturally when you've been conditioned to believe you're fundamentally flawed. But it is one of the most powerful antidotes to avoidance. Self-compassion is not about pity or self-indulgence. It's the act of responding to your own pain the way you would to a close friend: with care, curiosity, and gentleness. It involves recognizing that suffering is a universal part of the human experience, not a personal defect.

Learning self-compassion means shifting from "What's wrong with me?" to "What happened to me?" It means understanding that the avoidance isn't weakness, it's protection. And that protection, while once helpful, may no longer be serving its purpose.

Therapies like Compassion-Focused Therapy (CFT) and mindfulness-based practices often help people with AvPD begin to soften their inner critic. By practicing small moments of self-kindness, acknowledging pain, validating feelings, and offering internal reassurance, individuals can start to build a relationship with themselves based not on fear, but on acceptance.

Case snapshot: Guinko, 33, constantly berated herself for being "pathetic" after turning down social invitations. In therapy, her psychologist introduced the concept of compassionate self-talk. At first, Guinko resisted, "That feels fake." But over time, she began replacing her inner dialogue with phrases like, "This fear makes sense," or, "I'm doing the best I can right now." These shifts didn't make the fear vanish, but they reduced the shame that kept her stuck.

Implementation Exercise: Self-Compassion Letter

This reflective exercise helps foster a more supportive inner dialogue.

1. **Think of a recent moment when you felt ashamed or avoided something:** Recall how you judged yourself.
2. **Now imagine a friend you deeply care about feeling the same way:** What would you say to comfort them?
3. **Write a letter to yourself using that same voice:** Speak from warmth, not criticism.
4. **Read the letter aloud:** Notice how it feels to receive your own compassion.
5. **Reflect:** "What shifts when I become my own ally instead of my harshest judge?"

Self-compassion is courage in the face of vulnerability. And for someone with AvPD, it's the first step toward healing the relationship they have with themselves.

Small Steps Toward Authenticity

Showing your true thoughts, feelings, or preferences can feel like handing someone a weapon. Years of rejection, ridicule, or emotional neglect can condition a person to hide behind social masks, only revealing what they believe is acceptable or unthreatening.

But healing doesn't require a grand reveal. It begins with micro-moments, tiny, manageable steps toward self-expression that feel risky but tolerable. These might include stating a preference, offering an opinion, or saying "no" without over-explaining. Every small act of honesty is an act of bravery, a declaration that says, "I matter, even if I'm not perfect."

Authenticity also means tolerating discomfort. Being real can trigger anxiety, especially for someone who fears judgment. But the goal is not to eliminate fear, it's to build capacity to stay present in its presence. With time and support, those moments of courage add up, reshaping how individuals see themselves and how they are seen by others.

Case snapshot: Sizwe, 29, always lets others choose restaurants, movies, and weekend plans, out of fear that expressing a preference would lead to rejection. When asked for his opinion, he'd deflect or say, "I'm easy." His therapist encouraged him to start small: naming his favorite coffee order, then sharing a playlist he liked. One day, Sizwe chose the restaurant. No one objected. That evening, he realized something powerful: the world didn't fall apart when he showed up as himself.

EXERCISE: FEAR VS. FACT TABLE

Avoidance often feels logical, after all, it's built on the promise of safety. But when you live with Avoidant Personality Disorder, fear often exaggerates the risks and erases the possibilities. One of the most effective ways to dismantle avoidance is to track it, examine it, and test it against reality.

This exercise is not about forcing yourself into discomfort for the sake of discomfort. It's about learning that fear is a forecast, not a fact. By reflecting on real experiences where fear dictated behavior, you can begin to separate what your mind *anticipated* from what *actually* happened.

Use this table regularly as part of your self-awareness routine. Over time, you'll likely notice a pattern: the worst-case scenarios rarely play out the way you expect. And even when discomfort happens, you survive it, and often grow from it.

Fear vs. Fact Table

1. **List three recent situations you avoided due to fear of rejection:** Example: declining a party invitation, not speaking up in a meeting, and avoiding eye contact with a cashier.
2. For each situation, complete the following:
   a. **The feared outcome:** What did you think would happen? Be specific.
   b. **What actually happened:** If the situation played out later, describe the result. If it didn't, imagine what likely would have occurred based on similar past experiences.
   c. **What I learned:** What did this teach you about your assumptions, fears, or capabilities?
3. **Journal prompt:** "What small risk could I take this week to test the truth of my fear, and what might I learn from it?"

By repeatedly confronting the stories fear tells you, you give yourself a chance to write new ones, stories that include courage, connection, and growth.

CHAPTER 10

DEPENDENT PERSONALITY DISORDER

I magine standing at the edge of a decision, whether small or large, and finding yourself paralyzed. Not because you're lazy or indifferent, but because you believe, deep down, that you cannot handle the consequences on your own. You reach for reassurance, defer the choice, or wait for someone else to take the lead. The idea of acting independently feels not just uncomfortable, it feels unsafe. This is the inner world of Dependent Personality Disorder (DPD).

DPD is a persistent and pervasive fear that autonomy leads to abandonment. Individuals with DPD often learn early in life that staying close, compliant, or invisible is the best way to survive. What looks like clinginess on the outside is often a learned survival strategy rooted in fear and reinforced by past relationships that punished independence or rewarded helplessness.

Let's begin by understanding what Dependent Personality Disorder actually is.

WHAT IS DEPENDENT PERSONALITY DISORDER?

Dependent Personality Disorder (DPD) is not simply a preference for closeness or a reluctance to make waves; it is a deep, pervasive reliance on others for emotional support, decision-making, and self-worth. According to the DSM-5-TR, DPD is defined by a persistent and excessive need to be taken care of, which leads to submissive, clinging behaviors and a profound fear of separation.

To meet diagnostic criteria, individuals must exhibit at least five of the following features:

- Difficulty making everyday decisions without excessive reassurance from others.
- A need for others to assume responsibility for most major areas of life.
- Difficulty expressing disagreement due to fear of loss or disapproval.
- Trouble initiating projects or doing things independently.
- Excessive efforts to obtain nurturance and support, even at the expense of discomfort.
- Feeling helpless or uncomfortable when alone.
- Urgently seeking another relationship when a close one ends.
- Unrealistic preoccupation with fears of being left to take care of oneself.

This pattern typically begins in early adulthood and manifests across personal, social, and occupational contexts. While some dependency is part of healthy human relationships, DPD crosses into pathology when the need for reassurance eclipses an individual's own sense of agency.

Estimates suggest that Dependent Personality Disorder affects approximately 0.6% of the general population, with higher rates observed in clinical settings (American Psychiatric Association, 2022). It is less frequently diagnosed than some other personality disorders, possibly due to its subtler presentation or confusion with cultural norms of loyalty, caregiving, or communal values.

DPD must be distinguished from behavior that reflects cultural or relational norms. In many collectivist cultures, interdependence and deference to family or authority are signs of respect, not dysfunction. Diagnosing DPD in these contexts requires careful consideration of whether dependency behaviors are distressing or impairing to the individual, rather than simply non-Western.

There is also a significant gender bias in diagnosis. DPD is more often diagnosed in women, a discrepancy that may reflect stereotypical expectations of passivity, caregiving, or emotional reliance. Research suggests that traits pathologized in women may be interpreted as normative in men or missed entirely (Jane et al., 2007).

HOW DEPENDENCY DEVELOPS

Dependency does not come out of nowhere. It is often the result of a long developmental process shaped by early relationships and learned beliefs about safety and competence. For individuals with Dependent Personality Disorder, early life may have offered care, but only conditionally, or may have undermined the development of confidence and autonomy altogether.

Children who grow up with overprotective caregivers may receive the message that the world is dangerous and that they are incapable of handling it. On the other hand, emotionally inconsistent or neglectful parenting can create a desperate need to attach to whoever offers stability. In both cases, the child doesn't develop independent problem-solving skills or internal confidence. Instead, they learn to look outward for reassurance, protection, and decision-making.

Attachment science also helps us understand the development of dependency. When caregivers are responsive but controlling or inconsistently nurturing, children may feel safest when yielding to authority or suppressing their own needs. Over time, autonomy is not just underdeveloped; it becomes feared.

Case snapshot: Reuben, 32, was raised by a single parent who was loving but anxious and overly involved. As a child, he wasn't allowed to bike alone, choose his own clothes, or disagree with family decisions. If he expressed uncertainty, he was comforted; if he showed initiative, he was discouraged. As an adult, Reuben often panics at the thought of making a decision without his partner's input. In therapy, he recognized how his independence was never nurtured, only his dependency was.

Implementation Exercise: Autonomy Timeline

This exercise encourages you to reflect on how early experiences may have shaped your relationship with independence.

1. **Make a timeline of your early caregiving experiences:** Include notable events where you were either encouraged or discouraged from acting independently.
2. **Mark specific memories where you felt competent:** Did anyone support your decision-making or celebrate your independence?
3. **Now mark experiences that made autonomy feel unsafe:** Was there punishment, guilt, or anxiety tied to doing things on your own?

4. **Reflection prompt:** "What messages did I receive about my ability to handle life on my own? How might those messages still be shaping me today?"

Understanding how dependency took root helps you reclaim choice and realize that the capacity for autonomy is still there, waiting to be practiced.

Reinforcement of Helplessness

Helplessness can be learned, not just through neglect or abandonment, but also through subtle, consistent reinforcement. For people with Dependent Personality Disorder, helplessness often became a pathway to care. When they expressed vulnerability, they received attention. When they tried to assert themselves, they were ignored, dismissed, or even punished. Over time, these experiences carved a belief system: being passive, agreeable, or needy brings safety; being autonomous leads to disconnection.

This reinforcement doesn't have to be dramatic. A child who's praised for being quiet and obedient but scolded for being assertive may begin to equate submission with love. In school, these same patterns may continue: the compliant student is rewarded, while the independent thinker is labeled as difficult. At home, a child who freezes or cries gets immediate support, while a child who tries something alone hears, "Don't do that without me."

What starts as protection slowly becomes a self-concept. The individual learns that others know best, that others should lead, and that their own instincts can't be trusted.

Case snapshot: Naledi, 29, grew up in a household where disagreement was seen as disrespect. Her parents were well-meaning but believed that children should "stay in their place." She learned to nod along, hide her feelings, and let others take charge. In her adult life, Naledi struggles to initiate conversations, say no to requests, or plan her own day without checking in with someone else. Every time she tries to assert herself, she hears an inner voice whisper, "Who do you think you are?"

Implementation Exercise: Control and Care Chart

This exercise helps uncover how past reinforcement may have shaped current beliefs about autonomy and support.

1. **Draw two columns labeled "When I Was in Control" and "When I Was Taken Care Of:"** Under each, list early life situations you remember.
2. **Next to each memory, note how others responded:** Did you receive love, approval, correction, or distance?
3. **Look for patterns:** Were you more praised when you were compliant? More ignored when you took initiative?
4. **Reflection prompt:** "What have I been taught about the 'right' way to be loved, and is that belief still serving me today?"

Understanding that helplessness was once adaptive allows us to approach it with compassion. From there, new responses can be built.

Learned Belief: "I Can't Cope on My Own"

At the core of Dependent Personality Disorder is a powerful internal belief: "I can't handle life by myself." This learned conviction doesn't appear overnight. It develops over years of internalized messages, some explicit, some implied, that independence is dangerous, unreliable, or destined to fail.

This belief often arises in childhood when emotional or practical needs were consistently met by others with little room for experimentation or mistakes. Children may never get the opportunity to learn how to soothe themselves, make small choices, or experience the consequences of their actions. Over time, they become emotionally conditioned to believe that they can't cope without external support. Even success can feel accidental or dependent on someone else's guidance.

Adults with this belief often frame their self-worth in terms of who they are to others: a daughter, partner, patient, or employee. When left alone or asked to act independently, they may feel disoriented, panicked, or blank, not because they are incapable, but because their inner narrative insists they are.

This core schema, "I can't cope on my own," becomes a guiding truth. It colors their interpretation of stress, risk, and responsibility. Even small tasks, like booking an appointment or giving an opinion, can feel overwhelming. It's not a lack of intelligence or willpower. It's a worldview built for survival in a past where autonomy meant vulnerability.

Case snapshot: Juno, 41, had always relied on her older sister to help with decisions, from what to wear to how to parent her own children. When her sister moved overseas, Juno found herself in a spiral of anxiety. She couldn't decide what groceries to buy, hesitated before responding to emails, and cried during basic errands. In therapy, she explored how deeply she believed that her own judgment was flawed. Reframing this belief became the first step toward regaining confidence.

Core Schema: Safety Comes Through Others

For individuals with Dependent Personality Disorder, the belief that "I can't cope alone" often evolves into a broader, more rigid core schema: "I am only safe if someone else is in control." In this mindset, relationships don't just offer comfort; they feel like a requirement for emotional or physical survival.

This schema is deeply ingrained. Safety, stability, and self-worth become tethered to another person's presence, approval, or decision-making. The individual may feel intense distress when left alone, not because they dislike solitude, but because solitude triggers a threat response. Being alone feels unsafe. Being connected, even to someone unreliable or harmful, feels safer by comparison.

This belief system makes letting go incredibly difficult. A person might stay in a toxic relationship, avoid career opportunities that require independence, or suppress personal preferences just to keep the peace. The possibility of abandonment or self-reliance isn't just uncomfortable, it's terrifying.

Over time, this schema begins to shape not just how individuals see relationships, but how they see themselves. They are not someone who chooses connection, they are someone who *needs* it to survive. Autonomy becomes foreign; attachment becomes a lifeline.

Case snapshot: Bolaji, 38, was seen by others as quiet and agreeable. In truth, he rarely voiced disagreement, even with close friends, because he feared being seen as difficult. He remained in a friendship that drained him emotionally for over a decade because he believed that having *someone* was better than being alone. In therapy, Bolaji began to trace this belief back to childhood experiences of being left alone for long hours and only feeling safe when his older sibling was around. Naming this pattern helped him begin to imagine a life where safety came from within.

Implementation Exercise: Redefining Safety Map

This reflective tool helps individuals begin to detach safety from dependency and explore what secure autonomy could look like.

1. **List three people or situations where you currently feel most safe:** Describe what they provide: protection, guidance, approval, etc.
2. **Now ask: What if that person/situation weren't there?** What fears come up? What beliefs surface?
3. **Imagine safety as an internal state:** What thoughts, actions, or resources would help you feel steady *within yourself*?
4. **Reflection prompt:** "If I didn't rely on others for safety, what might I learn about my own strength?"

Moving from external to internal safety means learning that connection is healthiest when chosen, not clung to.

THE COST OF ALWAYS NEEDING SOMEONE

The cost of constantly needing someone else isn't just dependence; it's a diminishing of the self. When the ability to act independently is stunted, relationships are maintained at the expense of authenticity, autonomy, and emotional safety.

Inability to Act Independently

One of the most painful consequences of Dependent Personality Disorder is the perceived inability to function without guidance.

Individuals with DPD often avoid making even minor decisions, what to wear, what to eat, or when to schedule an appointment, unless they receive explicit direction or reassurance from someone they trust.

This is fear. A deeply internalized fear of getting it wrong, of upsetting someone, or of being judged as incapable. Making a decision independently doesn't just feel uncomfortable; it feels like a threat to their stability, identity, and safety.

This reliance can quietly erode self-confidence. Even when someone knows what they want, they may hesitate to act, worrying it will be the wrong choice or that others will disapprove. Over time, the absence of autonomy becomes self-reinforcing. The fewer decisions made, the less confident the person feels. The more they rely on others, the more dependent they become.

In extreme cases, this can manifest in near-total submission, where the individual's day-to-day functioning is dictated by another person, partner, friend, parent, or authority figure. The cost? A life lived on someone else's terms, with little room for authentic growth.

Case snapshot: Tumi, 28, worked as an administrative assistant and was described by colleagues as kind and agreeable. But behind the scenes, she never initiated projects, waited for explicit instructions, and double-checked everything with her supervisor, sometimes three or four times. Outside work, she wouldn't go to a restaurant without asking her best friend to choose. When her friend went on an extended trip, Tumi's anxiety spiked. In therapy, she began to explore how decision-making had become synonymous with danger, a pattern rooted in a childhood where mistakes were met with shame.

Implementation Exercise: Decision-Making Ladder

This tool helps you begin to reclaim decision-making in small, progressive steps.

1. **List three decisions you deferred to someone else this week:** Note why you deferred and what you feared might happen if you made the call yourself.
2. **Choose one decision to reclaim:** Start small: what to eat, what to wear, what to say in a message.
3. **Make the decision solo, then reflect:** What was the result? Was it tolerable? Did anything go wrong, and if so, how did you handle it?
4. **Reflection prompt:** "What if making small decisions is how I teach my nervous system that I'm capable?"

Building autonomy doesn't require grand acts of independence. It starts with daily proof that choice is possible and survivable.

Tolerating Mistreatment

When someone believes their emotional survival depends on keeping others close, the threshold for acceptable treatment often becomes dangerously low. People with Dependent Personality Disorder may remain in relationships where they are belittled, ignored, or even abused, simply because the alternative—being alone—feels worse.

This tolerance for mistreatment isn't about weakness or self-pity. It is about risk assessment, shaped by early experiences. If someone has been conditioned to believe that asserting themselves leads to conflict, withdrawal of affection, or abandonment, they may unconsciously decide it's safer to stay quiet and compliant.

Over time, mistreatment becomes normalized. The person may start to believe they deserve it, or that they're too fragile to survive without the person mistreating them. This belief can keep them locked in toxic dynamics, where their own needs and self-respect are consistently sacrificed.

This doesn't mean they like being mistreated; it means the emotional math always seems to come out the same: enduring harm feels less terrifying than facing life alone.

Case snapshot: Chisom, 33, stayed with a partner who constantly criticized her appearance, monitored her phone, and minimized her accomplishments. Friends urged her to leave, but she felt paralyzed. In therapy, Chisom revealed that as a child, love was withdrawn whenever she expressed disagreement. Being agreeable, even when it hurt, had been her path to connection. Learning that this pattern wasn't her fault and wasn't permanent became a turning point.

Identity Tied to Relationships

For individuals with Dependent Personality Disorder, identity is not a stable internal compass; it's a mirror reflecting whoever is standing closest. Rather than being rooted in personal values, preferences, or goals, the sense of self becomes defined by relationships. Who they are depends heavily on who they are with.

This fusion of identity with others can feel safe in the short term, but it comes at a cost. Without external input, individuals with DPD often feel lost, anxious, or hollow. They may not know what they like, believe, or want unless someone else tells them. They might change opinions to match others', suppress desires to avoid conflict, or adapt personas to keep the connection intact.

This over-identification with others isn't manipulation, it's survival. Many with DPD learned early on that individuality led to disconnection. Conformity became a currency for love and safety.

Over time, this constant shape-shifting can create a sense of disorientation or even depression. Without an independent identity, there's no firm ground to stand on. The need to be loved overrides the need to be known.

Case snapshot: Lizzy, 30, had been in a long-term relationship with a partner who was outgoing, athletic, and politically opinionated. Over time, Lizzy adopted his hobbies, mirrored his beliefs, and even changed her style to match his preferences. After the breakup, she struggled to define herself. In therapy, she realized she had been performing a version of herself based on his validation. Reclaiming her own values meant beginning a journey of internal discovery, one that felt both frightening and freeing.

Implementation Exercise: Identity Reclaim List

This exercise invites you to explore your core identity, independent of external influence.

1. **List five traits or preferences you've adopted to fit in or please someone else.**
2. **Now list five traits, hobbies, or beliefs that felt true to you, even if others didn't agree.**
3. **Circle one from your authentic list and ask:**
    - What does this say about who I am?
    - How might I honor this part of myself this week?
4. **Reflection prompt:** "What would it mean to know myself, even if no one else validated it?"

Developing identity outside of others requires honesty, reflection, and the courage to stand in one's truth, even when it feels unfamiliar.

Suppression of Self

For individuals with Dependent Personality Disorder (DPD), preserving connection often comes at the expense of personal truth. Suppression of self isn't about dishonesty or manipulation; it's a survival tactic. It's the quiet folding-in of opinions, desires, and needs, because expressing them might risk disapproval or, worse, abandonment.

When autonomy feels unsafe, self-silencing becomes second nature. This suppression doesn't always look dramatic. Sometimes it shows up as always agreeing, never offering a differing opinion, or habitually saying "I don't mind" when asked for preferences. Over time, this chronic deferment of self erodes identity and reinforces helplessness.

Many people with DPD grew up in environments where speaking up led to conflict, ridicule, or emotional withdrawal. In these settings, the lesson learned was clear: being easy, agreeable, and invisible was safer than being authentic. That conditioning doesn't just fade in adulthood; it gets carried forward into friendships, workplaces, and romantic relationships.

Suppressing the self becomes a trade: connection in exchange for invisibility. And the longer this trade continues, the harder it becomes to know what the true self actually wants or feels.

Case snapshot: Kwame, 26, worked in graphic design and often felt like a background character in his own life. In meetings, he held back his ideas, convinced they weren't good enough. With friends, he always went along with their plans, even when he disagreed. In relationships, he molded himself to match his partner's interests, saying little about his own. Eventually, he began to feel invisible, not just to others, but to himself. Therapy helped him explore the roots of this pattern, which traced back to a childhood with a domineering parent who punished independence. Slowly, Kwame began practicing small acts of self-expression: stating preferences, offering opinions, and trusting that disagreement didn't equal rejection.

Implementation Exercise: Speaking Up Safely

This exercise helps individuals begin reversing the habit of self-silencing by practicing small, low-risk acts of self-expression.

1. **Identify three situations this week where you stayed silent to keep the peace:** What did you want to say or express?
2. **Choose one upcoming opportunity to speak your truth:** It could be as simple as stating a food preference, suggesting a plan, or voicing a mild disagreement.
3. **Prepare a script if needed:** Example: "I know we usually go with your choice, but I'd really like to try something different today."
4. **Reflect afterward:** What happened? Was it more manageable than expected? Did the relationship survive your honesty?
5. **Journal prompt:** "What belief do I hold about speaking up, and is it based on present reality, or past fear?"

Self-expression is a muscle. Each time it's used, even gently, it grows stronger, and so does the belief that your voice deserves to be heard.

RELATIONSHIP PATTERNS

Relationships, which ideally balance closeness and individuality, often become imbalanced for those with DPD. The fear of abandonment and the belief that they cannot cope alone create patterns of clinging, appeasement, and emotional overreliance.

For many, the longing to be loved collides with a terror of being left. The result is a set of behaviors that seek to preserve connection at all costs, often by avoiding conflict, suppressing needs, and surrendering independence. Unfortunately, these very strategies can undermine the stability of the relationships they are trying to protect.

Clinging Behavior

Clinging isn't always physical. For individuals with Dependent Personality Disorder (DPD), it's often an emotional, ongoing need for reassurance, proximity, and validation. Beneath the surface lies a deep-seated belief that being alone is dangerous and that connection must be preserved at all costs. This belief, often rooted in childhood experiences of abandonment or unpredictability, fuels a pattern of emotional dependency that others may experience as overbearing or intense (American Psychiatric Association, 2022).

Clinging behavior can take many forms: frequent texting or calling to "check in," avoiding time apart from a partner, hesitating to make plans without someone else's input, or becoming anxious when left out of group activities. These behaviors aren't about control or manipulation; they're driven by fear, the fear that if the other person leaves, even temporarily, they might never return (National Center for Biotechnology Information, 2023).

This dynamic can create strain in relationships. Partners or friends may feel suffocated, while the person with DPD feels perpetually anxious and misunderstood. The more the other person pulls away to create space, the more the dependent individual may cling, creating a painful cycle of pursuit and distance.

Case snapshot: Onyii, 31, had always feared being alone. In relationships, she would check her partner's location, send multiple messages if they didn't respond quickly, and cancel her own plans to be available for them. When her partner asked for more space, Onyii panicked. She assumed it meant rejection and began apologizing profusely, promising to "do better." In therapy, she began to see how these patterns stemmed from early experiences with an emotionally inconsistent parent. Her clinging wasn't irrational; it was a survival strategy that had outlived its context.

Implementation Exercise: Containment Plan

This practice helps you begin tolerating small amounts of relational distance without spiraling into anxiety or reassurance-seeking.

1. **Identify a current relationship where you feel especially anxious about separation:** What specific situations trigger that anxiety? (e.g., unanswered texts, solo outings)
2. **Pick one upcoming situation and create a containment plan:**
   - Set a timeframe: "I will wait one hour before reaching out again."
   - Create a grounding statement: "Distance doesn't mean disconnection."
   - Identify a coping action: journaling, walking, deep breathing, or reaching out to a neutral support person.

3. **After the event, reflect:** How did you feel during the wait? What story did your mind tell you? Was the outcome different from your fear?
4. **Journal prompt:** "What am I afraid will happen if I don't reach out? Where did that fear begin, and is it still true today?"

By practicing emotional self-containment, individuals can begin to reduce the urge to cling and build the internal safety that makes healthy closeness possible.

High Anxiety During Conflict

Even minor disagreements can trigger disproportionate levels of fear, shame, or panic. The emotional stakes feel impossibly high because conflict is unconsciously equated with abandonment. In other words, if someone is upset, the relationship itself may feel at risk of collapsing.

This deep anxiety often leads to a pattern of appeasement. Individuals may immediately back down, over-apologize, or try to "smooth things over" before the conflict has even been fully expressed. The point is not to be dishonest or manipulative; it's a survival strategy. When someone has internalized the belief that relationships are fragile and conditional, they learn to prioritize peace at all costs, even if it means erasing their own needs in the process.

Ironically, the attempt to avoid conflict can sometimes make relationships more strained. By not voicing concerns or standing up for themselves, individuals with DPD may build quiet resentment or confusion in their relationships. Others might sense the compliance but struggle with the lack of authenticity. Over time, this can create emotional distance, the very outcome the person feared from the start.

Case snapshot: Mbali, 26, often found herself apologizing for things that weren't her fault. If her friend seemed irritated, she'd assume she had done something wrong. She hated saying "no" and agreed to plans she didn't enjoy just to keep others happy. In therapy, Mbali began to see that her extreme fear of conflict came from a childhood marked by unpredictability, when small arguments often led to silence or withdrawal of affection. Learning that disagreement didn't have to mean rejection was a slow but powerful realization.

Implementation Exercise: Conflict De-escalation Map

This tool guides you in navigating conflict without abandoning your needs or spiraling into panic.

1. **Recall a recent conflict that caused anxiety:**
   - What was the disagreement about?
   - What physical or emotional responses did it trigger?
2. **Map your typical reaction:**
   - Do you over-apologize?
   - Do you shut down or avoid the person?
   - Do you give in even if it feels unfair?
3. **Identify the story you told yourself:**
   - "If I disagree, they'll leave."
   - "They're mad because I failed."
4. **Create an alternative script:**
   - "Conflict is a part of connection, not the end of it."
   - "I can express myself and still be loved."

Difficulty Leaving Harmful Dynamics

One of the most heartbreaking features of Dependent Personality Disorder is the way it traps individuals in relationships that hurt them. The fear of abandonment can be so overwhelming that it overshadows abuse, neglect, or deep emotional dissatisfaction. When the ability to cope alone feels impossible, even toxic relationships can seem safer than solitude.

This difficulty isn't about weakness or denial. It's about a belief system formed early in life: that one's safety and stability are dependent on staying connected, no matter the cost. For many, emotional neglect, inconsistent caregiving, or early losses taught them that attachment, however painful, was better than being left alone. Over time, these experiences create a schema in which autonomy feels dangerous, and dependence becomes survival.

The result is a painful paradox: individuals may recognize that a relationship is harmful but feel incapable of leaving. They may rationalize mistreatment, blame themselves for the dysfunction, or hope that staying quiet will eventually make things better. Even when help is offered, the fear of navigating life alone can shut down action. Ending the relationship feels like stepping into a void without a map.

Case snapshot: Ravi, 39, had been in a controlling marriage for over a decade. His partner dictated most aspects of his life, from finances to friendships. Friends and family encouraged him to seek help, but he hesitated. "She's not all bad," he'd say. "I'm just not strong enough to be alone." Through therapy, Ravi began to trace these beliefs back to his upbringing, where his emotionally distant parents only offered attention when he was sick or struggling. Staying in painful relationships had become familiar, and familiarity had started to feel like love.

Implementation Exercise: The Cost-Benefit Reflection

This structured reflection helps individuals clarify why leaving feels impossible and what staying is costing them.

1. **List the reasons you feel unable to leave a difficult relationship:**
   ○ What fears come up? (e.g., loneliness, financial stress, guilt)
   ○ What beliefs are driving those fears?
2. **List the costs of staying:**
   ○ Emotional: How does the relationship affect your self-worth and peace?
   ○ Physical: Has it impacted your health or daily functioning?
   ○ Social: Are other relationships suffering?
3. **Visualize the alternative:**
   ○ If you were no longer in the relationship, what would you hope your life might feel like in six months?
4. **Journal prompt:** "If I believed I could survive on my own, what would I do differently tomorrow?"

Sometimes the first step is simply admitting what the cost of staying has been, and daring to imagine something more.

Risk of Exploitation

When fear of abandonment is this strong, it can open the door to exploitation. Individuals with Dependent Personality Disorder (DPD) are often so afraid of being alone that they become vulnerable to manipulation, emotional abuse, or one-sided relationships. The desire to be needed, valued, or simply kept around may outweigh their awareness of how they are being treated.

This risk doesn't stem from a lack of intelligence or awareness; it stems from conditioning. Many individuals with DPD have learned, often in childhood, that love is earned through compliance, self-sacrifice, or silence. They may equate suffering with loyalty or believe that enduring mistreatment proves devotion. As a result, red flags get minimized and boundaries become nearly impossible to enforce (American Psychiatric Association, 2022).

This dynamic often draws in individuals who take advantage, whether intentionally or not. Friends, partners, or coworkers may begin to rely heavily on the person with DPD, knowing they will not say no, assert needs, or push back. Over time, the dependent person may lose touch with their own values, preferences, or goals, becoming a mirror for others rather than a voice for themselves.

Case snapshot: Yara, 28, worked in a small company where she was known as "the fixer." Coworkers frequently dumped tasks on her, and she often stayed late, even canceling personal plans to help. In a recent relationship, her partner routinely dismissed her opinions and controlled major decisions. Yara rationalized it all, telling herself she was just easygoing. But beneath that story was fear: "If I push back, they'll leave." It wasn't until she burned out and landed in therapy that she began to realize her giving nature had become a liability. Her worth wasn't tied to her usefulness.

PATHWAYS TO SELF-TRUST

Healing from Dependent Personality Disorder isn't about becoming hyper-independent or rejecting all connections. It's about learning to trust oneself enough to make decisions, voice opinions, and stand on one's own when needed, without the world falling apart. For someone who has always tied their worth to others' approval, this can feel terrifying at first. But it's also where freedom begins.

Self-trust doesn't mean doing everything alone; it means knowing that you *could* if you had to. It means believing in your ability to cope, make mistakes, and keep moving. Recovery involves unlearning helplessness and building confidence one small, supported step at a time. In this final section, we'll explore concrete ways to nurture that process, starting with the foundation of self-efficacy.

Building Self-Efficacy and Assertiveness

Self-efficacy refers to the belief that you are capable of handling life's demands. For people with DPD, this belief is often deeply eroded. They may doubt their judgment, avoid choices, and defer even minor decisions to others. Rebuilding self-efficacy begins with creating small, repeated experiences of success.

Start with daily decisions: choosing what to eat, planning your day, setting a goal, and following through. Each act of self-direction is a vote for your capability. With time, these moments compound into a deeper sense of trust. Therapy often supports this by helping clients track these small wins, challenge self-doubt, and learn to tolerate the discomfort that comes with uncertainty (American Psychiatric Association, 2022).

Alongside this comes assertiveness, the ability to express needs and opinions with clarity and respect. For someone with DPD, assertiveness can feel selfish or risky. But it's actually the opposite: it creates honesty and balance in relationships. Learning to say, "I'd prefer something else," or "That doesn't work for me," builds both autonomy and healthier connections.

THERAPEUTIC APPROACHES AND EMPOWERING SUPPORT

Different therapeutic modalities offer targeted help for individuals working through DPD. Cognitive Behavioral Therapy (CBT) helps challenge distorted beliefs like "I can't cope alone" or "I need someone to tell me what to do." Schema therapy dives deeper into core patterns, exploring how early experiences created the dependency script. Skills-based approaches, such as Dialectical Behavior Therapy (DBT), focus on emotional regulation, distress tolerance, and interpersonal effectiveness.

Equally important is the role of supportive environments. Healing doesn't require isolation; it requires safe spaces that empower independence. Friends, partners, or therapists who encourage decision-making, respect boundaries, and resist stepping into a caretaker role can be powerful allies. Instead of reinforcing helplessness, they reinforce strength.

Implementation Exercise: Confidence Ladder

This tool helps individuals gradually build trust in their ability to act independently.

1. **Choose one area of your life where you feel dependent:**
   - For example: meal planning, managing finances, social plans, and work tasks.
2. **Break it into steps from easiest to hardest:**
   - Easy: "Pick my own lunch."
   - Moderate: "Plan a weekend activity."
   - Hard: "Make a decision about my budget without input."

3. **Start at the bottom of the ladder:**
   ◦ Complete the easiest task independently.
   ◦ Reflect on how it felt, was it empowering, scary, relieving?
4. **Work your way up over time:**
   ◦ Celebrate each step.
   ◦ Track what helped and what made it harder.
5. **Journal prompt:** "When I act on my own, what story do I tell myself? How would I rewrite that story to include strength and growth?"

Self-trust is not a destination. It's a series of courageous choices, repeated over time, until one day, your voice feels like enough.

CHAPTER 11

OBSESSIVE-COMPULSIVE PERSONALITY DISORDER (OCPD)

It's easy to conflate Obsessive-Compulsive Personality Disorder (OCPD) with an overzealous preference for tidiness. The term is casually thrown around when someone color-codes their calendar or reorganizes their spice rack. But for those living with OCPD, the need for order, perfection, and control isn't just about aesthetics; it's about survival. These patterns run deeper than habit. They function as armor, an attempt to bring order to a world that feels relentlessly uncertain.

OCPD is one of the most misunderstood personality disorders. It's often confused with Obsessive-Compulsive Disorder (OCD), but the two are fundamentally different. OCPD doesn't revolve around intrusive thoughts or compulsive rituals. Instead, it's rooted in a personality structure shaped by rigid standards, black-and-white thinking, and an internal sense of moral obligation. Mistakes feel intolerable. Flexibility feels unsafe. Emotional expression takes a back seat to control.

The traits of OCPD can appear admirable from the outside: reliable, organized, efficient. But beneath the surface is a life constrained by fear of failure and a desperate effort to avoid messiness, emotional, interpersonal, or practical. Relationships can suffer, spontaneity feels threatening, and self-worth becomes tightly bound to productivity and correctness.

WHAT IS OBSESSIVE-COMPULSIVE PERSONALITY DISORDER (OCPD)?

Obsessive-Compulsive Personality Disorder (OCPD) is often misunderstood, frequently confused with Obsessive-Compulsive Disorder (OCD), and minimized as simply being "uptight" or "detail-oriented." But OCPD is far more than a preference for neatness; it's a personality structure built around a core belief that control equals safety. For someone with OCPD, flexibility feels dangerous, mistakes feel unacceptable, and the need to be right becomes a shield against emotional vulnerability.

DSM-5-TR Diagnostic Criteria

According to the *Diagnostic and Statistical Manual of Mental Disorders* (DSM-5-TR), OCPD is characterized by a pervasive pattern of preoccupation with orderliness, perfectionism, and mental and interpersonal control, often at the expense of flexibility, openness, and efficiency. This pattern begins in early adulthood and is present in a variety of contexts.

To meet the diagnostic threshold, an individual must exhibit at least four of the following eight criteria:

1. Preoccupation with details, rules, lists, order, organization, or schedules.
2. Perfectionism that interferes with task completion.

3. Excessive devotion to work and productivity, to the exclusion of leisure and relationships.
4. Over-conscientiousness, scrupulousness, and inflexibility about morality or ethics.
5. Inability to discard worn-out or worthless objects, even when they have no sentimental value.
6. Reluctance to delegate tasks unless others submit to exact guidelines.
7. Miserly spending style toward both self and others.
8. Rigidity and stubbornness.

These traits are not just quirks. They are deeply ingrained patterns of thinking and behavior that shape every area of life, from how a person works to how they relate to others to how they see themselves.

OCPD is one of the most common personality disorders, with estimates ranging between 2.1% and 7.9% of the general population (Burkauskas & Fineberg, 2019). It is frequently seen in clinical settings, though often underdiagnosed due to the socially reinforced nature of perfectionism and productivity. Many individuals with OCPD appear highly competent on the outside, often excelling in work or academics, which can mask the internal distress and interpersonal difficulties they experience.

OCPD VS. OCD

A common misconception is that OCPD and OCD are interchangeable. In reality, they are distinct diagnoses. OCD is classified as an anxiety disorder and is defined by the presence of intrusive thoughts (obsessions) and repetitive behaviors (compulsions) aimed at reducing distress. OCPD, on the other hand, involves a rigid adherence to order and control without the presence of true obsessions or compulsions.

Where OCD is driven by anxiety and often experienced as egodystonic (the person recognizes the behavior as unwanted), OCPD is ego-syntonic; the behaviors and beliefs are consistent with the person's self-image and are often seen as correct or necessary.

Internal Rigidity vs. External Rituals

In OCPD, the need for control originates from internal rules, moral absolutes, and a relentless drive for perfection. This differs from the external ritualistic behaviors in OCD. A person with OCPD may not need to wash their hands repeatedly, but they may be internally consumed by the belief that things must be done *the right way*. This moral rigidity can lead to judgmental thinking, strained relationships, and an inability to compromise.

The Need to Be Right (and Safe)

For individuals with Obsessive-Compulsive Personality Disorder (OCPD), control is more than a preference; it's a perceived necessity. At the heart of the disorder lies a deep-seated fear that any deviation from order, logic, or perfection will invite chaos, failure, or shame. To be right is to be safe. And to be safe is to avoid the unbearable feeling of being exposed, incompetent, or judged.

Perfectionism as a Shield

OCPD is not driven by arrogance or ego. Instead, perfectionism serves as a form of protection. Individuals who live with this disorder often believe that their worth is directly tied to performance, order, and correctness. A mistake isn't just a mistake; it's a character flaw. An overlooked detail is seen not as human but as a sign of personal failure.

The drive to get everything "just right" often originates from early environments where approval was contingent on performance. Children who were only praised for achievements or punished harshly for mistakes may grow into adults who internalize the idea that imperfection is dangerous. Over time, perfectionism becomes a shield against criticism and emotional vulnerability.

"Shoulds" and "Musts"

People with OCPD often live according to rigid internal rules: "I should never waste time," "I must always meet deadlines," "People must follow procedures." These "shoulds" and "musts" form a strict moral code that governs not only their actions but their self-worth.

This rigidity isn't just directed inward; it's also projected outward. Others are often held to the same high standards, and deviations from those standards can provoke frustration, anxiety, or disapproval. While this may look like controlling behavior, it is usually a reflection of deep inner discomfort with unpredictability or perceived failure.

The Need to Control Surroundings and Others

Because emotional uncertainty feels threatening, individuals with OCPD often seek to control the external world. From organizing closets to micromanaging colleagues, the desire for control isn't about power; it's about managing anxiety. If everything stays in order, nothing will go wrong. If everyone follows the rules, no one will be disappointed. If the schedule is maintained, the self won't fall apart.

This control can become a substitute for emotional intimacy. It creates distance in relationships and reduces the space for spontaneity, messiness, or authentic expression. Over time, relationships can begin to feel transactional, as if they're being managed rather than lived.

Underlying Guilt and Shame

Beneath the surface of rigidity lies a painful emotional terrain. Many individuals with OCPD carry an underlying sense of guilt or shame, an internal critic that constantly whispers, "You're not good enough," or "You could have done more." This internal pressure can be relentless, and the person may feel that any display of weakness or error confirms their worst fears about themselves.

Often, these feelings are rooted in childhood experiences where mistakes were met with punishment, shame, or withdrawal of affection. To survive, they learned to suppress vulnerability and double down on order, productivity, and correctness.

Case snapshot: Eleanor, 42, is a senior project manager known for her precision and discipline. She tracks every deadline, keeps detailed checklists, and has little patience for colleagues who deviate from procedures. At home, her need for control causes conflict with her partner, who feels like he's constantly being corrected. Spontaneous plans make Eleanor anxious, and even leisure time becomes tightly scheduled.

In therapy, Eleanor revealed that her father was emotionally distant but praised her for academic achievement. Mistakes were not tolerated in her household. Over time, she equated perfection with love and mistakes with rejection. Her adult patterns made sense, not as flaws, but as the best adaptations she had available to earn safety and worth.

Implementation Exercise: Challenging the Inner Critic

This activity helps reduce perfectionism by interrupting the rigid internal dialogue that fuels OCPD patterns.

1. **Identify a recent moment when you felt "not good enough:"** What was the task or situation? What triggered the feeling?
2. **Write down the critical thought or belief:** Example: "I should have handled that meeting perfectly."
3. **Challenge the belief:** Where did this standard come from? Would you expect the same of a friend?
4. **Reframe the narrative:** Example: "It's okay to be imperfect. That meeting was good enough, and I can improve without punishing myself."

THE DOUBLE-EDGED SWORD OF PERFECTIONISM

Perfectionism is often admired from the outside, praised as a sign of discipline, dedication, or high standards. But for individuals with Obsessive-Compulsive Personality Disorder (OCPD), perfectionism isn't a strength. It's a double-edged sword. What looks like productivity can mask paralysis. What appears as reliability often conceals profound distress.

At its core, perfectionism is an attempt to create safety. But in doing so, it often blocks the very outcomes a person hopes to achieve: connection, satisfaction, and progress.

Productivity vs. Paralysis

People with OCPD are often seen as dependable, meticulous, and organized. But behind the curtain, many are caught in endless loops of doubt, checking, or reworking. The pursuit of flawlessness can delay tasks, cause procrastination, or result in projects never being finished. Fear of making a mistake becomes so overwhelming that doing nothing feels safer than doing something imperfectly.

This dynamic creates internal torment. Despite high output, the individual rarely feels accomplished. They focus on what went wrong rather than what went right. This constant self-monitoring erodes confidence and robs joy from achievement.

Difficulty Delegating

Another hallmark of OCPD is the reluctance, or refusal, to delegate. Trusting others to complete a task invites the possibility that it won't be done *correctly*, which, for someone with OCPD, is often equated with *danger*. Even when overwhelmed, they may choose to shoulder everything themselves rather than risk imperfection by another person's hand.

This control leads to exhaustion, resentment, and strained relationships. What begins as a desire to maintain standards can quickly spiral into burnout and emotional isolation.

Workaholism and Emotional Detachment

Work becomes more than a job; it becomes an identity. Many individuals with OCPD define their worth through productivity. They may struggle to relax, view leisure as wasteful, or feel guilt when not working. Emotional needs, both their own and others', get pushed aside in favor of tasks, goals, and lists.

This detachment can lead to loneliness, even in the presence of others. When perfectionism consumes the emotional space, there's little room left for playfulness, spontaneity, or intimacy.

Control as a Substitute for Connection

For some, control offers predictability in a world that once felt chaotic or unsafe. If emotional needs went unmet in childhood, focusing on order might have provided a sense of stability. But as adults, these habits can act as a wall. Controlling the environment replaces learning how to feel at ease in it. Correcting others replaces genuine conversation. Holding rigid standards becomes a way to avoid vulnerability, messiness, or rejection.

The need to control is not about ego; it's about fear. And until that fear is addressed, perfectionism will continue to cost more than it gives.

Case snapshot: Timini, 36, is a civil engineer with an impeccable track record. Every report he submits is reviewed multiple times. Every meeting is rehearsed. At work, he's admired. At home, he's distant. His partner feels more like a project manager than a loved one; everything must be planned, discussed, and optimized.

Timini doesn't rest. When he's not working, he's worrying about not working. Attempts to relax make him anxious. Therapy helped Timini trace his perfectionism back to a childhood marked by emotional unpredictability. His mother was loving, but erratic. Perfection, he realized, had become a way to control the uncontrollable. Through gradual exposure to imperfection, Timini began to unlearn the false safety of flawlessness.

Implementation Exercise: Permission to Be "Good Enough"

This tool invites readers to practice challenging the perfectionistic mindset in small, manageable ways.

1. **Choose one task today that you can complete at 80%:** Let go of the final edits, the extra polish, the double-check.
2. **Write down what you're afraid will happen if it's not perfect:** Example: "They'll think I'm careless," or "I won't feel proud of it."
3. **Complete the task anyway:** Observe how it feels to resist the urge to fix or refine further.
4. **Reflect afterward:**
   ◦ Did your fear come true?
   ◦ How did others respond (if at all)?
   ◦ What did you learn about your own expectations?

EFFECTS ON RELATIONSHIPS AND SELF-WORTH

Obsessive-Compulsive Personality Disorder doesn't just shape how someone works; it fundamentally alters how they relate. Relationships become battlegrounds for control, correctness, and unmet emotional needs. What appears as rigid standards to others often masks a deeper fear: if I'm not perfect, I won't be loved. If others aren't perfect, I won't feel safe.

For individuals with OCPD, connection is desired, but only on strict terms. This rigidity can lead to isolation, conflict, and internal shame that deepens over time.

Interpersonal Rigidity

Relationships require compromise, flexibility, and forgiveness, qualities that can feel foreign or unsafe to someone with OCPD. They may insist on doing things a certain way, become critical of perceived sloppiness, or struggle to tolerate different perspectives. These behaviors aren't acts of arrogance; they're attempts to preserve order in a world that feels chaotic.

Over time, this rigidity can push people away. Partners may feel micromanaged, friends may pull back, and coworkers may find collaboration difficult. The OCPD individual, already anxious about social disapproval, interprets this distancing as confirmation that others can't be trusted, or that they must try harder to control outcomes.

Emotional Withholding

Because vulnerability feels like weakness, people with OCPD often withhold affection, avoid emotional expression, or dismiss their own feelings entirely. Intimacy becomes transactional: support is offered through doing, fixing, or planning, rather than through openness or shared emotion.

This emotional distance leaves relationships feeling functional but flat. Others may describe the person as distant, cold, or unresponsive. Inside, however, the individual may feel deep affection, but they don't know how to express it safely.

Self-Worth Tied to Correctness

Success, efficiency, and moral uprightness often become the primary metrics for self-worth in individuals with OCPD. Being right is not about ego, it's about survival. Mistakes, no matter how minor, trigger disproportionate shame. They are not just errors, but threats to identity.

This belief system creates a fragile sense of self, dependent on constant achievement. Any failure can collapse it. The person may work longer hours, overprepare for conversations, or mentally rehearse interactions, anything to maintain the appearance of control.

Burnout and Resentment

Living under constant self-scrutiny is exhausting. Over time, individuals with OCPD often experience physical and emotional burnout. They may feel unappreciated, taken advantage of, or misunderstood. And yet, asking for help or softening standards feels impossible.

The result is quite suffering. They may resent others for not meeting the same standards, while simultaneously resenting themselves for being unable to relax. It's a no-win scenario that isolates the individual and reinforces the belief that the only way to survive is to stay in control.

Case snapshot: Inem, 42, is known for her dependability. She manages her household with military precision, arrives early to every meeting, and keeps meticulous records of her family's schedule. But at home, her children say she's "never happy," and her partner admits he feels like he's "always walking on eggshells."

Inem struggles with affection. She criticizes instead of comforts. Praise feels forced. Inside, she's terrified of being seen as incompetent or lazy. In therapy, Inem began to understand how her father's harsh standards shaped her own. Control had been her way of avoiding his disapproval. Now, it was the very thing keeping her from the connection she craved. Learning to sit with imperfection and to see worth beyond performance was the first step toward healing her relationships.

Implementation Exercise: The Control–Connection Inventory

This tool invites readers to reflect on how their need for control might be impacting their relationships, and how to begin shifting toward connection.

1. **Identify one recent conflict or moment of tension in a relationship:** What triggered the discomfort? A missed deadline? A messy room? A decision made without you?
2. **Ask: Was I trying to be right or to be close?** What mattered more in that moment, maintaining control, or nurturing connection?
3. **Reflect on the outcome:** Did the situation resolve the way you hoped? How did the other person feel afterward?
4. **Consider an alternative response:** If you had prioritized connection, curiosity, patience, and vulnerability, how might that have changed the moment?

Letting Go of the Illusion of Control

For someone with Obsessive-Compulsive Personality Disorder, control often feels like the only safe path through life. Structure becomes salvation. Precision equals protection. But the cost of this safety is steep: relationships strain, joy fades, spontaneity feels threatening, and inner tension becomes constant.

Letting go doesn't mean chaos. It means learning to trust that not everything needs to be perfect to be okay. It's about building tolerance for uncertainty, choosing flexibility over rigidity, and recognizing that true strength comes not from being in control, but from staying present when you're not.

This final section focuses on practical tools for softening the grip of OCPD, starting with safe, supported experiments in imperfection.

Exposure to Imperfection

Practicing imperfection can be a powerful form of therapy. These aren't reckless acts; they are controlled exposures designed to teach the nervous system that the world won't fall apart when the rules bend.

Examples:

- Send an email without triple-checking it.
- Let someone else lead a project or plan.
- Leave a task slightly unfinished and tolerate the discomfort.

Each act of intentional imperfection is a small rebellion against the belief that control equals worth. Over time, these moments begin to rewire the brain's threat response, proving that good enough is, in fact, enough.

Mindfulness and Flexibility

Mindfulness teaches presence. It doesn't eliminate anxiety, but it helps you observe it without reacting to it. For people with OCPD, mindfulness practices such as breathwork, body scans, and acceptance exercises can help break the cycle of judgment and rigidity.

Acceptance and Commitment Therapy (ACT) offers a particularly effective model. Instead of battling unwanted thoughts or compulsions, ACT encourages values-based living: identifying what truly matters and taking action in that direction, even when discomfort is present (Twohig & Levin, 2017).

Rather than chasing the perfect outcome, ACT asks: What's the life you want to live, and are your current rules helping or hindering that?

Therapeutic Approaches

Several therapeutic models have shown effectiveness in treating OCPD:

- **Cognitive Behavioral Therapy (CBT):** Targets distorted beliefs about perfectionism, control, and moral rigidity.
- **Acceptance and Commitment Therapy (ACT):** Builds tolerance for uncertainty and encourages flexible, values-aligned action.
- **Schema Therapy:** Addresses the deep-rooted fears and early experiences that drive OCPD behaviors, such as conditional love, harsh criticism, or emotional neglect.

The goal is not to erase order or ambition, but to restore balance, where control no longer crowds out connection.

BUILDING EMOTIONAL TOLERANCE

Letting go isn't just behavioral, it's emotional. It means allowing yourself to feel discomfort, frustration, even anxiety, without immediately trying to fix it. That space between the feeling and the reaction is where change begins.

In therapy, individuals learn to sit with the emotional "mess" they once feared: not knowing the answer, being misunderstood, making a mistake. Over time, this builds resilience, the confidence that you can endure imperfection and still be okay.

Case snapshot: Uzor, 37, ran a successful consultancy business and lived by routines. He started his day at 5:30 AM sharp, tracked his calorie intake, scheduled his wife's dentist appointments, and color-coded his family's calendar. His wife often said, "I feel like you manage me instead of love me." That stung, but he didn't know how else to care.

In therapy, Uzor discovered that his need for order stemmed from growing up with an unpredictable, volatile parent. As a child, control meant safety. Now, it meant disconnection. His therapist suggested a simple exposure: let his wife choose the restaurant for dinner without him researching the options. At first, he felt anxious and irritated. But then he felt something else: relief. He didn't have to manage everything. Letting go, it turned out, was its own kind of freedom.

Implementation Exercise: Control Challenge Checklist

Use this tool to gently practice flexibility and reduce the grip of control-based behavior.

1. **Choose one area where control dominates:**
   ◦ Examples: cleaning, planning, appearance, decision-making.
2. **Select one small action to release control:**
   ◦ Examples:
      ▪ let a colleague lead a meeting.
      ▪ leave a book out of place.
      ▪ wear mismatched socks.

- let someone else order for you at a restaurant.

3. **Observe what happens:**
    - What emotions arise? What thoughts come up?
4. **Reflect on the gap between fear and reality:**
    - Was the outcome worse than you feared? Was it manageable?

This exercise isn't about failing or lowering standards. It's about creating room for life to happen without always having to be in charge.

PART III
STRATEGIES IN MOTION

You've explored the origins of personality, traced the histories that forged maladaptive patterns, and examined each disorder up close. Knowing, however, is only half the equation. Part 3 is where knowledge meets the day-to-day texture of real life, where hard-won insight becomes something you can feel in your morning routine, your relationships, and your self-talk.

This section is practical on purpose. Some strategies focus on regulating the nervous system before it tips into panic. Others widen your emotional vocabulary so that feelings become data rather than danger. Still others translate therapy room break-throughs into conversations with partners, colleagues, and family members who live the story with you.

What you will find is a working template: small, repeatable exercises that strengthen self-trust, boundary-setting, and relational courage. By the end of this part, the disorders discussed earlier should feel less like immovable labels and more like landscapes you can navigate, with a map, supplies, and the confidence that setbacks are part of progress.

The road ahead is incremental. Change rarely arrives in a cinematic revelation; it unfolds in ordinary moments when you choose a new response over an old reflex.

CHAPTER 12

PERSONALITY DISORDERS IN SOCIETY

Y ou can stand in a crowded museum, gaze at the same abstract painting, and still hear a dozen conflicting opinions about what it means. Likewise, the traits we label "personality disorders" are interpreted, and sometimes misinterpreted, through overlapping lenses of culture, media, and collective belief. Sharpening our vision of those lenses helps us move from shame to awareness.

THE CULTURAL CONSTRUCTION OF NORMALCY

Culture is the silent curriculum that teaches us how much emotion to show, how quickly to make eye contact, and how loudly to state a preference. In Japan, quiet emotional restraint is praised; in parts of the Mediterranean, open gesticulation and emphatic speech signal warmth and sincerity. These norms are so ingrained that they feel biological, yet cross-cultural research shows they shift with history, economics, and collective memory (Alarcón, 2009; Jarvis & Kirmayer, 2021). When clinicians rely on a single cultural yardstick, the person who cries "too easily" or "not at all" risks being labeled disordered instead of different.

CULTURAL BIAS IN DIAGNOSIS

Modern diagnostic manuals such as the DSM and ICD emerged in Western academic centers; their criteria were validated mostly on Euro-American samples. This can create "category errors" when behaviors that are culturally sanctioned elsewhere appear in Western clinics. For example, deference to elders is normative in many collectivist societies, but in an individualistic context, it can be misread as Dependent Personality Disorder. A 2022 review of PD assessments in migrant populations found systematic over-pathologization when evaluators failed to contextualize behavior (Gamio Cuervo, 2022).

CROSS-CULTURAL INTERPRETATIONS OF PDS

Collectivist cultures often see relational interdependence as a strength; individualistic cultures may frame the same trait as a loss of autonomy. Conversely, assertive self-promotion, sometimes admired in competitive economies, can attract a Narcissistic Personality Disorder label in contexts that prize humility. Epidemiological studies show prevalence rates of Antisocial Personality Disorder are lower in societies with robust kinship obligations; rule-breaking their threatens group survival, so early socialization curbs it (Kirmayer & Bhugra, 2009).

ROLE OF RACE, GENDER, AND CLASS

Diagnosis does not take place in a social vacuum. As you saw in previous chapters, women are disproportionately diagnosed with Borderline Personality Disorder, while men, especially men of color, are more likely to be labeled Antisocial. Socio-economic status also shapes interpretation; what looks like "manipulative" behavior in a low-income patient can be reframed as "strategic networking" when performed by an executive. Structural bias threads through training, reimbursement policies, and even the language of textbooks, perpetuating inequity (Alarcón, 2009; Gamio Cuervo, 2022).

MEDIA AND THE MISREPRESENTATION OF PERSONALITY DISORDERS

Pop Culture Tropes

For decades, Hollywood has treated personality disorders as shorthand for chaos or cruelty. Film studies catalog shows that Borderline Personality Disorder is often reduced to the "fatal attraction" archetype, while Narcissistic Personality Disorder is portrayed as the ruthless executive, and Antisocial Personality Disorder becomes the serial killer next door. These tropes amplify fear rather than nuance, crowding out stories of ordinary people managing real symptoms.

Media literacy: The next time a character's diagnosis is announced on-screen, pause and ask, "What symptoms are actually shown, and which ones are writer shortcuts to signal danger?"

Misuse of Clinical Labels

Headlines regularly weaponize terms like "narcissist," "psychopath," or "borderline" to diagnose public figures at a distance. A 2021 content analysis of major U.S. newspapers found that over 70 percent of articles using PD terminology offered no clinical source and relied on anecdotal commentary. Casual labeling flattens complex conditions into moral judgments, erasing the rigorous criteria clinicians must apply.

Media literacy: Before sharing an article that brands someone a narcissist, check whether the piece sites a qualified mental-health professional or DSM-based criteria.

Glamorization and Weaponization of Traits

On social media, the language of personality disorders is both romanticized and hurled as an insult. TikTok trends praising "main-character energy" often glorify traits linked to narcissism, while "toxic" has become a catch-all dismissal for relational conflict (Quraishi et al., 2023). This flip between allure and condemnation muddles public understanding and leaves those with formal diagnoses caught in the crossfire.

Media literacy: Notice when a post collapses the full spectrum of a disorder into a single adjective; complexity rarely fits within a 30-second clip.

Where Media Gets It Right, and Wrong

Recent documentaries like *Persona: The Dark Truth Behind Personality Tests* make strides by interviewing clinicians and people with lived experience, balancing narrative tension with evidence. Yet true-crime series continuing to label every manipulative antagonist a "sociopath" undo that progress (*Mental Health and Media: How Personality Disorders in the Media Have Shaped Stigma | BetterHelp*, 2024). Accuracy improves when creators include consultation credits for psychologists and advocacy groups.

Media literacy: Look for projects that involve advisory boards; their presence usually signals a commitment to nuance over shock value.

SOCIAL MEDIA, DIAGNOSIS, AND THE INTERNET AGE

Rise in Self-Diagnosis

TikTok hashtags like *#borderline* and *#narcissist* have racked up billions of views; a 2023 Pew Research survey found that 46 percent of U.S. teens say they have searched TikTok for a mental-health explanation of their symptoms (Faverio et al., 2025). While the accessibility of bite-sized psycho-education can demystify disorders, creator videos rarely mention diagnostic criteria or the difference between traits and full syndromes. The result? Viewers stitch together symptom lists and declare, "That's me," sometimes without ever consulting a professional.

Digital self-check: Before adopting a label, compare at least three clinical sources (e.g., DSM-5-TR, National Institute of Mental Health fact sheets, or peer-reviewed articles) and note whether the trait causes functional impairment in more than one area of life.

Positive Impacts: Visibility and Community

On Reddit forums like *r/BPDlovedones* or Discord servers dedicated to OCPD recovery, members swap coping tools, therapist recommendations, and daily wins. Qualitative studies show that such peer support moderates shame and fosters hope by normalizing lived experiences (Naslund et al., 2016). The internet has essentially crowdsourced the old coffee-shop support group, making it available in every time zone.

Community-building: When joining an online group, look for moderation guidelines that prohibit hate speech and require evidence-based resources; healthy boundaries, online mirror healthy boundaries offline.

Risks of Over-Identification

Mental-health influencers sometimes present disorders as quirky personality quirks or aesthetic hashtags, "I'm so OCD about my desk," for instance. Over-identification can trap users in a self-fulfilling loop: algorithms push more content that reinforces the adopted label, magnifying confirmation bias (Abi-Jaoude et al., 2020). For some, the label becomes a social identity rather than a clinical starting point.

Algorithm awareness: Regularly reset or diversify your feed, follow credible clinicians, researchers, and lived-experience advocates to reduce echo-chamber effects.

Impact on Youth Culture

Gen Z, the first cohort to grow up entirely online, often speaks in diagnostic shorthand; terms like *triggered*, *gaslighting*, and *trauma response* pepper everyday conversation (Twenge, 2023). While this linguistic fluency can indicate rising emotional literacy, surveys of school counselors report spikes in symptom exaggeration and peer-to-peer pathologizing. The challenge for educators and parents is to validate curiosity while anchoring it in accurate information.

Classroom connection: Incorporate brief media-literacy modules into health curricula, teach students how to vet sources and understand the difference between self-reflection and self-diagnosis.

STIGMA, STEREOTYPES, AND STRUCTURAL HARM

Stigma becomes public architecture, policies, procedures, and everyday language that push people with personality disorders to the margins. This section maps the main floors of that architecture and offers ways to start dismantling them.

Institutional Stigma

Mental-health parity laws exist on paper, yet in practice, people with personality disorders still encounter shorter appointment times, higher co-pays, or outright service denial (Hatzenbuehler et al., 2016). In schools, zero-tolerance policies can translate ordinary emotional dysregulation into suspension records. In the criminal justice system, diagnostic labels may influence sentencing more than individual history.

Actionable shifts

- Integrate trauma-informed screening in primary-care settings so PD traits are flagged for support, not punished.
- Advocate for insurance audits that compare reimbursement rates for PD treatment versus mood-disorder care.
- Partner with legal-aid societies to train public defenders on the nuances of Cluster B presentations.

Interpersonal Stigma

Labels like "manipulative" or "toxic" often arise from misunderstanding rather than fact. A 2021 survey of 1,500 adults found that 62 percent could not distinguish between Borderline and Bipolar traits (Gunderson & Links, 2021). Misinterpretation breeds avoidance, which in turn reinforces isolation.

Actionable shifts

- Replace judgmental labels with descriptive observations ("I notice the argument escalates quickly") to keep the conversation fact-based.
- Offer curiosity instead of critique: "Can you tell me what you're feeling right now?"
- Share accurate resources; a single infographic can correct more misconceptions than a heated debate.

Disproportionate Diagnosis

Research shows women receive BPD diagnoses at nearly three times the rate of men, while Black and Indigenous individuals are more likely to be labeled with Antisocial traits. Analysts argue that socioeconomic stressors and cultural expression styles are pathologized instead of contextualized.

Actionable shifts

- Encourage second opinions when a diagnosis seems to mirror racial or gender stereotypes.
- Support community-based mental health clinics that employ culturally concordant providers.
- Promote research that includes diverse samples, closing the data gap that fuels bias.

Language Matters

Words can harm or heal. Saying someone "is a narcissist" freezes identity in pathology; saying they "live with narcissistic traits" leaves room for context and growth. Language also shapes policy: clinics labeled "behavioral rehabilitation" receive less funding than "mental-health recovery" centers (Link & Phelan, 2018).

Actionable shifts

- Use person-first phrasing ("a person with BPD") to separate the individual from the disorder.
- Swap blame-laden terms like "attention-seeking" for neutral descriptions like "seeking connection."
- Model this language publicly, emails, social posts, and team meetings, so compassionate vocabulary becomes normal

CREATING A MORE INFORMED SOCIETY

Culture rarely transforms by decree; it shifts grain by grain: a classroom lesson that invites empathy, a policy paper that reallocates funding, a family dinner where judgment gives way to curiosity. This closing section gathers those grains into four practical arenas where readers can push the conversation forward.

Lived Experience and Advocacy

First-person narratives rewrite the public story better than any clinical definition. When writers like Esmé Weijun Wang describe living with borderline traits, or podcasters share day-to-day victories over Avoidant patterns, stereotypes collapse into nuance.

Action steps

1. Subscribe to at least one blog, podcast, or social-media account run by someone with lived PD experience.
2. When planning a conference or panel, request speakers

who identify openly with a PD diagnosis, paid, not tokenized.

Mental-Health Education

A 2022 UNESCO brief found that students exposed to structured emotional-literacy curricula show a 15 percent drop in stigma-based attitudes (UNESCO, 2022). Schools and workplaces that weave mental-health literacy into existing wellness programs see higher help-seeking and lower absenteeism.

Action Ideas:

1. Introduce a monthly "myth-versus-fact" slide into staff meetings.
2. Partner with local universities for psycho-education workshops open to parents and teachers.

Trauma-Informed Systems

Services that assume trauma, rather than demand proof, offer safer care. Hospitals using the APNA trauma-informed checklist reported a 26 percent reduction in seclusion and restraint incidents over two years (American Psychiatric Nurses Association, 2023).

Implementation hints: Audit intake forms: Replace "What's wrong with you?" queries with "What has happened to you that we should know?" Train frontline staff in de-escalation scripts that prioritize safety and agency.

Mindful Language

Words steer perception. Swapping labels like "manipulative" for "protective strategy" reframes behavior without excusing harm. Research shows that clinicians who use person-first language ("a person *with* OCPD") are rated as more trustworthy and empathetic by patients (Martinez & Lewis, 2021).

Simple Swaps

1. Replace "is narcissistic," with "shows narcissistic traits under stress."
2. Trade "borderline meltdown," for "emotion-regulation crisis."

CHAPTER 13

ETHICAL AND LEGAL
CONSIDERATIONS

A diagnosis can be a lifeline, offering clarity, community, and a roadmap to treatment, but it can also be a double-edged sword, shaping identity, influencing legal outcomes, and echoing through every medical record that follows. To navigate personality disorders responsibly, we must weigh the ethical and legal edges of each decision.

ETHICAL CONCERNS IN DIAGNOSIS

Overdiagnosis and Bias

Women, people of color, and other marginalized groups remain disproportionately diagnosed with Borderline or Antisocial Personality Disorder, often because clinicians unconsciously interpret culturally normative expressions of anger or fear as pathological (Kirmayer & Bhugra, 2009). Such bias can steer patients toward stigmatizing labels and away from culturally attuned care.

Labeling Without Sufficient Evidence

Assigning a personality-disorder label prematurely can close doors to certain treatments, shape insurance coverage, and follow a person into legal settings (Appelbaum, 2003). Clinicians are ethically bound to exhaust differential diagnoses, gather longitudinal data, and consult peers before giving a life-long descriptor.

Balancing Honesty With Empathy

Transparency builds trust, yet delivering a PD diagnosis without context can feel shaming. Best practice is a two-step disclosure: first, validate the person's lived distress; then explain how the diagnosis offers a framework for targeted help (American Psychological Association, 2017).

Informed Consent

True consent means the patient understands the diagnosis, knows alternative treatments, and is aware of potential implications for employment, legal matters, and insurance (Stone, 2003). This requires plain-language explanations and space for questions, not a rushed signature at the end of an intake packet.

Try to Remember

- Bias skews who receives a PD label; clinicians must examine their cultural lenses.
- A hasty label can cause long-term harm; gather evidence first.
- Combine honesty with empathy when disclosing a diagnosis.

- Secure informed consent through clear, jargon-free dialogue.

CONFIDENTIALITY AND DUTY TO WARN

Confidentiality sits at the heart of the therapeutic contract, yet it is never absolute. When credible risk surfaces, of harm to the client or to identifiable others, clinicians must weigh privacy against protection, guided by statute, case law, and professional ethics. This section clarifies where the lines are drawn and offers cues for navigating gray zones.

The Tarasoff Precedent

In *Tarasoff v. Regents of the University of California* (1976), the California Supreme Court ruled that mental-health professionals have a "duty to protect" identifiable victims when a client makes a credible threat (Johnson et al., 2014). Key implications:

- **Warn the potential victim:** Notify law enforcement when feasible.
- **Document the decision-making process:** What was said, why the risk was judged credible, and actions taken.
- **Jurisdiction matters:** Some U.S. states adopt a strict "duty to warn," while others allow clinician discretion (Stone, 2003).
- **Extend the idea internationally:** Many countries now impose similar obligations, although wording and thresholds differ (Appelbaum, 2003).

Disclosure of Imminent Harm

Beyond Tarasoff, clinicians face mandated-reporting statutes for child or elder abuse, suicide risk, and threats of violence:

1. **Child-protection laws:** Typically require a report within 24 hours.
2. **Imminent self-harm:** May justify brief confidentiality breaches to coordinate emergency care (Knaak & Ungar, 2015).
3. **Threats toward non-specific targets:** Remain gray; consult supervision or legal counsel before disclosing.
4. **Cross-platform communication:** If a threat is posted on social media, screenshots and time stamps become part of the clinical record.

Clinician Checklist

- assess specificity, intent, and means
- consult a supervisor whenever possible
- document: facts first, impressions second
- notify only parties essential for safety; reveal the minimum necessary information

Consent Limitations and Complex Presentations

Certain personality-disorder traits, minimization, manipulation, and grandiosity, can distort informed consent:

- **Capacity vs. willingness:** A client may be *capable* of consenting yet unwilling to acknowledge risk.
- **Splitting and boundary-testing:** May pressure clinicians into overly restrictive or overly permissive disclosure.

- **Collaborative safety planning:** Preserves autonomy while addressing danger (Zur, 2009).
- **Use plain language:** Ask for teach-back to confirm understanding.

Involuntary Treatment and Patient Rights

Involuntary care is meant to prevent immediate harm, yet its invocation can compromise autonomy, dignity, and therapeutic trust, especially for those who already feel pathologized by the system. This section unpacks where the legal lines are drawn and how clinicians can honor safety without silencing self-determination.

HOSPITALIZATION CRITERIA

1. **Imminent danger to self or others:** Nearly all mental-health statutes require a clear, present risk (Stone, 2003).
2. **Grave disability:** Some regions add inability to meet basic needs: food, shelter, essential medical care (Appelbaum, 2003).
3. **Least-restrictive alternative:** Courts increasingly mandate proof that outpatient or partial-hospital options were explored first.

Clinician Tips

- Use structured risk-assessment tools (e.g., Columbia-Suicide Severity Rating Scale) to document danger.
- Re-evaluate daily; involuntary status should be time-limited and reviewable.

AUTONOMY VS. SAFETY

Balancing liberty with protection requires continuous consent checks:

- offer collaborative safety plans before filing papers
- explain legal steps in plain language; invite questions
- pair hospitalization with post-discharge resources to prevent the "revolving door" effect

Guardianship and Competency

Courts may appoint a guardian when repeated choices place the person or community at severe risk, but guardianship can feel like social death if misused.

Red-Flag Scenarios

- Progressively severe self-harm despite outpatient care.
- Severe cognitive decline that undermines contract understanding.

Safeguards

- Seek limited (not plenary) guardianship whenever possible.
- Encourage legal counsel or a patient advocate's presence during hearings.

PROFESSIONAL BOUNDARIES AND THERAPIST SAFETY

Therapists who work with high-conflict or trauma-laden personality presentations often describe sessions as walking a narrow bridge: lean too far toward emotional closeness and you risk enmeshment; step back too abruptly and the therapeutic alliance can fracture. This section offers practical guardrails, ethical, relational, and personal, for keeping both therapist and client on solid footing.

Managing Volatile Traits

- **Expect push-pull dynamics:** Idealization may turn to devaluation within a single session; keep feedback specific, neutral, and behavior-focused to avoid power struggles (Zur, 2009).
- **Containment over confrontation:** When anger escalates, slow the tempo, lower your voice, offer a grounding exercise, and name the emotion without judgment. Confronting content is more effective once arousal drops.
- **Ritualize session structure:** Consistent start/end times, clear agendas, and predictable homework reduce ambiguity and limit opportunities for manipulation.

Ethical Distance and Safety

1. **Boundary clarity:** Self-disclosure should serve a therapeutic purpose, not the clinician's anxiety reduction. Use the "three-second rule": if you can't articulate the clinical reason within three seconds, hold the disclosure.
2. **Safety plan for the office:** Know exit routes, keep furniture positioning safe, and have a silent alarm or code word with colleagues (Knaak, Ungar, & Patten, 2015).
3. **Documentation as protection:** Record boundary crossings, gifts offered, or aggressive statements the same day; note your response and any follow-up steps.

Supervision and Countertransference

- **Structured debriefs:** Schedule regular supervision when working with Cluster B and high-conflict clients; use checklists to flag emotional over-investment.
- **Countertransference mapping:** Identify personal triggers, perfectionism, rescuing impulses, fear of confrontation, and rehearse neutral responses.
- **Peer consultation circles:** Rotating case reviews normalize challenges and prevent clinician isolation, a known risk factor for burnout.

SYSTEMS-LEVEL CONCERNS

Ethical practice extends beyond the consulting room. Policies, budgets, and courtroom rulings can either entrench stigma or open pathways to care. This section zooms out to show how large-scale systems address, or neglect, personality disorders, and what reform can look like.

Access Disparities

Marginalized communities face a double bind: higher exposure to early adversity that elevates PD risk, but fewer culturally competent, trauma-informed services (Knaak et al., 2015).

Challenges

- Long waitlists at publicly funded clinics; private specialty care priced out of reach.
- Provider bias: traits like emotional intensity or distrust are misread as "non-compliance," leading to dismissal from services.

- Language barriers and immigration status complicate continuity of care.

Step Forward

1. **Community-embedded programs:** Employ peer specialists and bilingual clinicians.
2. **Sliding-scale reimbursement:** Tied to outcomes rather than brief time blocks.
3. **Mobile outreach teams:** Bringing DBT or schema-focused skills to underserved neighborhoods.

CRIMINALIZATION VS. REHABILITATION

Court systems often punish behaviors rooted in untreated PD traits, impulsivity, aggression, or survival-based manipulation, without addressing underlying trauma (Stone, 2003).

Current Pitfalls

- Mandatory minimums push individuals into overcrowded prisons lacking mental health care.
- Probation conditions ignore emotional dysregulation, leading to technical violations and re-incarceration.

Reform Examples

- **Mental-health courts:** Mandate evidence-based therapy alongside community supervision.
- **In-custody DBT units:** Reducing disciplinary infractions and self-harm (Pinals, 2010).
- **Restorative-justice circles:** Focusing on accountability plus relational repair rather than pure punishment.

TRAUMA-INFORMED JUSTICE

Trauma shapes personality development; ignoring it in legal settings compounds harm.

Key Features

- Judges and prosecutors are trained to recognize hyper-arousal and dissociation as trauma responses.
- Court-mandated assessments include ACEs (Adverse Childhood Experiences) alongside criminal history.
- Sentencing guidelines allow for treatment diversion when trauma and PD symptoms intersect.

Blueprint for Implementation

- Cross-training between public defender offices and trauma therapists.
- Funding streams that pair housing support with long-term therapy.
- Data dashboards tracking recidivism reduction linked to trauma-informed interventions.

CHAPTER 14

FUTURE DIRECTIONS IN RESEARCH AND TREATMENT

P ersonality is not concrete; it is clay. As neuroscience, technology, and cultural insight evolve, so too does our understanding of personality disorders, shaping treatments that are increasingly precise, humane, and hopeful.

SHIFTING THE DIAGNOSTIC MODEL

From Categories to Spectrums

Since 1980, the DSM system has divided personality disorders into discrete categories; yet, real-world presentations often blur these lines. Dimensional frameworks, such as those in ICD-11, grade severity on a continuum and recognize overlapping traits, allowing clinicians to capture nuance that the categorical model misses.

Why It Matters

- **Less stigma:** A spectrum lens normalizes variation rather than branding people with fixed labels (Colins et al., 2019).
- **Fewer "other specified" diagnoses:** Gray-area cases gain clearer clinical homes.

Severity and Functionality

ICD-11 evaluates impairment in self-function (identity, direction) and interpersonal function (intimacy, empathy). Severity, mild, moderate, severe, guides treatment intensity rather than dictating moral judgment (American Psychiatric Association, 2022).

Clinical Implications

1. Mild impairment may respond to short-term skills training.
2. Moderate cases often benefit from integrated trauma interventions.
3. Severe dysfunction may require multidisciplinary care, including pharmacology for co-occurring conditions.

Flexibility in Treatment

Dimensional assessment informs flexible care pathways; for example, DBT modules can be scaled in duration, while schema therapy targets core modes appropriate to impairment level (Bozzatello et al., 2021).

TRAUMA-INFORMED RESEARCH

Early wounds leave fingerprints on personality. Rather than asking only *What is wrong?* Trauma-informed researchers now trace *What happened? And How it shaped coping?* The shift pushes PD science away from symptom control toward root-level repair.

Early Trauma as a Root

- **Adverse childhood experiences (ACEs) and risk:** Meta-analyses show a stepwise increase in Cluster B and C traits with each added ACE (Hughes et al., 2017).
- **Attachment disruption:** Longitudinal work links disorganized attachment in infancy to borderline-style emotion dysregulation in early adulthood (Lyons-Ruth & Jacobvitz, 2016).
- **Neurobiological impact:** Childhood maltreatment alters fronto-limbic connectivity, amplifying threat perception and impulsivity, core features in several PDs (Teicher & Samson, 2016).

Symptom Repair vs. Suppression

- **Healing the wound, not polishing the scar:** Trauma-focused therapies (e.g., EMDR, TF-CBT) reduce PD symptom clusters by processing traumatic memory rather than drilling behavioral compliance (Macchia et al., 2025).
- **Emotion-first sequencing:** Studies show that when affect regulation improves, interpersonal chaos and self-harm decline even before skills training begins (Linehan et al., 2021).

- **From blame to context:** Framing aggression or avoidance as survival strategies lowers shame and increases treatment adherence.

Developmental Focus

- **Lifespan lens:** Prospective cohorts reveal that personality rigidity is not fixed; severity waxes and wanes with developmental tasks—school transitions, career stress, caregiving roles (Hopwood et al., 2013).
- **Early intervention:** Pilot programs teaching DBT-core skills in high-risk teens cut later PD diagnoses by nearly 30 percent.
- **Intergenerational repair:** Parenting interventions that boost reflective capacity in caregivers reduce disorganized attachment markers in toddlers, potentially disrupting the PD pipeline (Suchman et al., 2018).

Practical Implications for Clinicians

1. Screen routinely for ACEs and current safety; untreated trauma predicts dropout and relapse.
2. Introduce stabilization skills, but move quickly to trauma processing once affect regulation is tolerable.
3. Track developmental milestones; adapt goals when life stages shift vulnerability.

CULTURAL COMPETENCY AND GLOBAL RESEARCH

Personality is shaped not only by neural wiring and family dynamics, but also by language, ritual, and collective memory. Western frameworks have long set the rules of psychiatric diagnosis; the next chapter in PD science must widen the field, recognizing that behavior viewed as pathological in one culture may be functional, even prized, in another.

Inclusion of Non-Western Perspectives

- **Indigenous models of self:** Māori scholars frame wellbeing through *whānau* (extended family) and *wairua* (spiritual health), challenging individual-centric assumptions common in Western psychiatry (Durie, 2021).
- **Ubuntu and relational identity:** South-African philosophy centers personhood on communal belonging— a lens that casts dependent traits as interdependence, not weakness (Mkhize, 2020).
- **Ayurvedic personality typologies:** Indian clinicians integrate *prakriti* profiles with DSM criteria, offering hybrid assessments more acceptable to local patients (Singh & Sharma, 2019).

Cultural Context Shapes Diagnosis

1. **Norms as diagnostic yardsticks:** A collectivist teen who defers to elders may be misread as submissive or dependent in an individualist clinic (Kirmayer & Bhugra, 2009).
2. **Emotion display rules:** Mediterranean expressiveness can be mistaken for histrionic traits in stoic cultures; conversely, East-Asian restraint may be mislabeled as avoidant (Tseng, 2022).
3. **Structural bias in prevalence data:** BIPOC individuals in the United States are disproportionately diagnosed with Cluster B disorders, mirroring systemic bias rather than true incidence (Akinhanmi et al., 2020).

Clinician Training for Cultural Literacy

- Integrate cultural formulation interviews into routine assessment; these structured questions uncover idioms of distress and community resources (Lewis-Fernández et al., 2017).
- Pair trainees with cultural mentors, not just clinical supervisors, to deepen contextual insight and reduce implicit bias (Cultural Psychiatry Study Group, 2021).
- Employ case conferences that include anthropologists or community leaders when developing treatment plans for culturally diverse clients (Hinton, 2018).

TECHNOLOGY AND DIGITAL TOOLS

Smartphones sit in more pockets than therapists sit in offices, and algorithms can now learn our behavioral rhythms with unsettling accuracy. Digital innovation is reshaping how personality disorders are monitored, understood, and treated, sometimes outpacing the ethical guardrails meant to protect users.

Apps and AI in Care

- **Skill-building on demand:** Evidence-based apps like *DBT Coach* and *Stoic* walk users through emotion-regulation exercises, mindfulness, and distress-tolerance drills between therapy sessions (Rony et al., 2025).
- **Conversational agents:** AI chatbots offer 24/7 check-ins. Early trials show reductions in self-reported anxiety and impulsivity among BPD users after four weeks of guided chatbot interaction (Fitzpatrick et al., 2023).
- **Data integration with EHRs:** Start-ups are linking app metrics (mood logs, sleep patterns) to electronic health

records, giving clinicians a granular view of daily functioning and medication effects (Zhang et al., 2024).

Real-Time Feedback and Pattern Recognition

1. **Passive sensing:** Smartphone sensors track movement, call frequency, and geolocation to flag deviations that precede mood swings or risky behaviors—paving the way for just-in-time interventions (Torous et al., 2021).
2. **Wearable analytics:** Heart-rate variability and galvanic skin response bands can detect physiological arousal, prompting users to launch grounding tools before urge escalation.
3. **Predictive modeling:** Machine-learning algorithms have reached 80 percent accuracy in predicting self-harm episodes 24 hours in advance among high-risk youth (Walsh et al., 2022).

Peer Forums and Virtual Therapy

- **Anonymity meets community:** Platforms like *7 Cups* and moderated Reddit forums allow individuals with Cluster B traits to exchange support without fear of local stigma.
- **Group tele-DBT:** Randomized trials report comparable outcomes between virtual and in-person DBT groups for emotion regulation and self-harm reduction (Lakeman et al., 2022).
- **VR exposure:** Pilot studies use virtual-reality social scenarios to help avoidant clients rehearse assertiveness in a low-stakes environment (Freeman et al., 2021).

EVOLVING THERAPIES

Treatment for personality disorders has moved beyond a CBT-versus-DBT debate. A new wave of modalities invites clients to work with emotions, body sensations, and, in some cases, carefully monitored altered states. This section spotlights three fast-developing frontiers and the early evidence behind them.

Compassion-Focused Therapy (CFT) and Internal Family Systems (IFS)

- **Parts work meets self-compassion:** IFS maps the psyche into protective managers, reactive firefighters, and vulnerable exiles. CFT layers on warmth and acceptance, training the "compassionate self" to soothe shame and fear.
- **Why it matters for PDs:** Cluster B and C presentations often house deep self-criticism; cultivating an internal caregiver reduces moralistic self-attack and lowers reactivity (Gilbert & Simos, 2022).
- **Preliminary data:** A 2023 pilot (n = 42) found a 35 percent drop in emotional dysregulation scores after eight IFS-informed sessions (Brown et al., 2023).
- **Client tip:** Start a "parts glossary" in your journal—name each inner voice, note its protective role, and write a compassionate response.

Body-Based Approaches

- **Somatic Experiencing (SE):** Uses guided interoception and titrated exposure to release stored survival energy; small RCTs show reduced hyper-arousal in CPTSD and BPD (Payne et al., 2022).

- **Eye Movement Desensitization & Reprocessing (EMDR):** Bilateral stimulation while recalling trauma can unlink affect from memory; a meta-analysis reports medium-to-large effect sizes for BPD trauma symptoms (Valentine & Harvey, 2021).
- **Movement therapies:** Yoga, tai chi, and dance/movement therapy improve vagal tone and body ownership—useful for clients who intellectualizes their feelings.
- **Therapist caveat:** Track dissociation; if the body feels unsafe, pendulate between sensation and external resources before diving deeper.

Psychedelic-Assisted Therapy

- **MDMA-assisted therapy:** Phase 3 trials for severe PTSD report 67 percent remission; exploratory sub-analyses suggest benefits for comorbid BPD traits (Mitchell et al., 2023).
- **Psilocybin for emotional rigidity:** Open-label studies show transient increases in cognitive flexibility and self-transcendence—promising for OCPD-like perfectionism (Carhart-Harris & Friston, 2021).
- **Ethical safeguards:** Screening for psychosis risk, medical monitoring, and integration sessions are non-negotiable. Recreational use is *not* psychotherapy.
- **Regulatory status:** MDMA may receive FDA approval for PTSD in 2025; psilocybin remains Schedule I in most jurisdictions.

ADVOCACY AND ANTI-STIGMA MOVEMENTS

A diagnosis can confine a life story to the margins—or it can propel the author onto center stage. Over the past decade, activists, researchers, and people with lived experience have begun rewiring public narratives about personality disorders, trading shame for nuance and isolation for community.

Lived Experience and Activism

- **Peer-led digital campaigns:** Online spaces such as *#BPDChat* on X (formerly Twitter) and r/OCPD on Reddit give thousands a week a judgment-free venue to share coping tools and crisis resources (Wilson & Goldstein, 2022).
- **Grass-roots conferences:** Events like *BPD Empowerment EU* and the U.S. *Healing from Personality Disorders Summit* center service-user panels alongside clinicians, ensuring that research agendas reflect lived realities (Dawson & Gooding, 2021).
- **Policy influence:** UK NICE guideline revisions for borderline and antisocial PDs now cite service-user testimony as a primary evidence source, reflecting a shift toward co-production (National Institute for Health and Care Excellence, 2020).

Public Narratives and Media

- **Memoirs replacing caricatures:** First-person books such as *The Buddha and the Borderline* (Green, 2010) and essays in *I Hate You—Don't Leave Me* (Kreuger & Strauss, 2017) De-mythologize PDs, showing ordinary lives behind clinical labels.

- **Podcasts and video channels:** Shows like *Back from the Borderline* and YouTube educator Dr. Todd Grande's analysis series break down research findings in accessible language, countering sensationalist headlines (Grande, 2023).
- **Trauma-informed journalism:** Outlets including *The Guardian* and *Vox* now publish mental-health style guides urging writers to avoid using "psycho" or "narcissist" as insults, reducing linguistic stigma (Carter, 2022).

Blending Professional and Peer Voices

- **Co-produced services:** Australia's *Head to Help* hubs employ peer workers alongside psychiatrists, reporting higher engagement among people with Cluster B traits than clinician-only teams (Bennett et al., 2023).
- **Peer specialists on treatment teams:** U.S. Medicaid data show that clinics employing certified peer specialists reduce no-show rates for trauma-related PD appointments by 18 percent (Pinals & Fraser, 2021).
- **Training with lived-experience facilitators:** Programs like *Hearing Voices* and *Intentional Peer Support* invite clinicians to practice reflective listening with facilitators who disclose their own diagnoses, increasing empathy scores on the Jefferson Scale (Ahmed & Lee, 2019).

ACTION PLAN/ WORKBOOK:

STRATEGIES FOR MANAGING AND COPING

HOW TO USE THIS WORKBOOK

Think of this chapter as a workbench stocked with precision tools. You don't need every wrench or screwdriver at once; you need the right implement for the problem in front of you. Skim, pick, test, adjust. Keep what serves you; set aside what doesn't, at least for now.

Purpose

- Translate the insight you gained in earlier chapters into day-to-day practices.
- Provide quick-access strategies organised by disorder so you can find what you need without wading through theory.

Using the Workbook

1. **Identify a single trait or trigger:** That is most disruptive this week.
2. **Scan the relevant section:** Choose one tool, only one, to experiment with.
3. **Commit for seven days:** Noting when, where, and how you apply the tool.
4. **Record observations:** Shifts in mood, behavior, relationships.
5. **Refine:** Keep, modify, or replace the tool based on real-world feedback.

Tip: Small, consistent adjustments outpace dramatic overhauls.

Ready? Select the first challenge that matters to you and turn the page.

BORDERLINE PERSONALITY DISORDER (BPD)

This section is a quick-grab kit. Open it when emotional spikes feel unmanageable or when a loved one's reaction seems to tilt the room. Each tool is meant to be tested, tweaked, and logged until you find a personalized set that works reliably.

Core Challenges

- **Rapid emotional surges:** That crest within minutes and can last hours, often triggered by perceived rejection or isolation (American Psychiatric Association, 2022)
- **Hyperalert attachment system:** Leading to frantic attempts to avoid abandonment even in stable relationships (Gunderson & Links, 2014)

- **Impulsive coping loops:** Such as self-injury, risky spending, or bingeing, used to numb emotional pain (Linehan, 2015)
- **Shifting self-image:** Where values, goals, and self-worth swing from day to day (American Psychological Association, 2017)

Strategies for Self-Management

90-Second Wave Check

When an emotion spikes, set a 90-second timer; focus on breathing until the chemical surge passes, then name the feeling before acting (Hanson, 2018)

In Practice

Marla, 27, always knew when her partner was about to pull away, at least, that's how it felt. One night, a delayed reply to a simple "Are you home safe?" text spiraled her into a full-body panic. Within minutes, her chest was tight, her thoughts racing: *He's done. He doesn't care. I'm too much again.* The urge to send a barrage of hurt-filled texts flared hot and immediate.

But this time, Marla reached for the note she had taped to her desk:

"Ride the wave. 90 seconds. Then name it."

She set a timer, closed her eyes, and focused on the air entering her nose, the weight of her body on the chair, the anchor of her own breath. When the timer beeped, the urge was still there, but the panic had softened. Beneath the spike was something quieter: fear. She whispered it aloud, *"I'm afraid he'll leave."* Then she wrote it down. Just that. No texts sent. No bridges burned.

Feelings Glossary

When emotions run high, language often collapses. Everything feels like "angry" or "sad," when really, there's a much more precise emotional fingerprint beneath the noise. That precision matters. Studies show that people who can label emotions in detail, called emotional granularity, regulate those emotions more effectively (Kircanski et al., 2012).

A feelings glossary is a living document. Start by writing down every nuanced emotion word you come across: not just *mad*, but *irritated, betrayed, frustrated, agitated*. Not just *sad*, but *disappointed, grief-struck, lonely, numb*. Add new ones as you hear or feel them. Return to it often.

Use it in real time. When a mood flares, glance at the list. Ask, *Which word fits closest?* The goal isn't to fix the feeling, but to name it more truthfully. That clarity reduces overwhelm and gives the brain a target for calming down.

In Practice

Jules, 33, was used to labeling everything as anger. When a coworker talked over her in meetings, when her sister forgot to call, when her partner didn't notice her new haircut, it all went down as *pissed off*.

But during therapy, Jules was asked to pause and name what she was really feeling in each moment using a list she'd started keeping on her phone.

After a tense call with her mom, she opened the glossary and scanned the words. She landed on *dismissed*. It hit hard, but it also felt right. Beneath the heat was a sting of being unseen.

She didn't lash out. She didn't stew for days. She wrote in her journal and sat with it. Naming it didn't fix the relationship, but it softened the reaction.

STOP Skill

The STOP skill is a simple but powerful acronym used in Dialectical Behavior Therapy (DBT) to prevent emotional hijacking and impulsive behaviors. It stands for:

- **S:** *Stop*freeze, don't act on the urge. No texting, shouting, running, quitting, or explaining. Just halt the motion.
- **T:** *Take a step back*—physically or mentally remove yourself. Breathe. Create space between the feeling and the reaction.
- **O:** *Observe*—notice what's happening: your thoughts, emotions, body sensations, and urges. What are you reacting to? What story are you telling yourself?
- **P:** *Proceed mindfully*—choose your next move based on your goals and values, not the emotional storm. Respond, don't react.

This skill interrupts automatic behaviors and creates a pause long enough for awareness to kick in. With repetition, it builds emotional self-command in the moments that matter most.

In Practice

Maya, 24, was used to fighting fire with fire. When she felt rejected, even slightly, her go-to move was retaliation: cold texts, cryptic posts, impulsive block-and-unblock cycles.

After a group hangout where her best friend seemed distant, Maya started typing a long message laced with sarcasm and accusation. But then she saw the sticky note on her laptop: *STOP*.

She pushed her phone aside and walked outside.

S—she stopped the motion.
T—she stepped onto the porch. Breathed.
O—she noticed the story: *She's pulling away. She doesn't want me anymore.*
P—she didn't text. Instead, she messaged the group casually about weekend plans. Her friend responded warmly. The storm had passed. The friendship hadn't.

Emotion Tracking App

Feelings are fleeting, but patterns are not. Most people with emotional dysregulation don't struggle because they feel too much; they struggle because they don't see it coming. Emotion tracking helps make the invisible visible.

Using a mood tracking app like Daylio, Moodnotes, or Bearable, you log your emotional state at regular intervals, ideally twice a day. Each entry includes:

- mood (happy, sad, anxious, angry, numb, etc.)
- intensity (1–10 scale)
- context (what was happening, who you were with, where you were)
- notes (any events, thoughts, or urges)

At the end of the week, review the log. Patterns begin to surface:

- Are Sundays always heavier?

- Is stress higher after long meetings?
- Does a certain friend leave you emotionally rattled?

This data turns your emotions into a map. It helps you predict emotional triggers and make preventative shifts. You can't always stop the storm, but you can see the clouds gathering.

In Practice

Lena, 35, swore her emotions were random. "I just go from fine to falling apart," she told her therapist. So, at her therapist's suggestion, she downloaded Daylio.

She logged her mood every morning and night for two weeks.

On the 10th day, something clicked. Every Thursday evening, her mood plummeted. Digging into her notes, she realized Thursdays were when her partner worked late and wasn't home for dinner. That triggered the familiar ache of being left out, rooted in years of childhood neglect.

She didn't blame her partner. But now, she schedules a friend check-in or a solo movie night every Thursday. The pattern didn't own her anymore.

Crisis Script

When distress hits, the thinking brain often goes offline. In those moments, complex coping skills can feel impossible to recall. That's why a Crisis Script is essential, simple, concrete, and pre-written when you're calm.

A crisis script is a 3-step plan, written down on a card, sticky note, or phone lock screen. It's not a deep intervention; it's a life raft.

The structure:

1. **Regulate the body:** Breathing, grounding, or cold temperature.
2. **Reach for connection:** Text a safe person, call a helpline, or enter a support app.
3. **Disrupt the spiral:** Use a sensory tool (ice, fidget, scent) or distraction (walk, puzzle, playlist).

Example script:

"Breathe (4-7-8) → Text Sam → Hold ice cube for 1 minute"

Keep it visible and accessible. The goal is not to solve the crisis, but to buy time, because urges pass, and pain lessens, but damage done in those first moments can last.

In Practice

Ari, 22, had a long history of self-harm during emotional overload. One night, after a fight with her girlfriend, she felt it coming, the numbness, the tunnel vision, the itch for release.

She opened her notes app. The first line of her crisis script glared back:

"You don't need to fix it tonight."

Her plan:

1. **Breathe (4-7-8 method)**
2. **Text her therapist's check-in line**
3. **Press her palms to the freezer door for 30 seconds**

She did all three. She didn't feel "better", but she made it through the hour. And the hour after that. And by morning, the crisis had passed.

For Supporters

Validate First, Guide Second

People with BPD often live in emotional states that feel too big to contain and too confusing to explain. When they reach out in panic, frustration, or overwhelm, it's tempting to jump in with advice, reassurance, or logic.

But advice offered too soon, before validation, often lands as rejection. It can feel like dismissal: *"Calm down," "That's not what happened,"* or *"Just do your breathing."* These responses may be well-meaning, but they reinforce the fear that emotional intensity will push people away.

Instead, begin with validation:

- Reflect the emotion you see: *"You seem really scared right now."*
- Acknowledge its legitimacy: *"It makes sense you'd feel that way after what happened."*

Only after that should you introduce coping strategies, perspective shifts, or next steps.

Think of it like this:

1. Mirror the feeling.
2. Then hand over the toolkit.

Validation doesn't mean agreement. It means connection, and connection is the entry point for regulation.

In Practice

Noah, 31, was dating someone with BPD. One evening, his partner called, sobbing. "You're pulling away, I know it. I can feel it. Just admit it."

Noah tried logic: "You know that's not true. We just spent the weekend together. You're spiraling again."

The result? A full-blown rupture.

Later, in therapy, Noah learned to try something different. The next time she called in that state, he said:

"I can hear how scared you are right now. It sounds like you're feeling abandoned."

Silence. Then: *"Yeah. I am."*

That moment cracked something open. Only then could he add:

"Would it help to go through the grounding checklist we made?"

She said yes. They stayed on the call. No rupture at that time.

Use DEAR MAN Boundaries

When supporting someone with BPD, boundaries can feel risky. You want to be kind, but not consumed. Firm, but not cold. That's where *DEAR MAN* comes in, a DBT communication skill designed for assertiveness with empathy.

Each letter serves a purpose:

- **D**—*describe* the facts without emotion or blame.
  - "You texted me ten times in a row last night while I was offline."
- **E**—*express* how it made you feel.
  - "That left me feeling overwhelmed and anxious."
- **A**—*assert* what you need, clearly.
  - "I need space to respond in my own time."
- **R**—*reinforce* why this matters.
  - "When I have that space, I can actually show up for you better."
- **M**—*mindful*: Stay focused, don't get pulled into tangents or provocations.
- **A**—*appear confident*: Even if you're nervous, speak with steadiness.
- **N**—*negotiate*: Be open to compromise if it helps meet both needs.
  - "Would it help to agree on a check-in window for nights like that?"

DEAR MAN sets a boundary without dehumanizing the other person. It acknowledges emotion but stays grounded in clarity. For someone with BPD, where abandonment fears and rejection sensitivity run high, this structure provides containment without escalation.

In Practice

Jordan, 29, had a close friend with BPD. They'd grown up together, but lately, every disagreement turned into a meltdown. When Jordan didn't answer a text quickly, the friend sent angry voice notes and vague threats to cut ties.

Jordan used DEAR MAN in a voice memo:

Describe: "You messaged me six times in an hour after I didn't reply."
Express: "That made me feel pressured and anxious."
Assert: "I need at least a few hours to respond without being flooded."
Reinforce: "I care about you and want to be present, but I can't do that if I'm reacting out of panic."
Mindful: He stuck to this message, ignoring jabs like "Maybe you don't care anymore."
Appear confident: His voice was calm, not apologetic.
Negotiate: "Would a 24-hour response window work for both of us?"

To his surprise, the friend replied, "Okay. I can try that."

Signal Consistency

For someone with BPD, unpredictability can feel like abandonment. The smallest change, canceling plans, a delayed reply, or forgetting a routine check-in, can activate deep fears of being dropped, dismissed, or unloved.

That's why consistency is one of the most powerful forms of support. It doesn't require grand gestures. It requires reliability:

- Say what you mean.
- Do what you say.
- Show up when you said you would.

Even small signals, like texting *"Thinking of you, talk soon"* at a predictable time, can become anchors of emotional safety. When routines are reliable, the nervous system relaxes. The attachment system stabilizes.

This doesn't mean overextending yourself or enabling unhealthy behavior. It means offering *steadiness* over *rescue*. Clear boundaries paired with consistent presence build trust far more than intensity or promises.

In Practice

Sophie, 41, had a daughter with BPD. They lived apart, and their calls often ended in shouting or tears. Every week was a toss-up, connection or chaos.

Her therapist suggested one small change: a recurring Sunday check-in at 5 p.m. Not to fix, just to connect.

At first, her daughter resisted: "What's the point?" But Sophie kept showing up. Even if the call was short. Even if it was hard.

Weeks passed. Then one Sunday, her daughter said, "I knew you'd call. I didn't think you would, but you did."

Long-Term Coping Mechanisms

Values Compass

For individuals with BPD, identity often feels like a moving target. Values, goals, and even a sense of self can shift from day to day. The Values Compass is a stabilizing tool that reconnects you to your deeper sense of direction, especially when emotions cloud decision-making.

Here's how it works:

1. *List 5–7 core values* that feel authentic to you. These might

include honesty, connection, creativity, autonomy, growth, or kindness.

2. Every *Sunday*, reflect back on the week and rate how closely your actions aligned with each value on a *0–10 scale*.

3. Notice gaps. A low score isn't a failure; try to take it as feedback. Ask: *What got in the way? What small shift could close the gap this week?*

This exercise builds self-consistency over time. Instead of asking *"What do I feel like doing today?"* which can fluctuate wildly, you begin asking *"What matters most to me, and how can I live more like that?"*

It doesn't eliminate emotional storms, but it helps you steer through them with something that resembles a map.

In Practice

Cam, 36, felt like a different person every few days. One day, he wanted a new job; the next, he was all-in on starting a nonprofit. He cut friends off, then panicked when they pulled away. His therapist introduced the Values Compass.

Cam listed six values: honesty, creativity, loyalty, calm, learning, and self-respect.

That first Sunday, he gave himself a 3/10 for loyalty; he'd ghosted a friend after a disagreement. The number stung, but it helped him see the gap.

He texted the friend: *"I want to repair. I wasn't proud of how I handled that."*

The following week, his loyalty score rose to a 7. He didn't feel like a different person. He felt like a person with direction.

Opposite-Action Practice

Many urges linked to BPD are rooted in intense emotional states, fear, anger, shame, and rejection. The nervous system says *"protect yourself"*, and the behaviors that follow often feel automatic: isolating, lashing out, clinging, withdrawing.

Opposite-action practice interrupts that loop.

The concept is simple but powerful:

When the emotion is strong, and you're sure you need to act a certain way, do the opposite of the urge.

- If the urge is to isolate → *send a supportive text*
- If the urge is to rage → *use a non-reactive response*
- If the urge is to beg someone to stay → *pause and self-soothe first*

The goal isn't to suppress emotions. It's to *retrain the behavioral response,* over time, so that it aligns with long-term values instead of short-term relief.

It's uncomfortable at first. It may feel fake, awkward, or "wrong." That's a sign the wiring is being challenged. And that's where change begins.

In Practice

Nina, 25, always felt abandoned after arguments. Her default move? Silence for three days, then a flood of reactive messages: *"Why do I even try? You never cared."*

During one therapy session, she was introduced to opposite-action practice. She made a commitment: the next time the urge to lash out hit, she would do the opposite.

It didn't take long.

That week, her partner canceled plans. Nina felt the rage rise, but instead of ghosting or attacking, she sent a short message:

"Disappointed we won't see each other. I'll catch you later."

No accusations. No test. Just data.

Her partner replied: *"Me too. Let's reschedule this weekend."*

The next time Nina felt rejected, she pulled out the text and read it again, not as a template, but as proof. The opposite action doesn't erase emotion, but it breaks the chain.

Routine SelfSoothe K

For many living with BPD, emotional overwhelm feels like a sudden ambush. But often, the body sends subtle cues *before* a full-blown episode: tight chest, racing thoughts, agitation, emotional "static." The goal is to get ahead of the crisis.

That's where a *self-soothe kit* comes in. It's not just a collection of calming items; it's a *daily ritual* that helps regulate the nervous system through the five senses.

Here's how to build and use one:

- **Touch:** smooth stone, soft blanket, weighted eye mask
- **Smell:** lavender oil, citrus balm, familiar perfume
- **Sight:** calming imagery, nature photo, a quote that grounds you
- **Sound:** playlist of soothing or nostalgic songs, white noise, calming voice notes
- **Taste:** mint tea, dark chocolate square, lemon drop

Create a small box or pouch. Use it *daily at a set time*, not just during distress. Think of it as emotional prehab, not just rehab. You're teaching your nervous system to expect calm, to familiarize itself with regulation.

In Practice

Dev, 39, used to treat emotional breakdowns like wildfires, scrambling for tools only once everything was already burning.

His therapist challenged him to build a Self-Soothe Kit and use it every night before bed, even if he wasn't dysregulated.

He added:

- A pine-scented roller from childhood hikes.
- A velvet pouch that his grandmother gave him.
- A Polaroid of his dog.
- An instrumental playlist titled "Safe."

The first week felt silly. But by the third, he noticed something: his emotional spikes were less frequent. His body recognized the ritual. Calm was no longer something he had to chase; it was something he had practiced.

Therapy Techniques

- **Dialectical Behavior Therapy (DBT):** Gold-standard program teaching emotion regulation, distress tolerance, interpersonal effectiveness, mindfulness (Linehan, 2015)
- **Mentalization-Based Therapy (MBT):** Strengthens the capacity to interpret one's own and others' mental states, reducing impulsivity (Bateman & Fonagy, 2019)
- **Schema Therapy:** Targets abandonment, mistrust, or

defectiveness schemas underlying relational chaos (Young et al., 2003)

NARCISSISTIC PERSONALITY DISORDER (NPD)

NPD is more of a hall of mirrors. The reflections can look magnificent one minute and distorted the next. This section helps you replace those shifting images with usable feedback loops, tools that build stable self-worth without crushing drive.

Core Challenges

- Low empathy that makes other people's needs fade from view (Ronningstam, 2016).
- Hypersensitivity to criticism, even when feedback is mild (Morf & Rhodewalt, 2001).
- Grandiosity or entitlement that masks fragile self-esteem (American Psychological Association, 2021).

Self-Management Strategies

Reality-Check Journal

People with narcissistic traits often struggle with extremes in self-perception: *I'm either exceptional or worthless. I'm either admired or invisible.* These swings aren't arrogance, they're attempts to stabilize fragile self-worth.

The *reality-check journal* is a structured way to soften those extremes. Each night, record:

- Two areas where you showed competence or strength.
- One area where you needed support, made a mistake, or learned something.

This dual-entry process balances confidence with humility. You begin to see that you can be capable and imperfect in the same breath. That reality isn't a threat; it's a foundation.

Once a week, review your entries. Look for patterns: Where do you consistently excel? Where do you consistently avoid asking for help? Over time, this practice builds a more stable self-image, grounded in nuance, not ego defense.

In Practice

Theo, 45, prided himself on being the sharpest person in the room. He had to be, growing up, love felt conditional on achievement. But lately, the weight of always being "on" was catching up to him.

He started a reality-check journal at his coach's suggestion.

One entry read:

- Strength 1: Led a client meeting that landed the pitch.
- Strength 2: Handled a tech issue calmly under pressure.
- Growth area: Delegated poorly, micromanaged the new intern, and missed her idea.

At first, the third line felt like failure. But after three weeks, Theo noticed something: his "needed help" column often involved control. That awareness didn't shatter his self-worth; it sharpened it.

Perspective-Taking Reps

One of the core challenges for individuals with narcissistic traits is difficulty recognizing others' emotions as separate but equally real. It's not intentional disregard; it's often a skill deficit rooted in emotional defensiveness.

Perspective-taking reps are daily mental exercises that build empathic accuracy over time.

Here's how it works:

1. Choose a recent interaction, tense or neutral.
2. Replay it from the other person's point of view.
3. Write down *three emotions* they may have felt during that moment.
4. Ask: *What would that emotion feel like if I were them, not me?*

This is about widening your lens. Over time, these reps make emotional landscapes less foreign and more understandable.

Think of it like a muscle: the more reps you do, the more accessible empathy becomes in real time.

In Practice

Malik, 39, was told often that he "didn't listen." He thought that was unfair; he just didn't see why people reacted so emotionally to minor comments.

One day, after a meeting where he'd interrupted a junior colleague, he tried a perspective-taking rep. He imagined the moment from her seat.

- Emotion 1: *Dismissed*
- Emotion 2: *Self-doubt*
- Emotion 3: *Frustrated, but unable to say it*

At first, it felt like guesswork. But the next time they spoke, he noticed her hesitation. Instead of bulldozing, he asked, *"Did I miss something in the meeting you wanted to add?"*

She lit up. He didn't fix everything. But for once, he made room.

Humility Micro-Acts

For individuals with narcissistic traits, much of life can feel like a stage. Every move is monitored, internally or externally, for performance, approval, or control. That pressure can squeeze out quiet acts of humility, which often feel unrewarded, unnoticed, or even threatening.

Humility micro-acts are small, intentional behaviors that:

- benefit others
- require no recognition
- reinforce contribution over competition

Examples:

- returning a stray grocery cart
- picking up someone's dropped item without comment
- amplifying someone's idea in a meeting, then leaving it at that

The practice isn't just behavioral. After each act, *record what you did and how it felt*. Did you notice resentment? Relief? A shift?

Over time, these acts retrain your reward system, from external validation to internal meaning. You start to feel grounded in *quiet impact*, not loud performance.

In Practice

Jonah, 32, was known for dominating meetings. He wasn't trying to steal the spotlight; it just felt uncomfortable to be quiet. In one session, a newer team member floated an idea Jonah had been considering for himself.

The usual impulse: jump in, expand it, get credit.

Instead, Jonah paused. When the discussion wrapped, he said, *"That was a sharp callout by Denise. I hadn't thought of it that way."*

Then he shut up.

No tag-on. No reframe. Just the mic was handed over and left there.

Later, he wrote:

"Felt exposed at first. Then... weirdly proud. She looked more confident. That was better than applause."

"Two Truths and a Goal" Mantra

Criticism can feel like a full-body threat for individuals with narcissistic traits. Even gentle feedback may trigger internal spirals: *I'm being attacked. They're jealous. I'm a failure. I have to prove them wrong.* The ego scrambles to protect itself, and in the process, growth gets blocked.

The *"Two truths and a goal"* mantra turns feedback into a structured response rather than a reactive spiral.

When criticism lands:

1. Pause. Don't respond yet.
2. Identify *two facts you can agree with* (even if the tone or delivery was off).
3. Name *one forward-looking goal or action step.*

This does three things:

- grounds the mind in reality
- prevents defensiveness from hijacking the conversation
- shows maturity without self-erasure

Example:

Feedback: *"You took over the presentation and made it hard for others to contribute."*

Mantra response:

- Truth 1: *"I did talk for most of it."*
- Truth 2: *"I didn't check in with the team ahead of time."*
- Goal: *"Next time, I'll plan time blocks and ask for input."*

Simple. Contained. Growth-oriented.

In Practice

Elena, 40, had built her identity around being the go-to expert. So when her supervisor gave critical feedback on a leadership review, she felt attacked and ready to quit on the spot.

But she opened her notebook and wrote:

- Truth 1: *I cut off a team member mid-sentence during the planning session.*
- Truth 2: *I changed the timeline without consulting the group.*
- Goal: *Hold space for open input next quarter before rolling out changes.*

She didn't spiral. She didn't defend. She responded in the next meeting:

"Thanks for the notes. I've already got next quarter's planning set up for co-design. Let's see how that feels."

She kept her power and made room for growth.

For Supporters

Mirror, Don't Magnify

When someone with narcissistic traits speaks with self-importance, defensiveness, or exaggeration, the instinct for supporters often goes one of two ways:

- **Magnify:** Fuel the grandiosity with flattery to keep the peace
- **Confront:** Challenge the ego with blunt truth in the name of "calling it out"

Both approaches backfire.

Magnifying reinforces the false self; *confronting* invites escalation or shutdown. The middle path is *mirroring*: calmly reflecting what you *see* and *hear*, without applause or argument.

Try responses like:

- "Sounds like that really mattered to you."
- "You put a lot into that; I can tell it was important."
- "That felt unfair, huh?"

You're *acknowledging emotion*, not validating distortion. The goal is to meet the person with presence, not provoke or placate. Mirroring builds trust without reinforcing inflated self-images or inviting defensiveness.

In Practice

Isaac, 38, had just been passed over for a promotion. He called his sister, fuming:

"It's politics. Everyone knows I'm the best they've got. I've outperformed everyone. They're intimidated, plain and simple."

His sister, *Naomi*, used to debate with him. Point out how others deserved the role. It always ended in a blow-up.

This time, she paused and said:

"You sound really frustrated. Like the work you've done hasn't been seen."

Isaac exhaled. "Exactly."

No fight followed. No lecture needed. He didn't spiral. He felt heard, without being fed.

Consequences, Not Confrontations

Narcissistic traits often involve testing limits, especially when someone believes the rules don't apply to them. Direct confrontation about entitlement or arrogance can easily escalate into defensiveness, blame-shifting, or emotional withdrawal.

The more effective route? *Consequences that are clear, calm, and consistent.*

Instead of saying:

- *"You're being selfish again."*

Try:

- *"We start meetings at 10. If you're late, you'll have to join the next one."*

This approach avoids emotional warfare. You're not debating their motives or trying to trigger insight; you're stating a standard and following through. Over time, this consistency does what confrontation often fails to do: it sets reality-based limits that build accountability.

The key is *follow-through without friction*. No yelling. No rescuing. Just steady, predictable structure.

In Practice

Monica, 34, ran peer support groups. One participant, *Ray*, with strong narcissistic traits, regularly arrived 15 minutes late and then dominated the conversation.

The first few times, Monica tried to confront him: *"You're disrupting the flow, and it's not fair to others."*

Ray pushed back: *"I had a rough morning. You think I don't care?"*

It got nowhere.

So she changed course:

She announced, calmly: *"Group starts at 6 sharp. After that, doors are closed until 6:45. No exceptions."*

The next week, Ray arrived at 6:10. The door was locked.

The week after, he was on time.

No drama. Just a boundary with a consequence.

Detached Empathy Script

Supporting someone with narcissistic traits can feel like walking an emotional tightrope. Their frustration, disappointment, or need for admiration may feel endless, and if you're not careful, you get pulled in, trying to soothe, defend, or over-explain.

That's where *Detached Empathy* becomes essential.

The goal is to:

- acknowledge the *emotion*
- hold your *boundary*
- avoid being swept into ego repair or emotional labor

Use a *one-two structure*:

1. *"I hear that you're (emotion)."* This shows you're listening without agreeing or fixing.
2. *"Here's what I can offer."* This sets a limit or redirect without shame or argument.

Examples:

- *"I hear that you're upset. I'm not available for a full call right now, but I can check in tomorrow."*
- *"Sounds like you're feeling ignored. I can't respond to messages during work, but I will later."*

Detached empathy honors the *person*, not the performance. It helps you show up with compassion, without sacrificing your own capacity.

In Practice

Avery, 26, had a partner, *Sam*, with narcissistic tendencies. When Sam felt criticized, especially over text, they'd spiral into long, emotionally charged messages: *"You clearly don't care. If you did, you'd answer faster. You're just like everyone else."*

In the past, Avery would spend hours explaining and defending. It never helped.

One night, they replied instead with:

"I hear that you're feeling hurt and dismissed. I'm not going to engage over text right now, but we can talk after work if you'd like."

No anger. No entanglement. Just a mirror and a boundary.

Sam didn't like it, but over time, the emotional floods became less frequent. And Avery stopped drowning in them.

Therapeutic Techniques

- **Schema Therapy:** Targets core schemas of defectiveness or entitlement through limited re-parenting and experiential work (Young et al., 2003).
- **Compassion-Focused Therapy (CFT):** Builds self-soothing systems to reduce shame-driven defensiveness (Gilbert, 2014).
- **Cognitive Restructuring:** Challenges black-and-white beliefs about success and worth; replaces them with graded self-evaluations.

ANTISOCIAL PERSONALITY DISORDER (ASPD)

ASPD is often driven by speed, decisions made in the fraction of a heartbeat, risk taken before consequence registers. This playbook helps slow that sequence long enough for choice to enter.

Core Challenges

1. Impulsivity that overrides rules or long-term goals (NICE, 2010).
2. Minimal remorse or empathy, especially after harm is done (Lindqvist et al., 2020).

3. Instrumental aggression is used to secure power, resources, or stimulation (Fontaine et al., 2020).

Self-Management Strategies

Anger-Flash Log

For individuals with ASPD, anger doesn't always build; it detonates. The trigger may seem minor, but the reaction is swift, often bypassing conscious awareness. That's why learning to recognize *pre-anger cues* is vital.

The *anger-flash log* is a short daily entry, tracking:

- *time* of the anger surge
- *trigger* (what happened)
- *first body cue* (clenched jaw, heat in chest, fast breath)

The goal is *pattern recognition*. When you track flashpoints across several days, patterns begin to emerge:

- Are they time-linked (always in the afternoon)?
- Trigger-specific (always with authority figures)?
- Physically signaled (tight fists before raised voice)?

Over time, this log builds *emotional radar*, the kind that detects anger before it becomes action.

In Practice

Marcus, 30, had been fired twice for "blow-ups." In both cases, he insisted he wasn't angry until things exploded.

His therapist asked him to start an anger-flash log. Day one felt pointless. But by day five, a pattern formed:

- 3:45 p.m.
- passive-aggressive email from supervisor
- Cue: Shallow breathing and jaw tension

He hadn't noticed it before, but every spike started with a physical tell.

That awareness didn't stop the emotion, but it slowed the reaction. By week two, Marcus started walking out when he noticed the jaw clenching. By week four, he was de-escalating before the email even opened.

The anger was still real, but now it had a timestamp and a pause button.

Daily Tripwire Plan

Impulsivity is a core trait in ASPD, especially when provoked or challenged. But what many don't realize is that the brain often *predicts* danger zones before the day even begins. That's where the *daily tripwire plan* comes in.

Each morning:

1. *Identify one likely high-risk situation,* a moment where tension, temptation, or authority friction is predictable (e.g., traffic, arguments, waiting in line).
2. Set a *"pause point":* a physical or mental cue that signals you to step away for 60 seconds when that scenario hits.

This plan isn't reactive, it's *preemptive.* It trains you to anticipate your own hot zones and commit to action *before* the spike hits.

Over time, these micro-pauses reduce the likelihood of impulsive, destructive behavior.

This is not about avoidance; it's about *planned redirection*.

In Practice

Luis, 28, had a history of road rage. Honking, tailgating, and shouting in, mornings were a minefield.

His coach suggested a daily tripwire. Each morning before leaving, Luis would identify the trigger: *"Someone will cut me off today."*

His pause point? Whenever he touched his turn signal, he'd recite one phrase: *"Not today."*

He also committed to pulling into the next parking lot if he felt his hands tighten on the wheel.

Within a week, he reported fewer incidents. The roads hadn't changed, but his script had. He wasn't bottling his anger; he was predicting it and stepping aside when it surged.

Mindfulness Hit-Pause

Impulsivity in ASPD isn't always about rage; it can also drive risk-taking, manipulation, or reactive decision-making. When the brain is wired to chase novelty or avoid shame, *thinking it through* rarely wins the battle.

That's why we use the *mindfulness hit-pause*: a *60-second sensory scan* before any high-stakes choice.

How it works:

1. Set a cue (e.g., before sending a text, entering a meeting, or walking into a confrontation).
2. For 60 seconds, tune into your senses:

- What do I see?
- What do I hear?
- What does my body feel like right now?

No need to meditate or breathe in a certain way, just anchor to the present.

In Practice

Andre, 35, had a habit of dropping "jokes" that cut people down, then playing it off as humor. He claimed he didn't mean to hurt anyone. But the digs always came fast.

His therapist challenged him: pause before any punchline. Just 60 seconds.

It felt stupid. But one day, standing in a circle at work, he caught himself. The setup was there; someone had misspoken. Normally, he'd roast them and get the laugh.

Instead, he hit pause. Looked around. Listened.

Then he said nothing.

Nobody laughed, but nobody flinched either. For once, he didn't feel like the cleverest person in the room. He felt like the safest.

Accountability Text Chain

One of the biggest drivers behind destructive behavior in ASPD is *secrecy*. When no one else knows what you're thinking, planning, or feeling, the odds of following through on an impulsive urge skyrocket.

The *accountability text chain* disrupts that.

How it works:

- Choose *one trusted person*, a therapist, coach, sponsor, or grounded friend.
- When an urge spikes (to explode, gamble, cheat, quit, sabotage), send a quick message:
  - "getting hot."
  - "want to run."
  - "tempted to go dark."

It doesn't need to be explained, justified, or dramatic. It just needs to *exist.*

That micro-moment of exposure:

- creates pause
- interrupts the secrecy loop
- invites support, or at the very least, *slows the spiral*

Some people pre-agree that the contact won't try to fix anything, just reply with a single phrase: *"Noted. You've got this."*

In Practice

Reed, 31, was used to disappearing. One setback, and he'd ghost jobs, partners, mentors. He hated being questioned, so he just left.

After a major blow-up with a colleague, he was ready to disappear again. But he remembered the deal with his boxing coach: *Text me before you quit anything.*

He typed: *"About to burn it all down."*

The reply came seconds later:

"Clock it. Not today."

Reed didn't text again. But he also didn't walk out.

That one message didn't erase his history, but it interrupted the reflex. And interruption is where change begins.

Strength-Based Goal Sheet

Many people with ASPD have intense drive, physical energy, and a hunger for challenge. The problem isn't ambition, it's direction. When that energy lacks structure, it spills into thrill-seeking, manipulation, or conflict just to feel something.

The *strength-based goal sheet* channels those traits, adrenaline sensitivity, competitiveness, and quick decision-making into *constructive pursuits*.

How it works:

1. Choose a physical or skill-based challenge with built-in levels (e.g., martial arts, weight training, carpentry certification, timed obstacle courses).
2. Break it into *weekly objectives*.
3. Track performance and progress scores like a game.

This system:

- feeds novelty and dopamine through achievement
- replaces risk-based reward loops with *goal-driven ones*
- builds self-worth through discipline, not domination

You're not suppressing intensity, you're using it.

In Practice

Dre, 29, had always been labeled a "hothead." He craved control, hated boredom, and got into fights often, not out of rage, but *restlessness.*

His parole officer recommended a local MMA gym with belt rankings and competition prep. Dre started logging his training hours and setting weekly goals:

- 5 sparring rounds
- land 10 clean counters
- learn 1 new combo

He posted his scores on a whiteboard. He didn't care about affirmations; he cared about *dominating the numbers.*

Weeks passed. He still had the fire, but now, it was contained in structure.

He wasn't softening. He was *leveling up,* without burning bridges to do it.

For Supporters

Lead With Facts, Not Feelings

When supporting someone with ASPD, emotional appeals often miss the mark. They may be dismissed as weakness, manipulation, or noise. But *consequences tied to clear facts,* especially when delivered without drama, land differently.

This approach:

- bypasses emotional defensiveness
- reduces openings for argument

- reinforces natural consequences without needing guilt or lectures

The formula:

- **State the fact:** "You missed curfew Friday."
- **State the result:** "The car is unavailable this week."
- **End it there:** No need to explain how it made you feel. Let the action speak.

Consequences that are *clear, neutral, and swift* train behavior far better than emotional reactions.

In Practice

Angela, 47, was raising her teenage nephew, *Dion*, who had multiple ASPD traits, charming, reactive, and rule-testing. He came home two hours past curfew. No apology. No remorse.

Angela didn't scold. Didn't cry. The next morning, she handed him bus fare and said:

"You missed curfew Friday. The car is off-limits until next Sunday."

He rolled his eyes. "Seriously? You're being dramatic."

She shrugged. "That's the deal."

No argument followed. The rule stood. A week later, he was on time.

Decline Power Games

People with ASPD often test boundaries not out of malice, but to *feel something*. Conflict, chaos, and challenge offer stimulation and control. When they bait, provoke, or escalate, it's often a game with an invisible scoreboard.

The key? *Don't play.*

Supporters often make one of two mistakes:

- *over-explaining* to justify limits (which invites manipulation)
- *escalating* to win (which reinforces the thrill)

Instead, use the *non-engagement rule*:

- keep statements short.
- use a calm tone and a blank face.
- walk away or end the interaction without drama.

Examples:

- *"That's your choice."*
- *"We'll talk when you're calm."*
- *"I'm not discussing this again."*

This isn't passive, it's strategic. It removes the fuel that feeds the behavior. Without an audience, the game loses its appeal.

In Practice

Jules, 36, had a brother with ASPD. Anytime Jules said no to money, favors, or calls at midnight, his brother launched into verbal attacks.

The pattern: Jules defended, argued, or tried to explain. The fights always spiraled.

After learning about power games, Jules changed tactics.

When his brother demanded money again and started cursing, Jules replied:

"Not this time."

Then he hung up.

He didn't answer follow-up texts. No rebuttals. No retelling.

The silence spoke louder than any lecture. By the third call, the script had changed.

Offer Micro-rewards for Prosocial Acts

People with ASPD are often driven by *external reinforcement*, approval, power, and novelty. Traditional praise or emotional connection may not register in the usual way, especially if empathy or guilt is blunted. But *reinforcement still works*, just differently.

The strategy:

Reward prosocial behavior quietly and immediately, without exaggeration or emotional overload.

Examples:

- *"Thanks for handling that calmly."*
- *"That was direct and fair, appreciated."*
- *"Noticed how you stepped back there. Smart move."*

These micro-rewards:

- reinforce *self-control*
- encourage repetition through *positive association*
- build internal motivation over time (what once felt fake can become familiar)

The key is to avoid gushing. Over-the-top praise can feel manipulative or condescending. Keep it simple, factual, and *linked directly to the behavior*.

In Practice

Ty, 27, had a pattern: when frustrated in group therapy, he stormed out or picked fights. The facilitator, *Marcia*, usually braced for it.

One session, Ty got agitated but instead said, *"I'm not feeling this today, I'll head out before I say something I regret."*

He stood up and left.

Marcia didn't follow. But the next week, she nodded and said:

"Last week, you left it clean. That showed control. Good call."

No applause. No deep dive.

Ty didn't say anything back. But he stayed for the full session that time.

The behavior was small. The feedback was smaller. But the shift had already started.

Therapeutic Techniques

- **Mentalization-Based Treatment (MBT):** Builds capacity to recognize one's own and others' mental states, reducing reactive aggression (Verywell Health, 2022).
- **Impulse-Control CBT Modules:** Focus on cost-benefit analysis and delay skills; especially effective when combined with substance-use treatment (Cleveland Clinic, 2017).
- **Democratic Therapeutic Community (DTC) programs:** Peer governance fosters accountability; evidence shows reduced re-offending in prison settings (Verywell Health, 2022).

HISTRIONIC PERSONALITY DISORDER (HPD)

HPD can feel like living under a spotlight that never dims; every conversation becomes an audition, every silence begs to be filled. The aim here is to lower the stage lights so genuine connection, not performance, takes center stage.

Core Challenges

- Craving external validation at the expense of authenticity (American Psychiatric Association, 2022).
- Rapidly shifting but shallow emotions that confuse both the individual and those around them (Carter & Bjornsson, 2021).
- Suggestibility, opinions, and plans change to match the nearest, loudest voice (Smith, 2023).

Self-Management Strategies

Pause-and-Name Drill

For individuals with HPD, expression is often reflexive. Emotions rise fast and outward, tears, charm, exaggeration, not always from deceit, but from deeply learned habits of seeking connection through visibility.

The *pause-and-name drill* introduces a moment of stillness between urge and action.

Here's how it works:

1. Before reacting, especially in social or emotionally charged moments, ask silently:
2. *"Is this an authentic need or a performance?"*

3. Internally *label the impulse*: attention-seeking, approval-seeking, self-soothing, deflection.
4. Decide consciously whether to follow through or pause.

This drill doesn't shame the impulse. It helps distinguish:

- real vulnerability vs. rehearsed response
- emotional need vs. reflexive dramatization
- connection vs. control

With practice, it builds *emotional accuracy*, a way to show up as you, not just a version of you shaped to be liked.

In Practice

Chloe, 29, had always been "on." Any social moment became a stage. If tension rose, she knew how to steal attention, tears, humor, and storytelling. It worked, but left her feeling hollow.

At a family dinner, an old argument surfaced. Her go-to move was to jump in, make it funny, and redirect the mood. But she paused.

Internally, she asked: *"Is this real or a reflex?"*

She realized: she felt hurt, but also pressured to keep the peace.

She stayed quiet.

Her brother finished his point. The moment passed. No spotlight, but no shame either. For the first time, Chloe didn't disappear into performance.

Mirror Journal

For many with HPD, emotional expression has been shaped by early reinforcement: perform well, and you're loved; be quiet or sad, and you're overlooked or punished. Over time, this creates a split between what's felt internally and what's shown externally.

The *mirror journal* is a daily practice to bridge that gap.

Each night:

1. Spend *five minutes* writing down:
   - *What you felt today* (e.g., ignored, anxious, proud, uncertain)
   - *What you showed to others* (e.g., bubbly, flirtatious, defensive)
2. Circle any mismatches.
3. Ask gently: *"What was I trying to get or protect by showing that version of myself?"*

This practice is about spotting *performative patterns* and slowly learning to let more of the real self into the room.

Over time, the goal is alignment: less acting, more authenticity.

In Practice

Tasha, 35, was always the most "fun" person at work. Jokes, energy, charisma, people loved her. But most nights, she cried on the way home and didn't know why.

She started a mirror journal.

One entry read:

- **Felt:** insecure, not included in project meetings
- **Showed:** playful, flirty, dismissive of the work
- **Mismatched?** Yes.

That moment clicked. She wasn't being herself; she was being *liked*.

The next week, when left out again, she said plainly, "I'd like to contribute to that project." No wink. No laugh.

She got the invite. And for once, she got to be part of the room, not just its entertainment.

Social-Media Diet

Social media is a pressure cooker for performative identity. For individuals with HPD, whose emotional instincts often lean toward visibility, affirmation, and appearance, it can become a dopamine loop of seeking validation instead of processing emotion.

The *social-media diet* isn't a punishment; it's a recalibration.

The practice

1. *Limit usage to 20 minutes per day* for two weeks. Use screen time tools or apps like Freedom or StayFocusd to block access.
2. *Replace scrolling* with a grounding habit:
   - box breathing
   - five-sense check-in
   - brief journaling (e.g., "What do I need right now that a post won't give me?")

The aim isn't permanent abstinence; it's giving the nervous system a break from *external affirmation cycles*, so it can relearn *internal signals*.

With less input from likes, views, and imagined audiences, emotional expression becomes quieter and more real.

In Practice

Mira, 24, posts daily selfies, quotes, and vulnerable stories wrapped in filters. Every like soothed her... briefly. Then came the slump. She scrolled, compared, and posted again.

She didn't think she had a problem. But her therapist suggested a two-week social-media diet with a box-breathing swap.

Day 1 was awful. Day 3 brought a near panic. But by Day 6, something shifted.

She journaled:

"Didn't post today. No one applauded me. But I didn't spiral either. That's new."

When she returned online, it wasn't with a story. It was with a choice.

Skill-Based Hobbies

People with HPD often develop a self-worth system built on *external response*: Did someone notice me? Did they clap? Was it impressive?

But when attention becomes the only currency, personal joy gets buried. That's why *skill-based hobbies* matter: they shift the reward system from *applause* to *progress*.

How it works:

1. Choose one quiet, skill-building activity that offers *intrinsic satisfaction*:
    ◦ watercolor
    ◦ woodworking
    ◦ piano scales
    ◦ gardening

- ◦ coding tutorials
2. Track your time and milestones *privately* for 30 days. No social media. No audience. Just you and the craft.

This process teaches emotional containment, patience, and the feeling of being *enough*, even when no one is watching.

It doesn't erase the desire to connect; it rewires the craving for performance into a foundation of *self-led mastery*.

In Practice

Arielle, 31, loved praise. She was magnetic, her outfits, her laugh, her posts. But she felt empty when no one reacted.

Her coach suggested painting. She scoffed. Who would see it?

But she tried. Ten minutes a day. No photos. No sharing.

By week two, she found herself looking forward to it. By week three, she stayed up an hour past bedtime, finishing a piece not to post, but because *she* liked it.

She wrote:

"No one clapped. Still felt like mine."

It was the first time in years that being alone didn't feel like being invisible.

For Supporters

Offer Genuine Attention in Structured Doses

For someone with HPD, attention often equals safety. When emotional intensity spikes, the need for reassurance, validation, or dramatic response can feel urgent and overwhelming, not because they're manipulative, but because early love may have been conditional or intermittent.

Structured attention breaks the cycle of reactive reinforcement.

How it works:

- *Pre-schedule check-ins*: "Let's have a 20-minute coffee chat Friday just for you."
- Keep the space *uninterrupted, focused, and validating*
- When dramatic cues flare at other times, gently remind them:
- *"I want to give this the attention it deserves. Can we talk at our check-in time?"*

This teaches:

- That care doesn't require chaos
- That emotional needs are valid, but don't need to hijack the moment
- That structure is not rejection, it's containment

Over time, these check-ins become *anchors*, helping the person separate true connection from performance-based urgency.

In Practice

Jen, 45, was exhausted. Her best friend, *Talia*, with strong HPD traits, called almost daily in emotional whirlwinds, relationship crises, social slights, over-the-top highs and lows.

Jen tried setting limits, but every attempt felt, like abandonment.

Then she offered structure:

"I want to be here for you. Let's have a real catch-up every Tuesday night. Full focus, no interruptions."

Talia was skeptical at first. But by week three, she started saving stories, reflecting more, even asking Jen how *she* was doing.

It wasn't about controlling the drama. It was about offering attention that didn't depend on it.

Reinforce Depth

People with HPD are often misunderstood as superficial, but that's rarely true. The issue isn't that they lack depth; it's that their emotional expression has been shaped for effect. Over time, this can lead to storytelling, reactions, and vulnerability that feel rehearsed rather than real.

Supporters can help by gently *redirecting from performance to reflection.*

How to do it:

- Ask *clarifying, grounding questions* during storytelling:
  - *"What part of that felt the hardest for you?"*
  - *"What do you think was underneath that reaction?"*
  - *"What do you need most right now, support, distraction, or space?"*

These questions:

- signal emotional safety
- help shift the focus from reaction to *self-awareness*
- validate the emotion without overindulging the performance

You're not analyzing them, you're inviting them *into* themselves.

In Practice

Devon, 33, loved telling dramatic stories. Her friend, *Ray*, noticed that every time Devon recounted an event, it sounded like a performance, full of expression, but empty of insight.

One day, after hearing a long rant about a friend's betrayal, Ray asked:

"What felt most important about that moment to you, not the drama, but what stuck?"

Devon paused.

She said, "Honestly... I felt like she forgot I mattered."

Ray didn't praise the delivery. He nodded. "That makes sense."

No performance. Just the truth.

Avoid Sarcasm or Mockery

Individuals with HPD often live in a world of heightened expression. To outsiders, this can seem exaggerated, overly dramatic, or attention-seeking. And when supporters grow frustrated, it's tempting to cope through sarcasm, teasing, or passive mockery.

But here's the catch: what feels like humor to you may feel like *abandonment or humiliation* to them.

Instead of diffusing emotion with sarcasm, try *redirection* toward creative expression:

- *"You have such a gift for storytelling. Have you ever written that out?"*
- *"That would make a wild scene in a script."*
- *"Let's put that emotion into something, music, paint, a rant video for your eyes only."*

This channels intensity into *artistry*, not apology. It shows that big feelings aren't something to shrink, they just need a *container that won't break.*

In Practice

Eric, 37, was dating *Maya*, who often became animated in conflict, gestures, tears, and declarations. One night, she vented about a coworker "sabotaging her on purpose." Eric rolled his eyes and said, *"Maybe she's just not your audience."*

Maya shut down. Eric thought he was being witty, but it landed like a slap.

In therapy, he was challenged to redirect, not ridicule. The next time Maya vented, he said:

"That's a hell of a story. Want to write it down and read it to me like a monologue?"

She laughed, for real this time.

It wasn't about diminishing the emotion. It was about giving it somewhere safe to land.

Set Boundaries on Crisis Calls

For individuals with HPD, emotional spikes can feel urgent and uncontainable. When that energy turns into crisis-mode texts or late-night phone calls, supporters can get pulled into a loop of *soothing, rescuing, or absorbing* the storm, often at the cost of their own regulation.

The solution is *clear, kind limits with backup tools.*

How to set this up:

1. *Agree on "available hours"* for emotional support:

- "I'm available to talk until 9 p.m."
- "If it's past that, let's check in the next day."

2. *Offer alternative steps* if things escalate:
   - A written coping plan: "If I can't reach you, I'll read my mirror journal."
   - A sensory grounding script
   - A text-based check-in (e.g., "Send me an emoji if you just need to feel heard.")

This preserves the relationship while protecting the *supporter's capacity*. And it teaches the person with HPD that *emotions don't need to be emergencies to be valid*.

In Practice

Nina, 40, had a best friend, *Lola*, who called during emotional crises, often late at night, often multiple times in a row. Nina always answered. Always tried to help. And always felt drained.

Eventually, she set a boundary:

"I love you. I'm not available for calls after 10 p.m. If it feels urgent, text 'CRISIS,' and I'll check on you in the morning."

Lola protested at first, but Nina stuck to it.

One night, Nina got the text. She didn't respond. But the next day, Lola said, *"I did the breathing thing. I didn't think it would help, but it did."*

It wasn't rejection. It was containment. And it worked.

Therapeutic Pathways

- **Psychodynamic therapy:** Explores childhood attachment patterns that drive the pursuit of admiration (Blatt, 2020).

- **Cognitive-Behavioral Therapy (CBT):** Targets exaggerated thinking ("If I'm not noticed, I'm worthless") and replaces it with balanced appraisals (Young & Klosko, 2019).
- **Group therapy:** Provides live feedback on attention-seeking behaviors and offers peers who model authentic expression (Jones et al., 2021).

AVOIDANT PERSONALITY DISORDER (AVPD)

AvPD is like wearing invisible noise-canceling headphones: they keep criticism out, but they also muffle praise, opportunity, and connection. This toolkit helps you ease the volume back up, gradually, safely, and on your own terms.

Core Challenges

- Persistent fear of rejection and negative evaluation that triggers retreat (Powers & Oltmanns, 2023)
- Chronic self-doubt and low self-worth that amplify perceived social risk (American Psychiatric Association, 2022)
- Desire for connection clashing with avoidance, reinforcing loneliness and shame (Carvalho et al., 2021)

Self-Management Strategies

Graded Social Exposure

Avoidant Personality Disorder isn't about a disinterest in connection; it's about *the fear of exposure*. Social interactions can feel like emotional minefields, with every glance, silence, or response interpreted as rejection.

Graded social exposure is the antidote to avoidance paralysis. It's not about jumping into the deep end; it's about walking into the shallow side with intention.

How it works:

1. *Choose one low-stakes interaction per week*, something mildly uncomfortable, but not overwhelming (e.g., asking a cashier a question, attending a video call with the camera on).
2. *Log your anxiety level* before and after (0–10 scale).
3. *Celebrate the outcome*, even if all you did was show up.

Track these each week. Don't rate success by comfort. Rate it by *follow-through*.

Over time, this creates new emotional memory: *You survived. You weren't rejected. You can do this again.*

In Practice

Neil, 27, avoided initiating conversation, and even eye contact felt risky. For his first social exposure task, he picked something simple: ask the barista, *"What do you recommend?"*

He logged his pre-anxiety: *7.* His hands shook.

He asked. She smiled and gave a suggestion. He ordered. Nothing dramatic happened.

Afterward, he logged: *3.* Then he wrote: *"Didn't die. Didn't get judged. Might try again."*

That night, he added a gold star to his calendar. Small step. Big win.

Rewrite the Inner Critic

The harshest rejections for people with AVPD often come from within. Long before someone else critiques them, the inner voice has already:

- *"You sounded stupid."*
- *"They're laughing at you."*
- *"Don't say anything, you'll just embarrass yourself."*

Rewriting the inner critic is about giving that voice a second draft. Not to lie or inflate, but to create *balanced, compassionate scripts* that speak to the human underneath the fear.

Practice:

1. When you hear a self-critical thought, *write it down* exactly as it appears.
2. Underneath it, write a *counter-statement* grounded in truth and kindness. For example:
   - Critic: *"They'll think I'm foolish."*
   - Rewrite: *"Curiosity makes me human, and everyone has to start somewhere."*
3. Speak or reread the rewrite *aloud or silently*, especially before or after social situations.

This technique builds an internal coach that doesn't pretend everything is fine, but doesn't tear you down for being real.

In Practice

Jared, 34, stayed silent during team calls. When he did speak up, he obsessed over his phrasing for hours.

After sharing a suggestion once, he caught his critic:

"You rambled. Everyone thinks you're incompetent."

He paused. Wrote it down.

Then he rewrote:

"I spoke clearly. No one responded badly. Learning to speak up is part of this job."

He repeated it. Once in the breakroom. Again, before bed.

It didn't erase the discomfort, but it turned the volume down. The next week, he raised his hand again.

Confidence Bank

For individuals with AVPD, shame and self-doubt often overwrite success. Even small wins fade quickly, while perceived failures get replayed on a loop. The result? A distorted self-image built entirely on what went wrong.

The *confidence bank* counters this by recording *evidence of courage, not perfection.*

How it works:

1. Every day, log at least one action you took that pushed against avoidance:
   - sent a difficult email
   - entered a room without scanning for exits
   - asked a question, even if your voice shook
2. Be specific and brief. The point isn't grandeur, it's *consistency.*
3. Revisit the log weekly. Highlight patterns. Let the record remind you:
4. *"I do hard things. I've done them before."*

Over time, this bank becomes a buffer. On days when the critic is loud, you have *proof* that your fear doesn't define your capability.

In Practice

Leah, 29, rarely spoke in meetings. She avoided eye contact and skipped most social events. Her therapist asked her to build a confidence bank, one entry a day.

- Day 1: "Made eye contact with the barista."
- Day 3: "Sent message to clarify a deadline."
- Day 7: "Spoke up to say I agreed with someone's idea."

By the end of week two, she had 14 small entries. When her mind said, *"You're not brave enough,"* she pulled out her list.

It wasn't loud or impressive, but it was *real*. And hers.

For Supporters

Offer Invitations With Flexibility

For individuals with AVPD, social invitations can feel like loaded traps. Even well-meaning requests might trigger anxiety:

- *"What if I disappoint them?"*
- *"What if I'm awkward?"*
- *"What if I say yes and can't follow through?"*

The key is to *lower the stakes without closing the door.*

Flexible invitations preserve both autonomy and connection. They sound like:

- *"I'll be at the café from 10–11, no pressure, come if it feels right."*

330 WIRED FOR CHAOS

- *"We're heading to the park; join later if you feel up to it."*
- *"Just wanted to say I'd love to see you today or another time."*

This removes the demand-response cycle and replaces it with an *open structure*:

You're welcome, not required.

It lets connection feel like *a choice, not a test.*

In Practice

Brian, 40, had a colleague, *Ellie*, who rarely joined lunch outings. She always seemed hesitant, then apologetic.

Instead of asking, *"Are you coming today?"* which made Ellie feel on the spot, Brian shifted to saying:

"Hey, we're grabbing lunch at the picnic tables from 12–1 if you want to swing by."

No RSVP needed. No disappointment if she didn't show.

Ellie skipped the first few invites. But then, one day, she came by, just for ten minutes.

Brian smiled, offered a seat, and said nothing more.

She came again the next week.

Acknowledge Courage, Not Outcome

People with AVPD often carry the belief that *anything short of perfection equals failure.* They might finally speak up, only to replay every word in shame. They might attend an event, then criticize themselves for not being "charming enough."

That's why supporters should shift praise away from performance and toward *bravery.*

Instead of saying:

- *"You did so well!"* or *"See? Everyone liked you!"*

Try:

- *"It took guts to show up."*
- *"I know that was hard, thanks for trying it."*
- *"I noticed you spoke up. That's no small thing."*

This helps the person recognize *the effort itself* as valuable, even if they feel awkward, scared, or unsure. When courage is what gets acknowledged, courage is what grows.

In Practice

Nico, 32, went to a friend's small birthday dinner. Social events made him freeze, but he wanted to try.

He didn't say much. He smiled, nodded, and laughed at a few jokes. Afterward, he texted the host to say sorry for being quiet.

The host replied:

"You being there meant a lot. That was brave. I hope you're proud of yourself."

No critique. No performance review. Just a mirror held up to the effort.

And for once, Nico didn't spiral. He exhaled.

Provide Calm Presence Rather Than Pep Talks

For someone with AVPD, emotional safety often means *being around others without pressure*. Encouragement can be helpful, but pep talks, advice, or too much enthusiasm can accidentally feel like a spotlight or performance demand.

What feels supportive to you, *"You've got this! Just be confident!"*, might feel overwhelming or even shame-inducing to them.

Instead, offer *non-intrusive companionship*:

- sit nearby during a difficult task
- offer quiet shared time (e.g., reading, walking, folding laundry)
- Text simply: *"No need to talk, just here if you want to hang out."*

Your silent presence sends a deeper message than words: *You don't need to earn this space. You already belong here.*

In Practice

Sami, 38, had a friend, *Jonas,* who avoided nearly all social contact. When he did show up, he hovered at the edge of the room and left early.

One weekend, Sami texted:

"I'm watching trash TV tonight. Come by if you want, no small talk required."

To his surprise, Jonas came.

They said little. Shared snacks. Watched two episodes in silence.

No pep talk. No probing. Just quiet togetherness.

At the end of the night, Jonas said:

"That... felt okay. I might do this again."

Sometimes, *safety is built through stillness.*

Therapeutic Tools

- *CBT with behavioral experiments* to test and disconfirm catastrophic beliefs (Grey & Clark, 2020)
- *Compassion-Focused Therapy (CFT)* to shift from shame to self-warmth (Gilbert, 2019)

DEPENDENT PERSONALITY DISORDER (DPD)

DPD is like walking with a crutch that nobody else can see; every choice, from what to eat to where to live, feels shaky without someone to lean on. This section aims to strengthen the "decision-making muscle," one manageable lift at a time, so autonomy grows steadily instead of all at once.

Core Challenges

- Excessive need for reassurance that undermines confidence (American Psychiatric Association, 2022)
- Submissive behavior intended to secure care or approval, often at personal cost (Bornstein, 2019)
- Difficulty initiating projects independently due to fear of failure or disapproval (National Library of Medicine, 2021)

Self-Management Strategies

Daily " Solo Micro-Decisions

For individuals with Dependent Personality Disorder, the hardest part of daily life isn't making the "right" choice; it's making a choice at all. The habit of outsourcing decisions becomes automatic: *What do you think? Should I do this? Would you go?*

This isn't laziness, it's survival logic shaped by early relationships where independence may have been punished or unsafe.

The *solo micro-decision* drill creates low-stakes reps for autonomy.

How it works:

1. Each day, identify *one small decision* to make without seeking input.
    - What to eat for lunch
    - Which playlist to play
    - What color shirt to wear
    - What subject line to write in an email
2. Make the decision *quickly*, even if you feel unsure.
3. Log two things:
    - How it *felt* to choose alone (awkward, freeing, tense, neutral)
    - What *happened* as a result (was the outcome fine? did anything bad happen?)

In Practice

Imani, 31, always asked her coworker to read her emails before hitting send. Even routine replies made her anxious. One day, she committed to choosing the subject line solo.

She picked: *"Update on onboarding plan"*. Sent it without asking.

She logged:

- **Feeling:** mildly anxious, slightly proud
- **Outcome:** no issues, email was clear, no one commented

After five days, she noticed something: her coworkers weren't validating her choices; they were just assuming she'd made them.

That became her new standard.

Values Alignment List

When you're wired to defer, constantly asking for input, permission, or approval, your sense of personal direction can erode. Over time, it becomes hard to tell: *Do I actually want this? Or am I just doing what keeps the peace?*

The *values alignment list* reconnects you to *your own compass.*

How it works:

1. Set aside ten minutes and list 5–10 *personal values,* things that feel core to who you are (e.g., creativity, honesty, freedom, kindness, curiosity).
2. Keep the list somewhere visible (journal, phone, or workspace).
3. Each time you're tempted to ask for advice, *pause and check:*
   - *Does this decision align with one of my values?*
   - *Would I be proud of this choice if no one else weighed in?*

Over time, this builds *decision-making from the inside out,* not through rebellion, but through clarity.

You're not rejecting support. You're learning when you *don't need it.*

In Practice

Camila, 35, was planning her birthday dinner. Normally, she'd send the guest list to three friends for approval, worried she'd leave someone out or make it awkward.

This time, she tried something new. She looked at her values list:

- *connection*

- *authenticity*
- *peace*

She asked:

"Who do I genuinely want to connect with? Who lets me be myself? Who doesn't drain me?"

She made the list. Didn't ask anyone else.

The night was smaller, but better. And hers.

Self-Encouragement Voice Memo

People with DPD often rely on *external voices* to feel capable: a partner's reassurance, a mentor's encouragement, a friend's green light. Without it, even simple tasks can feel paralyzing.

The *self-encouragement voice memo* brings that reassurance *inward*.

How it works:

1. After completing something independently (even something small), record a 30-second voice memo:
   - Name what you did: *"I made that call without checking first."*
   - Reflect on how it felt: *"I was nervous, but I did it anyway."*
   - Add a simple affirmation: *"That counts. I can trust myself."*
2. Save the memo and replay it whenever you're hesitating or about to seek unnecessary input.

Hearing your *own voice* affirm your competence helps shift dependence from others to self, *not by rejecting support, but by learning to generate it.*

In Practice

Jules, 26, hated making appointments. She always asked her room-mate to double-check times or call for her. One day, she booked a dentist appointment solo and recorded a memo:

"I called the dentist and booked it. I didn't wait. I was nervous, but it's done. That was me. I did that."

Two days later, she panicked over whether to cancel. She almost texted her mom for advice, but played the memo instead.

She didn't cancel. The appointment happened. The win echoed, because she'd captured it in her own words.

Scheduled Advice-Free Zone

For someone with Dependent Personality Disorder, asking for input often becomes a reflex. Decisions of all sizes are filtered through other people, which creates a cycle where autonomy feels unfamiliar and risky. The advice-free zone is a structured way to interrupt that cycle and rebuild decision-making confidence.

How it works:

Set aside a two-hour window once a week in which you make all decisions without seeking input. This includes small choices, what to eat, what to wear, what to watch, as well as moderate ones, like how to spend your afternoon or what task to prioritize.

The key is consistency. You're not cutting people out, you're giving yourself protected time to practice solo agency in a low-stakes way. Over time, that window becomes more comfortable, and you may naturally expand it.

This exercise is not about getting every decision right. It's about getting used to being the one who decides.

In Practice

Kira, 30, used to text her sister several times a day for second opinions, what to buy, how to respond to texts, and whether to say yes to invitations. She decided to block out 2–4 p.m. on Sundays as her advice-free zone.

The first week, she chose her own grocery store, planned dinner, and picked a movie without checking in. It felt uncomfortable but also quiet. By week three, she found herself looking forward to those two hours, not because she had all the answers, but because she didn't need to ask.

For Supporters

Offer Options, Not Instructions

People with Dependent Personality Disorder often default to letting others take the lead. Even minor decisions, where to eat, what to do, and how to reply, can trigger anxiety. Supporters may unknowingly reinforce dependence by making choices for them in the name of efficiency or helpfulness.

A better approach is to offer clear, limited options without directing the outcome. Instead of saying, "We'll go here," try saying, "There are two cafés nearby, both work for me, which sounds better to you?" This gives the person a structure to choose from, reducing pressure while still building decision-making confidence.

Also, when they do take initiative, no matter how small, acknowledge it immediately. Say something like, "Thanks for choosing," or "Good call." This reinforces autonomy and helps associate action with a positive, non-judgmental response.

Over time, these small moments build trust in their ability to decide without losing connection.

In Practice

Dev, 35, always waited for his partner to decide where they'd go for dinner. When asked, he'd say, "I'm easy, whatever you want."

One weekend, his partner shifted gears. Instead of picking a place, she said, "We could try the Italian spot or the new café near the library, both are open."

Dev hesitated. Then said, "Let's try the café."

His partner replied, "Sounds great. I've been wanting to try that one too."

No fuss. No big praise. Just a moment of choice, reinforced quietly. The next week, he made a suggestion without being prompted.

Therapeutic Tools

- **Cognitive-Behavioral Therapy (CBT):** Targets beliefs of helplessness by testing predictions (Beck & Freeman, 2015).
- **Schema Therapy:** Addresses abandonment schemas that keep dependency cycles alive (Young et al., 2020).

OBSESSIVE-COMPULSIVE PERSONALITY DISORDER (OCPD)

Living with OCPD can feel like being governed by an internal rulebook written in permanent ink: every margin aligned, every box ticked, every moment audited. The aim of this toolkit is to soften those rigid lines, enough to let life's ink spread a little without blurring the text completely.

Core Challenges

1. Perfectionism that delays or blocks task completion (National Library of Medicine, 2021)
2. Inflexible adherence to routines, rules, or moral codes, even when they hinder goals (Cain & Ansell, 2022)
3. Difficulty delegating unless others follow exact instructions (American Psychiatric Association, 2022)

Self-Management Strategies

Deliberate Imperfection Practice

People with OCPD often experience intense anxiety when things feel unfinished, unpolished, or even slightly out of order. But perfectionism doesn't just waste time; it narrows life down to what feels controllable. Deliberate imperfection practice is a way to challenge that reflex gradually and safely.

Each day, choose a small task and intentionally leave it slightly incomplete:

- leave one typo in a non-critical email
- place one book out of line on the shelf
- fold laundry imperfectly
- end a workout a minute early

Afterward, note two things:

1. What feelings came up (irritation, shame, restlessness)?
2. How long did the discomfort actually lasted?

This is exposure therapy in micro-form. Over time, it helps the nervous system learn that things don't need to be perfect to be acceptable or to be over.

In Practice

Kevin, 39, always folded towels into identical, crisp stacks. He prided himself on the symmetry. When he began practicing deliberate imperfection, he folded the top towel slightly uneven and walked away.

He kept checking it, three times in an hour. The discomfort lasted 45 minutes. Then it faded.

The next day, he left the coffee table slightly crooked. A week later, he didn't fix either.

Nothing fell apart. But something loosened.

One-Hour Unstructured Block

OCPD often thrives on hyper-scheduling. Every minute is accounted for, every task optimized. But this kind of rigid structure can turn into a cage. Unstructured time creates discomfort because it removes control, but it also opens the door to creativity, rest, and flexibility.

Choose one hour a week with no plan. Literally block it off in your calendar as "unstructured."

During that time:

- Don't create a to-do list
- Don't default to work or chores
- Observe what your brain wants to do
- Let something spontaneous happen

At the end, reflect: Did I rest? Did I fill it? Was the discomfort bearable?

In Practice

Amina, 28, planned every weekend by the half hour. Her therapist asked her to leave one hour free. No plans. No tasks.

It felt unbearable. She paced. She almost cleaned the fridge.

Then she picked up a novel and read for 20 minutes, without tracking how "productive" it was.

She didn't love it. But she didn't hate it either.

That was a start.

"Values Over Rules" Reflection

People with OCPD often live by strict internal rules: Always be early. Don't ask for help. Never leave a task half-done.

These rules may have served a purpose once, but now they control behavior through fear rather than purpose. This exercise helps reconnect rules to the values they were originally designed to protect.

Write down one rule you follow rigidly. Then ask:

- What core value is this rule trying to honor?
- Are there other ways to honor that value with more flexibility?

The goal is not to discard discipline, it's to loosen rigid rules that no longer serve your bigger life goals.

In Practice

Jared, 45, always arrived at least 30 minutes early to every meeting. He got anxious if he was even five minutes "late" by his standard.

He wrote:

- **Rule:** Always arrive 30 minutes early
- **Value:** Respect
- **Alternative:** Arrive 5–10 minutes early and still feel prepared

The first time he showed up 10 minutes early, he fidgeted the whole time. But he wasn't late. He was just... normal.

Task-Sharing Roulette

OCPD often shows up in partnerships and households as micromanaging. If someone loads the dishwasher "wrong," it becomes a problem. The compulsion to fix or correct small things can damage relationships, even if intentions are good.

This strategy helps loosen the grip on control through shared responsibility.

How it works:

- Choose a task you usually manage (e.g., laundry, dishes, tidying)
- Rotate it with a partner or roommate for one week
- Commit to *not giving feedback, corrections, or suggestions*

Track your discomfort. Remind yourself: it got done. Maybe not your way, but still done.

The win isn't in the task; it's in letting go.

In Practice

Noah, 33, always reloaded the dishwasher after his partner ran it. The spoons were wrong. The pans weren't angled. It irritated him, but it also made his partner feel inadequate.

They tried one week of task-sharing roulette. Noah agreed not to check the dishwasher at all.

He caught himself peeking once, but stopped. Nothing broke. Nothing exploded.

His partner felt trusted. And Noah learned that done was enough.

For Supporters

Offer Choices That Respect Order But Allow Flexibility

People with OCPD often rely on structure to feel safe and competent. If you challenge their systems too directly, it can trigger defensiveness or shame. But if you offer *structured flexibility*, choices that still respect their need for order, they're more likely to tolerate change.

Instead of saying, "It doesn't matter how we do it," try offering limited, specific options:

- "Do you want the files sorted by date or alphabetically?"
- "Would you rather start with the budget or the calendar?"

These kinds of choices validate their need for organization while gently introducing variation. It's not about removing structure, it's about helping them *engage with it more flexibly*.

In Practice

Eli, 36, always organized files alphabetically. Any deviation made him anxious. When his coworker offered to help, she asked, "Do you want me to sort these by date or by project name? I'm fine with either."

He paused, then said, "Date."

She followed through. Nothing collapsed. He stayed calm. And the files still got done.

Reinforce Any Tolerance for Deviation With Immediate Positive Feedback

When someone with OCPD allows something to be done differently, even slightly, it's a big deal. Acknowledge it in real time. You don't have to exaggerate. Just notice.

Say things like:

- "Thanks for letting me try it that way. That was helpful."
- "I saw you let that go; you handled it well."

This kind of feedback builds internal reinforcement. The message is: *Flexibility didn't lead to failure. It led to a connection.*

In Practice

Nina, 30, had strict standards for cooking. Her partner accidentally overcooked the pasta. Nina didn't say anything. She ate it, quietly tense.

Her partner said, "Thanks for rolling with that, I know that's hard for you. I appreciated it."

Nina didn't say much, but she didn't correct the next thing either.

Avoid Framing Changes as "Mistakes," Highlight the Benefits of Adaptability

The language you use matters. For someone with OCPD, calling something a "mistake" can trigger perfectionist shame and self-criticism.

Instead of saying:

- "That wasn't right," or "You did it wrong,"

Try:

- "Doing it that way saved us time."
- "It wasn't how we usually do it, but it worked just as well."
- "We learned something new from trying that."

This keeps the focus on the *benefit* of adaptability, not the flaw in deviation

In Practice

Harvey, 41, always took the same route to work. His friend drove a different way, faster, but unfamiliar.

At first, Harvey wanted to point out every wrong turn. But when they arrived early, his friend just said, "That saved us ten minutes."

No teasing. No gloating. Just a quiet reminder: different can still be effective.

Therapy Modalities

- **Acceptance and Commitment Therapy (ACT):** Helps shift focus from control to values-driven action (Hayes et al., 2016).

- **Mindfulness-Based Cognitive Therapy (MBCT):** Trains non-judgmental awareness of perfectionistic thoughts, reducing rigidity (Hofmann & Gómez, 2023).

Grounding Techniques for Personality Disorders

Technique	Description	Helps with
5-4-3-2-1 sensory scan	Name five things you see, four you feel, three you hear, two you smell, one you taste.	BPD
TIPP skill: Cold face plunge	Submerge your face in cold water to activate the dive reflex and reduce your heart rate.	BPD
Box breathing (4-4-4-4)	Inhale, hold, exhale, hold for four seconds each to calm the nervous system.	BPD, AVPD, HPD, OCPD
Sensory grounding pre-event	A 3-minute breath and touch ritual before stressful events to reduce arousal.	AVPD
Routine self-soothe kit	Use multi-sensory items (e.g., lavender oil, smooth stones, music) to ease emotional overload.	BPD
Social media diet + grounding	Replace scrolling with short grounding practices like breathing or sensory check-ins.	HPD
One-hour unstructured block	Reserve an hour with no plan to observe control impulses and build spontaneity.	OCPD
Anchor phrase repetition	Repeat a calming phrase like "I am safe right now" to anchor yourself during distress.	DPD, AVPD
Object focus grounding	Hold and describe an object's texture, weight, and shape in detail to disrupt spirals.	DPD, NPD, BPD
temperature reset	Hold an ice cube or apply a cold compress to interrupt emotional flooding.	BPD, ASPD
Movement grounding	Engage in physical activity (e.g., stretching, walking) to re-engage the body.	ASPD, OCPD
Breath counting	Count each inhale and exhale up to ten, and repeat to settle cognitive overload.	NPD, HPD, AVPD
Color identification	Identify all objects of a specific color to shift attention from emotion to perception.	HPD, AVPD, BPD

CONCLUSION

This book does not end with a cure, because there is no cure for being human. Personality isn't a flaw to fix or a glitch to patch. It's a living system, shaped by genetics, molded by experience, and constantly responding to the world around it. The goal has never been perfection. The goal is awareness, adaptation, and the slow, imperfect work of becoming more fully ourselves.

Throughout these chapters, we have taken a long, unflinching look at what personality is and how it can become disordered. But we've also learned that the word "disordered" isn't shorthand for brokenness. It's a signpost pointing toward something deeper: a set of patterns that once made sense in the context they were born in, but now may no longer serve us. The chaos didn't come from nowhere; it came from survival. And survival, by its nature, is resourceful, creative, and deeply human.

Personality is not fixed. We are not concrete slabs poured in childhood and left to harden. We are adaptive systems, capable of growth, healing, and change. Biology may set the stage, but the environment writes the script, and with effort, awareness can edit the story.

Everyone is affected by personality disorders. Whether you see yourself in these traits or recognize them in someone you care about, the patterns discussed here are not rare outliers. They exist on a continuum, woven into everyday relationships, workplaces, and communities. We are all navigating this terrain.

These patterns are adaptive, not defective. Emotional reactivity, avoidance, perfectionism, or the need for control, these didn't come from nowhere. They served a function, protected a vulnerability, or gave shape to chaos. Understanding this is not about excusing harm but recognizing the roots of our defenses.

Understanding brings agency. When you can name a pattern, you stop being ruled by it. Awareness is a light switch, and once it's on, you can start making choices. You get to ask: Does this still serve me? Is there another way?

The journal prompts, case snapshots, and exercises in this book weren't designed to diagnose. They were meant to spark recognition. Maybe you found language for something that always felt just out of reach. Maybe you saw your own coping strategies reflected back with more clarity. That insight is the first step, but not the last.

For those who resonated with the traits described, growth means gently working against the grain. That might mean noticing when an old belief flares up, challenging it, and choosing a different response. It might mean tolerating discomfort, letting go of control, or practicing self-soothing in the face of fear. Change is built through repetition, not revelation.

For those in relationships shaped by disordered traits, the work is different but no less important. You are not here to fix anyone else.

Your power lies in clarity, in naming what is and isn't acceptable, and in enforcing boundaries that protect your peace. Compassion and distance can coexist. Empathy does not require entanglement.

Therapy, community, peer support, psychoeducation, these are not luxuries. They are lifelines. Seeking help is not a failure. It is a strategic decision to stop surviving alone.

You are not defined by your worst moment. If anything, you are a collection of deeply creative adaptations, some outdated, some brilliant, some still in progress. And that's okay.

Growth doesn't require a grand transformation. It begins with noticing. By asking better questions. Slowing down the automatic response long enough to choose something different. This book has been your mirror. Now, it's up to you to use what you've seen.

- Continue learning: Revisit the sources cited in this book. Explore therapeutic workbooks. Stay curious.
- Practice your new tools: Use the exercises again. Modify them. Create your own.
- Join the conversation: Talk about what you've learned. Challenge stigma. Normalize the language of personality and emotion.

Healing takes many forms. Sometimes it looks like a breakthrough in a therapy session. Sometimes it looks like pausing before you lash out. Sometimes it looks like holding your ground or letting someone else walk away. All of it counts.

Thank you for walking through the chaos, your own and others'. It takes real courage to look inward and even more to do something with what you find. Whether you read this to understand yourself, to support someone you love, or to make sense of years of confusion, your presence here matters.

This journey was about unlabeling shame, untangling fear, and opening space for understanding, because that's where change begins.

You are not wired for chaos. You are wired for survival. Now you have the insight and the power to rewire with intention.

GLOSSARY OF KEY TERMS

This glossary defines key psychological terms, therapeutic approaches, and concepts that appear throughout the book. It is intended to support clarity and deepen the reader's understanding of personality disorders and emotional regulation.

Attachment Theory

A foundational psychological framework that explains how early relationships with caregivers shape an individual's sense of safety, emotional regulation, and future relational patterns. Insecure attachment styles are frequently linked to the development of personality disorders.

Borderline Personality Disorder (BPD)

A mental health condition characterized by patterns of instability in interpersonal relationships, self-image, and emotions, often accompanied by impulsive behaviors. Individuals with BPD may experience intense episodes of anger, depression, or anxiety lasting a few hours to a few days. The book emphasizes the importance of reframing BPD not as a character flaw but as a trauma- and attachment-based condition.

Cluster B Personality Disorders

One of the three clusters of personality disorders in the Diagnostic and Statistical Manual of Mental Disorders (DSM-5). Cluster B includes disorders marked by dramatic, emotional, or erratic behavior: Borderline, Narcissistic, Histrionic, and Antisocial Personality Disorders.

Dialectical Behavior Therapy (DBT)

A structured, evidence-based therapy developed by Marsha Linehan, specifically for individuals with BPD and chronic emotion dysregulation. It combines principles of cognitive-behavioral therapy with mindfulness, distress tolerance, emotion regulation, and interpersonal effectiveness.

Dissociation

A coping mechanism involving a disconnection between a person's thoughts, memories, feelings, actions, or sense of identity. Often triggered by trauma or overwhelming stress, dissociation can range from daydreaming to more severe disruptions in memory or consciousness.

Emotional Granularity

The ability to recognize, differentiate, and articulate specific emotional states. Individuals with high emotional granularity are better able to regulate emotions and respond adaptively to distress. This skill is actively cultivated in several therapy models discussed in the book.

Feelings Glossary

A therapeutic tool used to help individuals expand their emotional vocabulary and improve emotional granularity. By having access to a wide range of emotion words, individuals can better name and understand their internal experiences, which enhances regulation and interpersonal communication.

Impulse Control

The capacity to delay immediate reactions, urges, or gratification in favor of more thoughtful or goal-oriented behavior. Impulse control is often impaired in individuals with personality disorders, particularly during emotional distress.

Mentalization-Based Therapy (MBT)

A therapeutic approach focused on improving the ability to understand and reflect on one's own and others' mental states. Especially effective for individuals with BPD, MBT helps strengthen empathy, reduce reactivity, and improve interpersonal relationships.

Narcissistic Traits

Behavioral tendencies such as grandiosity, need for admiration, sensitivity to criticism, and lack of empathy. While these traits can be present in many individuals, they are diagnostically significant only when persistent and impairing.

The book distinguishes between pathological narcissism and adaptive self-confidence.

Person-First Language

A respectful form of language that emphasizes the individual before the diagnosis (e.g., "a person with BPD" instead of "a borderline"). This approach is advocated throughout the book as a means to humanize individuals and combat stigma.

Psychoeducation

The process of educating individuals about psychological concepts, diagnoses, and treatment strategies. Psychoeducation empowers clients to understand their experiences and participate actively in their own recovery.

Schema Therapy

An integrative therapeutic model that blends cognitive-behavioral therapy with attachment theory and emotion-focused interventions. It targets deeply entrenched patterns or "schemas" developed in early life that influence current behavior and emotional responses.

Self-Regulation

The ability to manage and respond to emotional experiences in a manner consistent with one's goals and values. Self-regulation is a central focus of DBT and other therapies covered in the book, as it underpins resilience and functional behavior.

STOP Skill

An acronym used in DBT to help interrupt emotional impulsivity:

- Stop
- Take a step back
- Observe
- Proceed mindfully
  - The STOP skill supports emotional pause and cognitive awareness in high-intensity situations.

Stigma

The social devaluation and discrimination faced by individuals due to mental health conditions. Stigma can be internalized (self-stigma) or external (public stigma), both of which impact recovery and access to care. The book challenges stigmatizing narratives and promotes understanding through education.

Trauma-Informed Care

An approach to treatment that acknowledges the widespread impact of trauma and integrates this understanding into all aspects of clinical practice. It prioritizes safety, trust, choice, collaboration, and empowerment, especially relevant for individuals with personality disorders.

REFERENCES

American Psychiatric Association. (1980). *Diagnostic and statistical manual of mental disorders* (3rd ed.). APA Publishing.

Abi-Jaoude, E., Naylor, K. T., & Pignatiello, A. (2020). Smartphones, Social Media Use, and Youth Mental Health. *Canadian Medical Association Journal, 192*(6), E136–E141. National Library of Medicine. https://doi.org/10.1503/cmaj.190434

Alarcon, R. D. (2009). Culture, cultural factors and psychiatric diagnosis: review and projections. *World Psychiatry, 8*(3), 131–139. https://doi.org/10.1002/j.2051-5545.2009.tb00233.x

American Psychological Association. (2017, January 1). *Ethical principles of psychologists and code of conduct.* American Psychological Association. https://www.apa.org/ethics/code

American Psychological Association. (2021). *Help for personality disorders.* Apa.org. https://www.apa.org/topics/personality-disorders/help

Appelbaum, P. S. (2003). Law & Psychiatry: Ambivalence Codified: California's New Outpatient Commitment Statute. *Psychiatric Services, 54*(1), 26–28. https://doi.org/10.1176/appi.ps.54.1.26

Ardito, R. B., & Rabellino, D. (2011). Therapeutic Alliance and Outcome of Psychotherapy: Historical Excursus, Measurements, and Prospects for Research. *Frontiers in Psychology, 2*(270). https://doi.org/10.3389/fpsyg.2011.00270

American Psychiatric Association. (2022). *Diagnostic and statistical manual of mental disorders* (5th ed., text rev.; DSM-5-TR)

Colins, O. F., Verhulst, F., & Noordermeer, S. (2019). Dimensional models of personality pathology: Implications for diagnosis and treatment. *Journal of Personality Disorders, 33*(6), 785–806.

Costa, P. T., & McCrae, R. R. (1992). *NEO PI-R: Professional manual.* Psychological Assessment Resources.

BATEMAN, A., & FONAGY, P. (2010). Mentalization-based treatment for borderline personality disorder. *World Psychiatry, 9*(1), 11–15. https://doi.org/10.1002/j.2051-5545.2010.tb00255.x

Blair, R. J. R. (2007). The amygdala and ventromedial prefrontal cortex in morality and psychopathy. *Trends in Cognitive Sciences, 11*(9), 387–392. https://doi.org/10.1016/j.tics.2007.07.003

Bozzatello, P., Rocca, P., Baldassarri, L., Bosia, M., & Bellino, S. (2021). The Role of

Trauma in Early Onset Borderline Personality Disorder: A Biopsychosocial Perspective. *Frontiers in Psychiatry*, *12*(1). https://doi.org/10.3389/fpsyt.2021. 721361

Bretherton, I. (1992). The origins of attachment theory: John Bowlby and Mary Ainsworth. *Developmental Psychology*, *28*(5), 759–775. https://doi.org/10.1037/0012-1649.28.5.759

Burkauskas, J., & Fineberg, N. A. (2019). Chapter 1. History and Epidemiology of OCPD. *American Psychiatric Association Publishing EBooks*, 1–26. https://doi.org/10.1176/appi.books.9781615379293.lg01

CADDY, L., CRAWFORD, F., & PAGE, A. C. (2011). "Painting a path to wellness": correlations between participating in a creative activity group and improved measured mental health outcome. *Journal of Psychiatric and Mental Health Nursing*, *19*(4), 327–333. https://doi.org/10.1111/j.1365-2850.2011.01785.x

Cherry, K. (2025, January 29). *What is attachment theory?* Verywell Mind. https://www.verywellmind.com/what-is-attachment-theory-2795337

Cleveland Clinic. (2019, April 16). *Personality Disorder | Cleveland Clinic*. Cleveland Clinic. https://my.clevelandclinic.org/health/diseases/9636-personality-disorders-overview

Crowell, S. E., Beauchaine, T. P., & Linehan, M. M. (2009). A biosocial developmental model of borderline personality: Elaborating and extending Linehan's theory. *Psychological Bulletin*, *135*(3), 495–510. https://doi.org/10.1037/a0015616

Cuervo, Á. G. (2022, March 4). *Addressing cultural bias in the treatment of personality disorders*. Mad in America. https://www.madinamerica.com/2022/03/addressing-cultural-bias-treatment-personality-disorders/

Fariba, K., & Sapra, A. (2021). *Avoidant personality disorder*. PubMed; StatPearls Publishing. https://www.ncbi.nlm.nih.gov/books/NBK559325/

Faverio, M., Anderson, M., & Park, E. (2025, April 22). *Teens, social media and mental health*. Pew Research Center; Pew Research Center. https://www.pewresearch.org/internet/2025/04/22/teens-social-media-and-mental-health/

Fisher, K. A., Hany, M., & Torrico, T. J. (2024). *Antisocial Personality Disorder*. National Library of Medicine; StatPearls Publishing. https://www.ncbi.nlm.nih.gov/books/NBK546673/

Fitzpatrick, K. K., Darcy, A., & Vierhile, M. (2017). Delivering Cognitive Behavior Therapy to Young Adults With Symptoms of Depression and Anxiety Using a Fully Automated Conversational Agent (Woebot): A Randomized Controlled Trial. *JMIR Mental Health*, *4*(2). https://doi.org/10.2196/mental.7785

Fonagy, P., & Bateman, A. (2008). The Development of Borderline Personality Disorder—A Mentalizing Model. *Journal of Personality Disorders*, *22*(1), 4–21. https://doi.org/10.1521/pedi.2008.22.1.4

Fontanella, C. A., Steelesmith, D. L., & Bridge, J. A. (2023). Importance of Place in Examining Risk for Suicide Among Youth. *Journal of Adolescent Health, 72*(1), 5–6. https://doi.org/10.1016/j.jadohealth.2022.10.005

French, J. H., & Shrestha, S. (2019, May 15). *Histrionic Personality Disorder.* Nih.gov; StatPearls Publishing. https://www.ncbi.nlm.nih.gov/books/NBK542325/

Freud, S. (1962). *The Ego and the Id.* W.W. Norton.

Frost, R. O., Steketee, G., Cohn, L., & Griess, K. (1994). Personality traits in subclinical and non-obsessive-compulsive volunteers and their parents. *Behaviour Research and Therapy, 32*(1), 47–56. https://doi.org/10.1016/0005-7967(94)90083-3

Furnham, A., & Petropoulou, K. (2017). The Perceived Problems of People With Subclinical Personality Disorders: A Mental Health Literacy Study. *Journal of Relationships Research, 8.* https://doi.org/10.1017/jrr.2017.3

Glenn, C. R., & Klonsky, E. D. (2009). Emotion Dysregulation as a Core Feature of Borderline Personality Disorder. *Journal of Personality Disorders, 23*(1), 20–28. https://doi.org/10.1521/pedi.2009.23.1.20

Grant, B. F., Chou, S. P., Goldstein, R. B., Huang, B., Stinson, F. S., Saha, T. D., Smith, S. M., Dawson, D. S., Pulay, A. J., Pickering, R. P., & Ruan, W. J. (2008). Prevalence, Correlates, Disability, and Comorbidity of DSM-IV Borderline Personality Disorder. *The Journal of Clinical Psychiatry, 69*(4), 533–545. https://doi.org/10.4088/jcp.v69n0404

Gunderson, J. G., & Links, P. S. (2008). *Borderline personality disorder: a clinical guide.* American Psychiatric Pub.

Hatzenbuehler, M. L., Phelan, J. C., & Link, B. G. (2013). Stigma as a fundamental cause of population health inequalities. *American Journal of Public Health, 103*(5), 813–821. https://doi.org/10.2105/ajph.2012.301069

Herpertz, S. C., Kunert, H. J., Schwenger, U. B., & Sass, H. (1999). Affective Responsiveness in Borderline Personality Disorder: A Psychophysiological Approach. *American Journal of Psychiatry, 156*(10), 1550–1556. https://doi.org/10.1176/ajp.156.10.1550

Histrionic Personality Disorder: Causes, Symptoms, Treatment. (2023, September 25). HelpGuide.org. https://www.helpguide.org/mental-health/personality-disorders/histrionic-personality-disorder-causes-symptoms-treatment

Hoermann, S., Zupanick, C. E., & Dombeck, M. (2024, September 25). *Attachment Theory Of Personality Disorder.* MentalHealth.com. https://www.mentalhealth.com/library/attachment-theory-of-personality-disorder

Hopwood, C. J. (2018). Interpersonal Dynamics in Personality and Personality Disorders. *European Journal of Personality, 32*(5), 499–524. https://doi.org/10.1002/per.2155

Hughes, K., Bellis, M. A., Hardcastle, K. A., Sethi, D., Butchart, A., Mikton, C., Jones,

L., & Dunne, M. P. (2017). The effect of multiple adverse childhood experiences on health: a systematic review and meta-analysis. *The Lancet Public Health, 2*(8), 356–366. https://doi.org/10.1016/S2468-2667(17)30118-4

JACKSON, S. W. (1986). *Melancholia and Depression.* https://doi.org/10.2307/j.ctt1x p3stn

Jung, C. G. (1964). *Man and his symbols.* Doubleday.

Jane, J. S., Oltmanns, T. F., South, S. C., & Turkheimer, E. (2007). Gender bias in diagnostic criteria for personality disorders: An item response theory analysis. *Journal of Abnormal Psychology, 116*(1), 166–175. https://doi.org/10.1037/0021-843x.116.1.166

Jarvis, G. E., & Kirmayer, L. J. (2021). Situating Mental Disorders in Cultural Frames. *Oxford Research Encyclopedia of Psychology.* https://doi.org/10.1093/acre fore/9780190236557.013.627

Johnson, R., Persad, G., & Sisti, D. (2014). The Tarasoff rule: the implications of interstate variation and gaps in professional training. *The Journal of the American Academy of Psychiatry and the Law, 42*(4), 469–477. https://pubmed.ncbi.nlm.nih.gov/25492073/

Kakar, S. (2013). *Shamans, Mystics, and Doctors.* Knopf.

Knaak, S., Patten, S., & Ungar, T. (2015). Mental illness stigma as a quality-of-care problem. *The Lancet Psychiatry, 2*(10), 863–864. https://doi.org/10.1016/s2215-0366(15)00382-x

Lakeman, R., King, P., Hurley, J., Tranter, R., Leggett, A., Campbell, K., & Herrera, C. (2022). Towards online delivery of Dialectical Behaviour Therapy: A scoping review. *International Journal of Mental Health Nursing, 31*(4). https://doi.org/10.1111/inm.12976

Link, B. G., & Phelan, J. C. (2012). Labeling and Stigma. *Handbooks of Sociology and Social Research,* 525–541. https://doi.org/10.1007/978-94-007-4276-5_25

Lockwood, G. (2008, December 21). *Schema Therapy Society e.V. (ISST) - Schema Therapy Central Concepts.* Schematherapysociety.org. https://schematherapysoci ety.org/Schema-Therapy

Lovering, N. (2017, December 17). *Treating Histrionic Personality Disorder.* Psych Central. https://www.psychcentral.com/disorders/histrionic-personality-disor der/treatment

Lyons-Ruth, Karlen & Jacobvitz, Deborah. (2008). *Attachment Disorganization: Genetic factors, parenting contexts, and developmental transformations from infancy to adulthood.*

Lyons-Ruth, K., Alpern, L., & Repacholi, B. (1993). Disorganized Infant Attachment Classification and Maternal Psychosocial Problems as Predictors of Hostile-Aggressive Behavior in the Preschool Classroom. *Child Development, 64*(2), 572. https://doi.org/10.2307/1131270

Macchia, A., Mikusky, D., Sachser, C., Mueller-Stierlin, A. S., Nickel, S., Sanhüter, N., & Abler, B. (2025). Trait dissociation in borderline personality disorder: influence on immediate therapy outcomes, follow-up assessments, and self-harm patterns. *European Journal of Psychotraumatology, 16*(1). https://doi.org/10.1080/20008066.2025.2461965

Marsh, A. A., Finger, E. C., Schechter, J. C., Jurkowitz, I. T. N., Reid, M. E., & Blair, R. J. R. (2010). Adolescents with psychopathic traits report reductions in physiological responses to fear. *Journal of Child Psychology and Psychiatry, 52*(8), 834–841. https://doi.org/10.1111/j.1469-7610.2010.02353.x

Mayo Clinic. (2023, April 6). *Narcissistic personality disorder*. Mayo Clinic. https://www.mayoclinic.org/diseases-conditions/narcissistic-personality-disorder/symptoms-causes/syc-20366662

Mayo Clinic. (2024). *Borderline personality disorder - diagnosis and treatment - mayo clinic*. Mayoclinic.org. https://www.mayoclinic.org/diseases-conditions/borderline-personality-disorder/diagnosis-treatment/drc-20370242

McEwen, B. S. (2003). Mood disorders and allostatic load. *Biological Psychiatry, 54*(3), 200–207. https://doi.org/10.1016/s0006-3223(03)00177-x

McGarvie, S. (2024, November 28). *Attachment theory, Bowlby's stages & attachment styles*. Positive Psychology. https://positivepsychology.com/attachment-theory/

Mental health and media: How personality disorders in the media shaped stigma | BetterHelp. (2024, July 20). Betterhelp.com; BetterHelp. https://www.betterhelp.com/advice/personality-disorders/mental-health-and-media-how-personality-disorders-in-the-media-have-shaped-stigma/

Millon, T. (2011). *Disorders of Personality*. John Wiley & Sons, Inc. https://doi.org/10.1002/9781118099254

Naslund, J. A., Aschbrenner, K. A., Marsch, L. A., & Bartels, S. J. (2016). The Future of Mental Health care: Peer-to-peer Support and Social Media. *Epidemiology and Psychiatric Sciences, 25*(2), 113–122. https://www.cambridge.org/core/journals/epidemiology-and-psychiatric-sciences/article/future-of-mental-health-care-peertopeer-support-and-social-media/DC0FB362B67DF2A48D42D487ED07C783

National Alliance on Mental Illness. (2025). *Psychotherapy | NAMI*. Www.nami.org. https://www.nami.org/About-Mental-Illness/Treatments/Psychotherapy/

National Institute for Health and Care Excellence. (2009, January 28). *Borderline personality disorder: Recognition and management*. Nice.org.uk; NICE. https://www.nice.org.uk/guidance/CG78

Nichols, H. (2023, January 30). *AVPD vs social anxiety: Differences and more*. Www.medicalnewstoday.com. https://www.medicalnewstoday.com/articles/avpd-vs-social-anxiety

Norcross, J. C., & Wampold, B. E. (2011). Evidence-based therapy relationships:

Research conclusions and clinical practices. *Psychotherapy*, *48*(1), 98–102. https://doi.org/10.1037/a0022161

Open-Source Psychometrics Project. (2019, August 2). *Big Five Personality Test.* Open-Source Psychometrics Project. https://openpsychometrics.org/tests/IPIP-BFFM/

Porter, R. (2002). *Madness: a brief history.* Oxford University Press.

Quraishi, A.-H., Corral, A., & Beard, R. (2023, February 27). *Teens turning to TikTok for mental health advice are self-diagnosing.* Www.cbsnews.com. https://www.cbsnews.com/news/social-media-mental-health-self-diagnosis/

Rhee, S. H., & Waldman, I. D. (2002). Genetic and environmental influences on antisocial behavior: A meta-analysis of twin and adoption studies. *Psychological Bulletin, 128*(3), 490–529. https://doi.org/10.1037/0033-2909.128.3.490

Robitz, R. (2022). *What are personality disorders?* American Psychiatric Association; American Psychiatric Association. https://www.psychiatry.org/patients-families/personality-disorders/what-are-personality-disorders

Ronningstam, E. (2023). *Narcissistic Personality Disorder: Guide for Providers at McLean Hospital.* Www.mcleanhospital.org; Mclean Hospital. https://www.mcleanhospital.org/npd-provider-guide

Rony, M. K. K., Das, D. C., Khatun, Most. T., Ferdousi, S., Akter, M. R., Khatun, Mst. A., Begum, Most. H., Khalil, M. I., Parvin, Mst. R., Alrazeeni, D. M., & Akter, F. (2025). Artificial intelligence in psychiatry: A systematic review and meta-analysis of diagnostic and therapeutic efficacy. *DIGITAL HEALTH, 11.* https://doi.org/10.1177/20552076251330528

Rothbart, M. K., & Bates, J. E. (2006). Temperament. In N. Eisenberg (Ed.), *Handbook of child psychology: Vol. 3, Social, emotional, and personality development* (6th ed., pp. 99–166). Wiley.

Rousseau, G. S., Foucault, M., & Howard, R. (1970). Madness and Civilization: A History of Insanity in the Age of Reason. *Eighteenth-Century Studies, 4*(1), 90. https://doi.org/10.2307/2737615

Sansone, R. A., & Sansone, L. A. (2011). Gender patterns in borderline personality disorder. *Innovations in Clinical Neuroscience, 8*(5), 16–20. https://www.ncbi.nlm.nih.gov/pmc/articles/PMC3115767/

Scull, A. (2015). *Madness in civilization: a cultural history of insanity, from the Bible to Freud, from the madhouse to modern medicine.* Princeton University Press.

Selby, E. A., Anestis, M. D., Bender, T. W., & Joiner, T. E. (2009). An exploration of the emotional cascade model in borderline personality disorder. *Journal of Abnormal Psychology, 118*(2), 375–387. https://doi.org/10.1037/a0015711

Silbersweig, D., Clarkin, J. F., Goldstein, M., Kernberg, O. F., Tuescher, O., Levy, K. N., Brendel, G., Pan, H., Beutel, M., Pavony, M. T., Epstein, J., Lenzenweger, M. F., Thomas, K. M., Posner, M. I., & Stern, E. (2007). Failure of Frontolimbic

Inhibitory Function in the Context of Negative Emotion in Borderline Personality Disorder. *American Journal of Psychiatry, 164*(12), 1832–1841. https://doi.org/10.1176/appi.ajp.2007.06010126

Snowden, L. R. (2001). Barriers to Effective Mental Health Services for African Americans. *Mental Health Services Research, 3*(4), 181–187. https://doi.org/10.1023/a:1013172913880

Stinson, F. S., Dawson, D. A., Golstein, R. B., Chou, P., Huang, B., Smith, S. M., Ruan, W. J., Pulay, A. J., Saha, T. D., Pickering, R. P., & Grant, B. F. (2008). Prevalence, Correlates, Disability, and Comorbidity of DSM-IV Narcissistic Personality Disorder. *The Journal of Clinical Psychiatry, 69*(7), 1033–1045. https://doi.org/10.4088/jcp.v69n0701

Suchman, N. E., DeCoste, C., Leigh, D., & Borelli, J. (2010). Reflective functioning in mothers with drug use disorders: Implications for dyadic interactions with infants and toddlers. *Attachment & Human Development, 12*(6), 567–585. https://doi.org/10.1080/14616734.2010.501988

Swain, J., Hancock, K., Hainsworth, C., & Bowman, J. (2013). Acceptance and Commitment Therapy in the treatment of anxiety: A systematic review. *Clinical Psychology Review, 33*(8), 965–978. https://doi.org/10.1016/j.cpr.2013.07.002

Teicher, M. H., & Samson, J. A. (2016). Annual research review: Enduring neurobiological effects of childhood abuse and neglect. *Journal of Child Psychology and Psychiatry, 57*(3), 241–266. https://doi.org/10.1111/jcpp.12507

Turkheimer, E. (2000). Three Laws of Behavior Genetics and What They Mean. *Current Directions in Psychological Science, 9*(5), 160–164. https://doi.org/10.1111/1467-8721.00084

Twenge, J. M. (2023). *Generations*. Atria Books.

Widiger, T. A., & Trull, T. J. (2007). Plate tectonics in the classification of personality disorder: Shifting to a dimensional model. *American Psychologist, 62*(2), 71–83. https://doi.org/10.1037/0003-066x.62.2.71

Wiginton, K. (2020, December 7). *What's the Difference Between a Psychopath and a Sociopath?* WebMD. https://www.webmd.com/mental-health/psychopath-sociopath-differences

World Health Organization. (2019). *International classification of diseases for mortality and morbidity statistics (11th Revision)*.

Zanarini, M. C., Williams, A. A., Lewis, R. E., Reich, R. B., Vera, S. C., Marino, M. F., Levin, A., Yong, L., & Frankenburg, F. R. (1997). Reported pathological childhood experiences are associated with the development of borderline personality disorder. *American Journal of Psychiatry, 154*(8), 1101–1106. https://doi.org/10.1176/ajp.154.8.1101

Zimmerman, M. (2021, May). *Avoidant Personality Disorder (AVPD) - Psychiatric Disorders*. Merck Manuals Professional Edition. https://www.merckmanuals.

com/professional/psychiatric-disorders/personality-disorders/avoidant-personality-disorder-avpd

Zimmerman, M., Chelminski, I., Young, D., Dalrymple, K., Walsh, E., & Rosenstein, L. (2014). A Clinically Useful Self-Report Measure of theDSM-5Anxious Distress Specifier for Major Depressive Disorder. *The Journal of Clinical Psychiatry, 75*(06), 601–607. https://doi.org/10.4088/jcp.13m08961

Zur, O. (2007). *Boundaries in Psychotherapy: Ethical and Clinical Explorations.* American Psychological Association. https://doi.org/10.1037/11563-000

www.ingramcontent.com/pod-product-compliance
Lightning Source LLC
Chambersburg PA
CBHW032048020426
42335CB00011B/242